C000161219

# Fashions in Eyeglasses

Fashions in Hair

Fashions in Makeup

Stage Makeup

RICHARD CORSON

# *Fashions in Eyeglasses*

PETER OWEN · LONDON

ISBN 0 7206 3282 X

Second impression with supplement
published 1980 by
PETER OWEN LIMITED
73 Kenway Road London SW5 0RE
First published 1967
© Richard Corson 1967, 1980

Book designed by Beatrice Musgrave

Composition and original printing by
R & R Clark Ltd Edinburgh
Reprinted by Clarke, Doble & Brendon Ltd Plymouth

# TO MITCHELL ERICKSON

*who asked the question*

In the more than six centuries since their invention, only one major work has been written about the form (as opposed to the function) of eyeglasses. That was published in Paris in 1911, when glasses were still a necessary evil, something to be slightly embarrassed, slightly apologetic about wearing. There was no hint then that one day hundreds of new styles would flood the market each year and that the fashion-conscious woman could choose her eyeglasses to match her dress, her eyes, her hair, or even her dog if she so wanted. With glasses now so much a part of the world of fad and fashion, it seems time for a look through history at their fascinating story.

My basic purpose in compiling such a work has been, as it was with *Fashions in Hair*, to provide for the benefit of costumers, make-up artists, actors, and illustrators a practical guide to styles of eyeglasses worn since their appearance in Europe nearly seven hundred years ago. A recent New York production of *Love's Labour's Lost*, in which a pair of silver oxford glasses on a chain were worn some three hundred years before they were invented, strengthened my conviction that such a book might be useful.

To this end I have provided, for each century, plates of drawings of eyeglasses, reproductions of old prints showing them in actual use, and text material giving historical and social background and, when possible, descriptions and comments by contemporary writers.

My work has been immeasurably simplified, my days of research brightened, and the book enriched by the enthusiastic co-operation of Miss Elizabeth Roth and Mr Wilson Duprey of the Prints Division of the New York Public Library. Through their extraordinary knowledge of prints and their endless patience, they have turned up treasures which I could never have found on my own, and I am most grateful.

I am also indebted to Bausch and Lomb, the American Optical Company, the Better Vision Institute, and the Fashion Eyewear Group of America for their co-operation. And I wish particularly to express my gratitude to Mitchell Erickson (who quite by accident made me aware of the need for such a book) for reading the manuscript and making many invaluable suggestions.

R. C.

*Habit de Marchand Mirvitier Lvnettier*

G. Valck excudit.

# Contents

# Contents

\* The extract from Aldous Huxley's 'The Monocle' published in *Two or Three Graces and Other Stories* appears by kind permission of Messrs Chatto and Windus Ltd.

# Illustrations

## Plates

## Figures in the Text

\* Figure 5 is reproduced by courtesy of the National Gallery, London ; Figures 8, 9, 15, 23, 26, 30, 33, 36, 41, 43, 46, 47, 50, 51, 52, 59, 60, 61, 63, 64, 68, 69, 70, 82, 86, 90, 115 by courtesy of the Prints Division, New York Public Library ; Figure 66 by courtesy of the National Portrait Gallery, London.

# Fashions in Eyeglasses

Den vordantz hat man mir gelan
Dann jch on nutz vil bücher han
Die jch nit lyß/ vnd nyt verstan

## Von vnnutzē buchern

Das jch sytz vornan jn dem schyff
Das hat worlich eyn sundren gryff
On vrsach ist das nit gethan
Vff myn libry jch mych verlan

THE SCHOLAR. Woodcut by Sebastian Brandt, from *The Ship of Fools*, 1494

# 1 · The Beginnings

It is difficult to imagine a world without books as we know them. It is even more difficult to imagine a world in which only a few educated men were able to read the precious manuscripts in the libraries and monasteries. But it is, perhaps, most difficult of all to imagine a world in which educated and gifted men with brilliant minds were denied years of reading through simple defects of vision which can now be corrected in a matter of minutes—in other words, a world without glasses.

Seneca, it is said, managed to read all the books in the libraries at Rome by peering through a globe of water to provide magnification; but most scholars with visual afflictions hired younger scholars to read to them. Yet lenses did exist in classical times. Ptolemy, in fact, mentions the general principle of magnification; but the lenses then available were evidently unsuitable for use in precise magnification.

The oldest lens we know of, found in the ruins of ancient Nineveh and still in existence, is of plano-convex type, made of polished rock crystal, an inch and a half in diameter, with a focal length of four and a half inches. Possibly it was used as a burning glass. Aristophanes in *The Clouds* refers to a glass for burning holes in parchment and also mentions the use of burning glasses for erasing writing from wax tablets. According to Pliny, physicians used them for cauterizing wounds.

It was formerly assumed, through uncertainties in the translation of Pliny, that Nero watched the combats of the gladiators through an emerald, presumably a lens. The assumption in this case would be that Nero was nearsighted. But since Pliny elsewhere clearly states that Nero had to squint in order to see near objects, a characteristic of longsightedness, it seems likely that he used the emerald as a mirror instead of a lens, especially since Pliny's preceding sentence refers to the reflecting qualities of flat emeralds: *Quorum vero corpus extensum est, eadem, qua specula, ratione supini imagines rerum reddunt. Nero princeps gladiatorum pugnas spectabat in smaragdo*—'As for flat emeralds, they reflect images in the manner of mirrors. The emperor Nero observed the combats of the gladiators in an emerald.'

According to the December 1925 issue of the *Bausch and Lomb Magazine*, 'Excavations by Count Byron Khun de Prorok on the site of ancient Carthage, Rome's greatest rival, have uncovered a pair of double convex lenses, originally mounted in a bronze frame, and unmistakably intended as an aid to human vision'. Photographs and further details were promised in a subsequent issue. A careful search through those issues has, however, revealed no further information about the discovery. Nor does it seem to have been mentioned by other writers. Surely such a remarkable discovery, had it actually been made, would have been well publicized. Therefore, we are probably justified in assuming that the announcement was unfounded and that Carthaginians did not wear eyeglasses while their Roman neighbours read through globes of water.

Then came the Dark Ages; and in the miasma of superstition surrounding human ailments, the help which might have been forthcoming was delayed for centuries. A favourite Anglo-Saxon remedy for lack of visual acuity has come down to us:

'The eyes of an old man are not sharp of sight; then shall he wake up his eyes with rubbings, with walkings, with ridings, either so that a man bear him or convey him in a wain. And they shall use little and careful meats, and comb their heads and drink wormwood before they take food. Then shall a salve be wrought for unsharp-sighted eyes; take pepper and beat it, and beetle nut and a somewhat of salt and wine; that will be a good salve.'

Other ailments of the eyes had equally intriguing remedies. In the latter part of the fourth century Marcellus recommended that in order 'to avoid inflamed eyes, when you see a star fall or cross the heavens, count quickly, for you will be free from inflammation for as many years as you count numbers'. Another reasonably simple remedy, and one not requiring waiting around for a falling star, involved immediate action: 'As soon as a man gets pain in his eyes, tie in unwrought flax as many knots as there are letters in his name, pronouncing them as you go, and tie it round his neck'.

More serious ailments required considerably more effort: 'For white spots, as cataracts, catch a fox alive; cut his tongue out; let him go; dry his tongue and tie it up in a red rag and hang it round the man's neck. If anything causing annoyance gets into a man's eye, with five fingers of the same side as the eye, run the eye over and fumble at it, saying three times, "Tetunc resonco, bregan gresso" and spit thrice.' As an alternative one might 'shut the vexed eye and say thrice, "In mon deromarcos axatison" and spit thrice'. Lacking success with either of these, the patient was advised to 'shut the other eye, touch gently the vexed eye with the ring finger and thumb, and say thrice, "I buss the Gorgon's mouth"'.

For hordeolum, 'which is a sore place in the eyelid, of the shape of a barley corn', the remedy seemed hardly designed to decrease the soreness: 'Take nine grains of barley and with each poke the sore, with each one saying the magic words, "Kuria kuria kassaria sourophbi", then throw away the nine and do the same with seven; throw away the seven, and do the same with five; and so with three and one'. Here also there was an alternative: 'Take nine grains of barley and poke the sore, and at every poke say "pheuge pheuge krithe se diokei": "flee, flee, barley thee chaseth"'. For a simpler and perhaps equally effective remedy the patient was advised to 'touch the sore with the medicinal or ring finger and say thrice, "Vigaria gasaria"'.

Thus were visual defects dealt with in the Dark Ages. It was not until the year 1268 that Roger Bacon, an English philosopher whose unorthodox views got him into endless trouble, wrote in his *Opus Majus*: 'If anyone examine letters or other minute objects through the medium of crystal or glass or other transparent substance, if it be shaped like the lesser segment of a sphere, with the convex side towards the eye, he will see the letters far better and they will seem larger to him. . . . For this reason such an instrument is useful to all persons and to those with weak eyes, for they can see any letter, however small, if magnified enough.'

To men who were literate but were condemned by blurred vision never again to read, such a device must have seemed an unbelievable reprieve, a gift from God; but to others it may have been no more than a mildly interesting observation. To no one, evidently, did it occur that knowledge of this simple fact of nature could help shape the course of history.

Bacon does not suggest that the idea was original with him, though the wording of his report does give the impression that this specific use for lenses was not widely known. Alhazen's *Opticae Thesaurus*, an eleventh-century Arabian work which mentions plano-convex lenses, was familiar through a Latin translation of 1266 in many convents and would certainly have been known to Bacon. But Alhazen's lenses, with a thickness greater than the radius, would not have been suitable for reading. Bacon, however, recommended lenses with a thickness smaller than the radius, a major step in the development of eyeglasses. His is the first concrete evidence we have that lenses were or could be used for reading.

At about the same time (between 1260 and 1284, according to Greeff) German poets mentioned the use of lenses for optical magnification. Von Rohr points out that since the manufacture of such lenses was sufficiently commonplace to be written about in German rather than Latin, it had probably begun in the first half of the century.

What use Bacon made of his knowledge about lenses we can only surmise. Did it, perhaps, occur to him that it would be easier to read with the lens close to the eye rather than resting on the page? And did it then or at some later date appear that for two eyes there ought to be two lenses and that the two lenses would be far easier to manage if attached to each other at the same distance apart as the two eyes?

That it did occur to someone is clear, for in 1289, in a manuscript entitled *Traité de conduite de la famille*, Sandro di Popozo wrote: 'I am so debilitated by age that without the glasses known as spectacles, I would no longer be able to read or write. These have recently been invented for the benefit of poor old people whose sight has become weak.' Thus, between 1268 and 1289 spectacles were evidently invented. It seems more than likely that the first eyeglass would have been a single lens in a frame with a handle and that later the two handles would have been joined. That this took less than seventy years we know, but beyond that we can only speculate. As to the date of the invention itself, whether of a single or a double lens, we can be more specific.

On Wednesday morning, the 23rd of February 1306, in the Florentine church of Santa Maria Novella, Fra Giordano di Rivalto, a monk of Pisa, delivered a sermon in which he stated : 'It is not yet twenty years since the art of making spectacles, one of the most useful arts on earth, was discovered. . . . I, myself, have seen and conversed with the man who made them first.' Although Fra Giordano neglected to say who the man was, his sermon does make it possible to place the date of the invention, at least in Italy and probably in the Western world, at about 1287.

Perhaps the most significant evidence of all is to be found in a document, still in existence in the monastery at Pisa, recording the death in 1313 of a Dominican monk by the name of Alessandro della Spina, described as 'a modest and good man' with the ability to reproduce any man-made article he had seen with his own eyes. According to the document, one of the things he had seen with his own eyes was a pair of spectacles invented by someone who did not wish to make his invention known. The 'someone' was, unfortunately, not identified. All we know for sure is that Spina, having seen the spectacles, made many copies which he 'distributed with a cheerful and benevolent heart'.

Over the centuries scholars have tried without success to trace the inventor. Most of the attention has centred on a Florentine named Armato degli Armati, the seeds of whose fame seem to have been planted by scholars whose eagerness outweighed their caution. Edward Rosen, in a detailed and scholarly study of the question published in 1956, argues convincingly that there was more involved than mere carelessness and that the whole Armati legend was a deliberate fabrication, including his relatively modern tombstone with the inscription:

> Here lies Salvino d' Armato deglie Armati, of Florence,
> the inventor of spectacles. May God forgive his sins.
> He died anno Domino 1317.

And then, of course, there is Bacon. It is interesting to note that in 1285, just before spectacles are supposed to have been invented in Italy, Henry Goethals, an intimate friend of Bacon's, was sent by the friars of his order to Rome with a petition to the Pope. But when Goethals learned of the death of Martin IV, he stayed for some time with the Dominicans in Pisa, awaiting the election of a new Pope. There, of course, he would have known Spina. And had he had with him a pair of spectacles, Spina could easily have copied them. But further speculation seems fruitless. Whoever may have invented spectacles in Europe, it is quite possible that he was not the first, for they seem to have been used in China about the same time, probably earlier. The difference in construction suggests that they were invented independently.

The first authentic reference to eyeglasses in China appears to have come from Marco Polo, who stated that elderly people used lenses for reading. This would have been at about the same time as their appearance in Italy. Rasmussen points out, however, that for the use of glasses to be established at that time, they would have had to be invented at least several decades earlier. He assumes, therefore, that the invention of spectacles in China preceded that in the Western world. Chinese historians claim that eyeglasses came to China from Arabia two centuries before Marco Polo observed them; but since at that time Alhazen was evidently unaware of the possibility of using lenses for reading, this seems unlikely. In any event, their development appears to have roughly paralleled that in Europe.

We do not know for certain how the earliest spectacles were received by the Chinese. But in Europe they must surely have been welcomed by ageing monks and scholars who were thus enabled once again to read clearly and to write their manuscripts. However, in these dark times before the rebirth of learning and the invention of printing, when few were able to read, there was no general rejoicing over the invention of something which seemed to be designed for a very small and élite minority and was far too expensive for the general public to buy. Not only that, but the Church in many instances encouraged the idea that afflictions sent by God were meant to be endured in silence for the good of one's soul and that any mechanical device which counteracted them must perforce be the work of the devil. The ignorant and the gullible, unable to afford glasses themselves, were only too eager to decry their use by others. Eventually, of course, their practical value could no longer be denied, and opposition to them died out.

And so it is that the inventor of eyeglasses, instead of having his name blazoned across the history books as a benefactor to mankind, is lost in obscurity; and the story of the benefaction begins falteringly and moves forward at a snail's pace for nearly two centuries.

Fig. 1 : Saint Peter with riveted spectacles.  From a fifteenth-century altarpiece by Wolgemuth (1434–1519) in the Church of St James in Rothenburg, Bavaria

# 2 · The Middle Ages

Povert a spectakel is, as thinkith me,
Thurgh which he may his verray frendes se.
GEOFFREY CHAUCER

The oldest known work of art portraying spectacles, and therefore our most reliable source of information about their appearance, is a portrait of Hugh of St Cher, Cardinal Ugone, who died before they were invented. The portrait (Figure 2) was painted at Treviso in 1352, a century after Hugh's death, by Tommaso da Modena. Another painting by the same artist in the same year shows a single magnifying glass (Plate 1-c).

The glasses in Hugh's portrait were included not because he wore them, as of course he could not have, but as a mark of respect. This practice continued for several centuries, particularly in religious paintings, in which saints were sometimes accorded the honour of wearing, or at least holding, a pair of eyeglasses (Figures 1, 4, 5). Presumably glasses were equated with learning and the ability to read and with contemporary persons of influence and importance.

Inasmuch as the earliest double eyeglasses were evidently made up simply of two single eyeglasses (or magnifying lenses) with the handles riveted together, it is hardly surprising that a Florentine monk should have been able to master the secret of the invention merely by seeing them. The problem which was not mastered then or for some centuries afterwards was that of keeping the glasses on the nose.

Since these early riveted spectacles, being completely rigid, had to be held by hand or very carefully balanced on the nose, they were never worn continuously but only when needed for close vision (Figures 1, 2, 4). Even those forms designed to rest a little more securely on the nose were still too unsteady for continuous wearing. But since they were designed for the longsighted, to be used only in reading or for close work, they would not normally have been worn continuously in any case. No attempt was made to provide help for the shortsighted for several centuries.

Variations in the form of the frames soon developed (Plate 1), but it was a long time before enough flexibility could be provided so that the glasses would cling to the nose without being balanced or held. Plate 1-B represents an early attempt dating from the late fifteenth century.

Various other means of securing the glasses were tried. Savonarola, speaking of an aged person, said that since his glasses frequently fell off, it became necessary to put a hook on his cap to secure them. At the end of the fifteenth century it was not unusual to hold spectacles in place with the aid of a vertical extension over the forehead.

Early spectacle frames were made of brass or iron, later of horn, bone, gold, nickel, silver, and, late in the fifteenth century, even of leather (Plate 1-E). In 1326 an inventory at Exeter Palace of the possessions of Walter de Stapledon, an English bishop, included a pair of spectacles framed in gilded silver and valued at two shillings. By at least the middle of the fifteenth century the frames of bone or horn were sometimes split to allow insertion of the lenses, then tied firmly together with thread (Plate 1-K).

The first lenses, always convex and designed only for farsightedness, were ground from berillus or beryl, a smoke-coloured stone, and from sections of quartz known as 'pebble'. Later they were made of glass, the best ones coming from Venice. After 1420 the ruling classes wore gold frames with lenses of crystal and beryl. Thompson mentions the record of a festival celebrating the marriage of the Austrian Duchess of Juta, in which it is stated that 'one Pietro Buonaparte, who was ambassador to the Austrian Court, caused a great sensation by appearing with glasses across his nose called "beryls", said to have been invented by the Florentine Salvino d'Amato'. From beryl came the French *béricle* and later *besicles*, meaning spectacles.

The manufacture of glasses was begun in France in the early part of the fourteenth century, perhaps at the end of the thirteenth in Italy. In 1363 Guy de Chauliac referred to a 'spectacle maker'; and Petrarch, his contemporary, mentioned both spectacles and spectacle makers.

The spectacle makers' guild appeared fairly early, and in 1465 they took part in a craftsmen's review before Louis XI, walking with the haberdashers and

Fig. 2 : Hugh of St Cher, Cardinal Ugone. Posthumous portrait by Tommaso da Modena, 1352. This is the earliest known portrait with glasses

Fig. 3 : DANSE MACABRE. French, 1465. Notice the spectacle case hanging from the man's belt

Fig. 4 : Saint Paul. From a drawing in an illuminated manuscript, 1380

upholsterers. According to Pflugk, spectacle makers are reported from Frankfurt in 1450, from Strasburg in 1466, and from Nürnberg in 1478. They engaged in free trade until 1507, when the guilds took over and regulations were established. Their original charter still exists.

Eyeglasses required cases; and since the glasses were valuable possessions, the cases were often works of art. They were usually made of wood, metal, or ivory, elegantly decorated. Often the precious spectacles were guarded in their case by grotesque masks, lions, unicorns, or strange monsters. At other times, especially in later centuries, they were embellished with graceful arabesques, Biblical scenes, or religious symbols. Common cases were made of leather, morocco, horn, or even paper.

Sometimes, for convenience, a receptacle for spectacles was constructed in the cover of a book. Records of 1403 refer to the forging of 'a gilded silver plate to be put into the cover of a book of the duc de Bourgogne where he might put his glasses so that they would not be broken'. Frequently the case was suspended from the belt (Figure 3).

Even after the invention of spectacles, the single lens continued to be used. The accounts of Queen Jeanne d'Évreux for 1372 list a paste jewel in the shape of an eyeglass, priced at twenty francs; and an inventory of Charles V for 1379 includes 'two eyeglasses, one of which has a wooden handle'.

In England the single eyeglass was called a *spectacle*, as in Chaucer's *The Wife's Tale* :

> Povert a spectakel is, as thinkith me,
> Thurgh which he may his verray frendes se.

Fig. 5 : SAINTS PETER AND DOROTHY. Cologne School.
Master of the Altar of St Bartholomew, active *c.*
1485–1510

This was about 1387. A quarter of a century later Hoccleve, having strained his eyes for nearly twenty-four years in the Privy Seal office and prevented by his pride from relieving the strain with glasses, wrote :

> Throw foul book, un-to my Lord seye also,
> That pryde ys un-to me so greet a fo,
> That the spectacle forbideth he me,
> And hath y-doon of tyme yore ago ;
> And, for my sighte blyve hastith me fro.
> And lackith that that sholde his comfort be,
> No wonder thogh thow have no beautee.
> Out up-on pryde, causer of my wo
> My sighte is hurt thrgh hir adversitee.

The single reading glasses, though primarily utilitarian, were not necessarily lacking in decoration. An account of 1454 lists money paid 'To Lubin de Dreux Orfèvre, living at Chinon, for two ounces of silver for making a circular ornament to embellish a reading glass for the Queen'.

But plain or fancy, single or double, these aids to vision were slow indeed in capturing the interest of the medical profession. Rosen considers the earliest

Fig. 6 : Canon George van de Paele. Detail
from *Saint George, the Virgin, and
Saint Donat* by Jan van Eyck, 1436

authentic mention of eyeglasses by a medical writer to be that of Guy de Chauliac, a professor at Montpellier. In 1363 he wrote in his *Chirurgia magna* : 'And if these things do not avail, recourse must be had to spectacles of glass or beryl'.

But most physicians, putting their faith in lotions and incantations, scoffed at the use of eyeglasses and refused even to suggest that they might be of any help. In 1377 a physician named John of Ardern wrote a manuscript entitled *De Cura Oculorum*, in which he gave a variety of remedies for conditions of the eye, among which was the following :

'For watery eyes, if the patient be aged and decrepit, this ointment provides the best cure (many times I have proved this) which is thus made : use a basin of brass, well greased with fresh butter, and let it stand overnight ; in the morning let the basin be inverted upon a pot or dish in which is the sour urine of a man, warmed that it may receive the most urine ; let the butter be melted and when cool take down the basin and thus let it stand for a whole day ; afterward let the butter be scraped out (it will appear green) and mix with it a little fat of a capon liquefied by the sun's heat or a fire and store it up in a waxed vessel. Let the eyelid be well anointed. Do not let it run down into the eyes ; the eyes should be bandaged, and thus let him lie all night. Of a surety let it be dissolved in the morning, but not washed, then it will be healthy. . . . This medicine was highly beneficial to my own eyes in

Fig. 7 : Drawing by Pisanello from the records of the Council of Constance, *c.* 1417

studying and writing until the seventieth year of my age, much having been undertaken. And know all men present and to come that I, Master John of Ardern, and the least of surgeons wrote this little book painfully with my own hand at London in the first year of King Richard the Second and in the seventieth year of my age.'

Glasses were largely unnecessary so long as there were few books and little education. But then came the invention of printing, making books available in large numbers, and with the books came the desire of more and more people to read them, leading, naturally, to an enormous increase in the demand for spectacles. Mass production methods were instituted to meet the demand. Prices fell drastically ; and by the end of the fifteenth century cheap spectacles, along with other kinds of merchandise, were distributed through peddlers. Finally, after two centuries, glasses could be bought by anybody who needed them.

But despite this general availability of spectacles and the skill of the spectacle makers, no one had as yet provided any help for the shortsighted. Only the longsighted (which usually meant the middle-aged and the elderly) could be fitted with glasses. For any of Columbus's crew who were afflicted with shortsightedness, the New World must have been only a vague blur until they were practically on land. But all that was soon to change.

PLATE I : THE MIDDLE AGES
1300–1500

A  1352, Italian. Riveted eyeglasses of horn. This is the earliest style known (see Figure 2).

B  *c.* 1490. The slightly flexible extension helps to clasp the glasses firmly on the nose.

C  1352, Italian. Reading glass. From a painting by Tommaso da Modena.

D  Fifteenth century. Bridged spectacles of horn.

E  Late fifteenth century, German. Frames of hard leather.

F  *c.* 1417 (see Figure 7).

G  1403, French.

H  1436, Flemish. This is the earliest example known of this style.

I  Late fifteenth century, German.

J  Late fifteenth century.

K  Mid-fifteenth century, Dutch. The projections are split to allow insertion of the lens, then bound with cord or thread to hold the lens in place (see Figure 1).

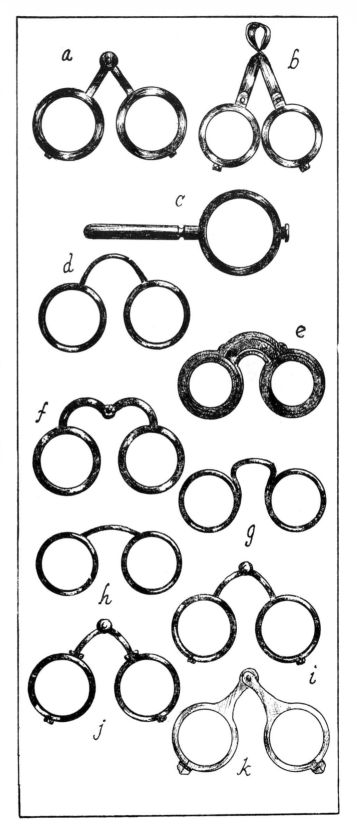

Fig. 8 : Pieter Brueghel (*c.* 1525–69).  Self-portrait

# 3 · The Sixteenth Century

It is much better and more useful that
one leaves spectacles alone. For naturally
a person sees and recognizes something
better when he has nothing in front of
his eyes than when he has something there.

DR GEORG BARTISCH

By the sixteenth century spectacles had achieved such importance and respect that they were even stamped on coins. The first of these we know of is an early sixteenth-century Danish gold ducat bearing the motto: 'Behold the Wonders of God'. A Brunswick *thaler*, dated 1589, bears the likeness of an old man carrying a torch, an hour-glass, a skull, and a pair of spectacles. The inscription reads: *Was hilft dem Alten Licht und Brill. Der sich selbst nicht hilft und kennen will*—Of what avail is lens and light, to him who lacks in mind and might?

Perhaps one of the most significant developments in spectacle making in the sixteenth century was the introduction, early in the century, of concave lenses for the shortsighted. Pope Leo X, who was very shortsighted, wore concave spectacles when hunting and claimed they enabled him to see better than his companions.

Until this time all lenses had been circular. But oval lenses, which can be traced to 1510, resulted from the need to look over the presbyopic lenses for clear distance vision—a difficult thing to do with the large, round lenses. In the Italian street scene in Figure 9, showing a spectacle maker with his many customers, it is clear that spectacles were selected by trial and error—it was up to the customer to choose the lenses which seemed to give the greatest improvement. Although this particular spectacle maker offered a choice of lenses, he evidently offered no choice in frames.

Bone was used for spectacle frames in France in 1582 and in Venice in 1585. But early in the sixteenth century in Germany horn was replacing bone for mountings, and leather was frequently used, as shown in Amman's woodcut of a spectacle maker (see dedication page).

Despite the spread of spectacles, single reading glasses were no less popular. By 1519 jointed eyeglasses which could be folded together and used as a single glass of increased power were being manufactured; and an inventory of Marguerite d'Autriche in 1524 lists 'a glass provided with a silver handle, surmounted with a small gilded lion, for reading a book'. In 1583 large numbers of single lenses mounted in horn were sold in Nürnberg for only three farthings when purchased

Fig. 9 : CONSPICILLA.  Engraving by Philip Galle, after Stradanus's *Nova Reperta*, 1600

in quantity.  Ordinary horn spectacles were the same price, leather ones were four farthings, and gilt horn cost nine and a half farthings.  As early as 1520 Albrecht Dürer paid less than ten farthings retail for a pair of reading glasses.

Although mass-produced German spectacles had become very inexpensive, much higher priced ones were to be had.  August, Elector of Saxony (1526–86), paid the equivalent of twelve guineas for a pair of Venetian spectacles with gold frames; and he ordered quadrilateral spectacle lenses from London for three pounds plus freight charges of one pound five shillings and sixpence.  In England, at the end of the century, the upper classes usually used a single glass for distance vision, whereas the lower classes used some form of spectacles.

The increased use of spectacles made it even more imperative to find some practical means of keeping them on.  Rabelais told how Panurge (in *Gargantua and Pantagruel*) wore his spectacles attached to his hat and how the Fredon brothers kept them on their noses even while asleep.  Sir Thomas More, like many others, evidently found the lower, fleshy part of the nose the most practical place for wearing the inflexible frames (Figure 11).

But the earliest glasses suitable for continuous wearing were probably those with lenses set into sturdy sole leather or horn with attached leather straps, which could be fastened around the head (Plate 2-E-F-G).  No further developments along this line seem to have taken place until late in the century, when glasses were sometimes tied on by means of cords around the ears—a Spanish-Italian style.

A painting by J. Rouyer, about 1581, shows Girolamo Capivaccio, a Paduan professor, wearing bridged eyeglasses attached to the ears by loops of cord (Figure 10). In 1596 El Greco painted his famous portrait of Cardinal Niño de Guevara (Figure 12) with his eyeglasses held on in the same way. In the 1580s the Spanish-Italian Jesuits, according to Jesuit historians, introduced this style of eyeglasses to the Chinese, who continued to wear them for about two hundred years. Instead of the loops (Figure 13-A), they sometimes wore weighted cords over the ears (Figure 13-B).

There are still in existence three pairs of spectacles which belonged to Saint Filippo Neri (1515–95)—one pair of horn, one of leather, and one of lead, the latter with the fragment of a frontal bow, to be inserted under the hat. But Saint Filippo was evidently not one to take chances, for on each side of the lead spectacles there was also a little ring through which a cord could be passed to encircle the ears.

According to Dr Bourgeois (in his *Besicles de nos ancêtres*, published in 1923), a form of binocle existed in the sixteenth century, constructed of two large round lenses mounted on long and slightly curved arms, joined at the opposite end, which

HIERONYMVS CAPIVACCEVS PATAVINVS PHILOS. ET MEDICINÆ PROFESSOR.

Fig. 10 : Girolamo Capivaccio, Paduan professor of philosophy and medicine. Engraving after a painting by J. Rouyer, *c.* 1580

F.E.—C

Fig. 11 : Sir Thomas More (1478–1535).
Painting by Holbein

was held in the hand. The binocle folded into a protective sheath which Dr Bour-geois thought was probably of horn. The two lenses could also be superimposed to form a single magnifying glass. No examples of this sixteenth-century glass have been found; but a manuscript of 1600, now in Nürnberg, does show drawings of double eyeglasses (Plate 3-E) similar to Dr Bourgeois's description. It seems more than likely, in fact, that this is the source of his information. These glasses may or may not ever have been manufactured. They were evidently of horn, they undoubtedly folded into a handle of horn, and there is a drawing to indicate that the lenses could be superimposed and used as a single glass. It seems, however, that they were actually held with the lenses downward, the handle in front of the forehead (see Jost Amman's woodcut on the dedication page).

In 1525 in France the spectacle makers and the mirror makers were combined into a single guild. In 1582 they were joined by the toy makers. After 1557, in Nürn-berg, locally made spectacles were permitted to be sold only in the shops of their manufacturers; and imported Venetian spectacles were to be sold only in the streets. The Venetian lenses were considered to be of very high quality, whereas the German frames were superior to the Italian.

Fig. 12 : Cardinal Niño de Guevara. Painting by El Greco, 1596. The glasses are
held on with loops around the ears

Fig. 13 : Chinese eyeglasses : (a) Tungusian woman. Forehead rest and ear loops. (After
Vereschagin.) (b) Chinese eyeglasses with weighted cords. (After a drawing in Davis's
*The Chinese*)

*Ecco la barqua delli mal Contenti*

Fig. 14 : REFRAIN OF THE MALCONTENTS. Anonymous Italian engraving, sixteenth century

An English book entitled *A Briefe Treatise touching the Preseruation of the Eie-sight, consisting partly in Good Order of Diet and partly in Use of Medicines*, evidently published in 1586, mentioned the usefulness of tinted glasses. In 1591 lenses of amber saturated in linseed oil were developed for protection against the sun.

Despite the widespread use of spectacles, they were still looked upon with suspicion by many physicians. Dr Georg Bartisch of Dresden, the most famous oculist of the sixteenth century, advised against their use, writing in 1583 :

'It is much better and more useful that one leaves spectacles alone. For naturally a person sees and recognizes something better when he has nothing in front of his eyes than when he has something there. It is much better that one should preserve his two eyes than that he should have four.'

PLATE 2 : THE SIXTEENTH CENTURY
1500–1600

A  1510, Italian.

B  First half, English.  Made of horn.

C  *c.* 1500, German.  Made of horn.

D  Early years, Flemish.

E  1583, German (Dresden).  Leather and horn.

F  *c.* 1600, German.  Leather and horn. From a manuscript in Nürnberg.

G  *c.* 1600, German.  Leather.  From a manuscript in Nürnberg.

(For Spanish styles with ear-loops, see Figures 10 and 12.)

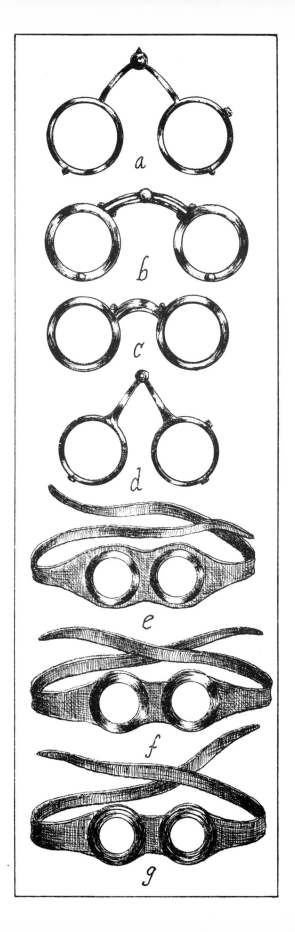

38

Plate 3 : The Sixteenth Century
1500–1600

A  German. Spectacle makers' 'master-piece'. The same designs for the master-pieces continued to be used in Nürnberg until 1723.

B  German. Spectacle makers' master-piece with the Regensburg coat of arms.

C  German. Spectacle makers' master-piece.

D  c. 1600, German.

E  c. 1600, German. Folding eye-glasses of horn. From a manuscript in Nürnberg. Whether or not the design was ever actually manu-factured is not certain. They were held with the lenses downward, the handle in front of the forehead.

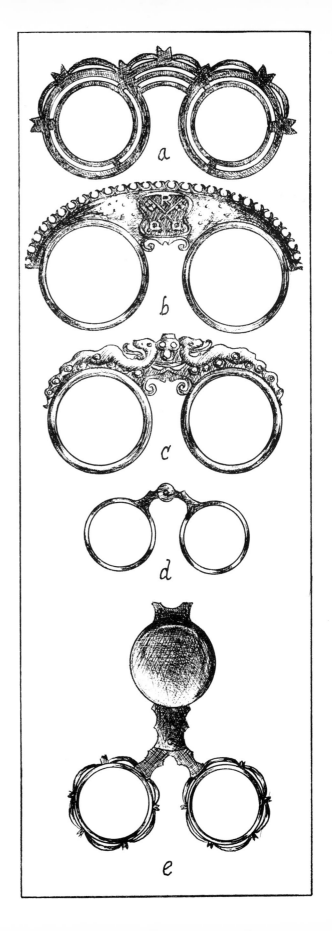

Fig. 15 : Knives Combs or Inkhornes.  Engraving by Mauron, published by Tempest,
1711

# 4 · The Seventeenth Century

Spectacles are for sight and not for shew;
Necessity doth spectacles commend;
Was't not for need, there is but very few
That would for wearing Spectacles contend.

JOHN BUNYAN

Although the seventeenth century did not bring dramatic developments in spectacles, at least in their outward appearance, it did bring notable refinements in workmanship in both frames and lenses. Along with the high-quality spectacles, there were also cheap ones for mass consumption. And now that spectacles, whatever the quality, were available to everybody, class distinctions among the styles inevitably arose.

## THE PERSPECTIVE GLASS

In the early days of spectacles, when they were still expensive and after they had become a sort of status symbol through being worn by men of learning, they were adopted by those who could afford to pay for them and thus came to symbolize social status as well. Then, when cheap spectacles became readily available, the rich and the fashionable, unwilling to give them up since they had nothing to replace them, demanded more expensive materials and finer workmanship.

But since nationalities other than the Spanish and the Chinese (and to some slight extent the Italian) did not like the idea of tying their glasses around their ears, some new style seemed to be required. The innovation turned out to be a reversion to the single glass—smaller than the early reading glass, usually with a lens for distance vision rather than reading, and often designed to be suspended from a cord or ribbon around the neck, as in Plate 4-E. This was known in England as a *perspective glass*. Once it had become established among the fashionable, spectacles were out of fashion, though never out of use, for more than three hundred years.

In Shakespeare's time the lower classes probably used nose-glasses mounted in leather, whereas the upper classes were more likely to use the perspective glass. We find, for example, that when Coriolanus (*c.* 1610) enters Rome triumphantly,

All tongues speak of him, and the bleared sights
Are spectacled to see him.

Fig. 16 : Gentleman with perspective glass.
Early seventeenth-century engraving by Piazzetta

But in the last act of *All's Well that Ends Well* (c. 1606) Bertram, a courtier, says :

> Admiringly, my liege, at first
> I stack my choice upon her, ere my heart
> Durst make too bold a herald of my tongue,
> Where the impression of my eye unfixing,
> Contempt his scornful perspective did lend me,
> Which warped the line of every other favour,
> Scorned a fair colour, or expressed it stolen,
> Extended or contracted all proportions
> To a most hideous object.

The perspective glass, if loaned to someone for whose eye it was not intended, might well distort or warp objects observed through it. Figure 16 shows a gentleman of the period using his perspective glass.

In 1644 there appeared a theological pamphlet bearing the following title : *A prospective Glasse, wherein The Child in understanding is enabled to see what the wicked*

*Counsellours did above twenty years ago (to maintain the Protestant Religion :) as clearly as the Man can see what they have done these 3. years past for the same pretended end, with the helpe of Chrystall Spectacles.* The 'prospective Glasse' is no doubt the same as a perspective glass—at least, it is so defined by the *Dictionary of Archaic and Provincial Words*. This same dictionary, however, defines *perspective* as a 'reflecting glass', not a lens. Which one is meant here it would be difficult to say. Certainly single lenses were much used, whatever the terminology. Frequently those lenses designed for distance viewing were referred to as *young* glasses (to be used by young people, that is), whereas the reading glasses, more often mounted in a double spectacle frame, were known as *old* glasses.

SPECTACLE FRAMES

For these 'old' glasses, light steel frames with round lenses were used early in the century. Silver, gold, brass, horn, and leather were also available. Randle Holme, in his *Academy of Armoury*, published in England in 1688, described spectacles as 'round glasses set in frames of siluer or bone, which according to the age of the person that useth them, are wrought thicker in the midle of the glasse then in the sides, which makes any thing bigger that is seene throw it'.

The first real attempt to establish rules for the numbering and selection of lenses seems to have been made by Valdés in Seville in 1623. Prior to that each maker simply scratched on each lens a number indicating the age for which he considered it most suitable. Valdés believed that women had weaker vision than men and required stronger lenses. Later, in the eighteenth century, lenses were graded according to radius of curvature.

The lenses were now often joined with a semi-circular spring, which kept the spectacles on the nose somewhat better than the rigid nosepiece which had been used previously (Plates 3-D, 4-A-D, 5-A). Sometimes cords were attached to the sides of the frames and looped over the ear in the Spanish style. But in most countries this was evidently not considered a satisfactory answer to the problem. The cords continued to be worn, however, by the Orientals (Figure 17).

One ugly and probably uncomfortable solution was the *forehead frame*—a metal band worn around the forehead. To this were riveted two round metal (usually steel) rings for lenses. Later the rings were made of horn instead of metal.

Since the books of the London Spectacle Makers' Company were burned in the Great Fire, we have almost no information as to the exact form of spectacles in use in London between 1629 and 1666. But in 1671 large numbers of French spectacles with tin mountings were imported into England. In Nürnberg at this time metal frames were the same price as leather and horn.

Since the early metal frames made in Nürnberg were hammered out by hand

Fig. 17 : Gouache by Tomokiyo, also known as Minenobu (1662–1708). Spectacles have green ribbons or cords attached for looping around the ears. The case is of black leather with a decorative gold border

and there was no way of putting the name and mark of the manufacturer on the frame itself, cards containing this information were printed first from woodblocks, later from copper engravings, and pasted on the boxes of spectacles. Even after machine manufacture made it possible to stamp the frames with the identifying name and symbol, the cards continued to be used.

In 1675, judging from Yarwell's shop print (Figure 20), horn frames, with the bridge slit for flexibility, were in use (see also Plate 5-F). Cuming describes a similar pair of about the same period : 'The frames are of tortoise-shell, the broad arched spring consisting of four lamina, formed by equidistant slits ; the lenses are plano-concave, with broad, unpolished margins. The case is almost as curious as the instrument. It is a flat oval box of beechwood, the interior sunk in the form of spectacles, and the surface of the cover stamped with a border of crosses, the centre being adorned with a dice pattern ; and it is secured by a brass hook and staple. From the make and style of decoration of the case, there can be little doubt that this specimen is of German origin.' Figure 21 shows several forms of spectacle cases in carved wood and engraved iron. All except number 3 date from the seventeenth century.

Although a great deal of money could be spent on elegant eyeglasses, as well as cases, ordinary ones were easily within the reach of most people. In an accounting of Claude Lestourneau, receiver, made in Paris in 1612–13, we find listed an

Fig. 18 : Drawing by Rembrandt, 1639

expenditure 'for nine spectacle cases at the rate of twenty sous each. For four and a half dozen glass spectacles at the rate of five sous each.'

According to the records of the Spectacle Makers' Company, late seventeenth-century black (presumably horn) frames were sold for 5d. per pair, black slit frames for 1s. 4d., four-slit frames for 2s. 1d., and ordinary white spectacles for 7d. The latter were probably of metal and of a type to be seen, von Rohr believes, in the lawyer's hands in Hogarth's *Marriage à la Mode*.

Towards the end of the century leather replaced horn in England. In J. Marshall's shop print (*c.* 1694) we are informed that he 'also makes very neat Leather Frames for Spectacles, which are not subject to break as Horn or Tortois Shell'. A later shop print indicates that J. Marshall 'was the first Maker of Neats-Leather Frames for Spectacles : they being the most serviceable of any other yet made'.

Protective glasses were made in several colours, including various shades of red, yellow, blue, and green. Valdés especially recommended light yellow and blue. He advised against single glasses, which he said would make the eyes unequal.

In December 1666 Samuel Pepys, who was having considerable trouble with his eyes, wrote in his diary that he intended to get some green spectacles. The following week he had still done nothing about it : 'I do truly find that I have over-wrought my eyes, so that now they are become weak and apt to be tired, and all

Fig. 19 : Carlo Dolci.  Self-portrait, 1674

excess of light makes them sore. . . . My Lord Bruncker do advise as a certain cure to use green spectacles, which I will do.'  Good as his word, he later added : 'I did this evening buy me a pair of green spectacles, to see whether they will help my eyes or no.  Then to the office and did business till my eyes began to be bad.'

After a good deal of experimenting with reading through tubes, he wrote in October of the following year : 'To several places to buy a hat and books and neck cloth, and several errands I did before I got home, and among other bought me two new pair of spectacles of Turlington, who, it seems, is famous for them ; and his daughter, he being out of the way, do advise me two very young sights, and promises me very great ease from them, and I will try them'.

A few weeks later he was still seeking help : 'From the Exchange I took a coach and went to Turlington, the great spectacle maker, for advice, who dissuades me from using old spectacles, but rather young ones, and do tell me that nothing can wrong my eyes more than for me to use reading glasses which do magnify much'. Unfortunately the glasses were of little avail, and eventually Pepys could no longer see well enough to continue his journal.

The Spanish, whose taste in eyeglasses as well as in hair styles, departed somewhat from that of other European countries, evidently had acquired a certain reverence for spectacles beyond their practical value.  Marie de Berneville, Countess d'Aulnoy, makes this clear in a letter written from Madrid in March 1679 :

'On my first visit to the Princess of Montelon I was surprised to see many young ladies with large spectacles on their noses and fastened to their ears.  But what seemed strangest to me was that they made no use of them where they were really necessary—they only talked while they had them on.  I asked the Marchioness de la Rosa the reason for it. . . .  She fell to laughing at my question and told me that it was done to make them look serious.  They did not wear them for necessity, but to draw respect.  "Do you see that lady ?" she said to me.  "I do not believe that since she was ten years old she ever left them off except when she was in bed." It is so common a thing to wear them that I understand there are different spectacles according to rank.  As a man increases the size of his fortune, he increases the size of his lenses.  The grandees of Spain wear them as broad as one's hand.  They fasten them behind their ears and leave them off as seldom as they do their collars.' This undoubtedly explains the unusual number of portraits of distinguished

Fig. 20 : Yarwell's shop print, showing slit-bridge spectacles, *c.* 1675

Fig. 21 : Spectacle cases.  Number 3 is an eighteenth-century case of carved wood ;  the others are of carved wood and engraved iron, seventeenth century.  From Heymann's *Lunettes et lorgnettes de jadis*

Spaniards of the period with their glasses. The Marquis d'Astorga (Figure 22) even commissioned a marble bust of himself wearing spectacles.

A Spanish manuscript by Daza da Valdés, entitled *On the Use of Glasses*, published in 1623, included an imaginary and enlightening dialogue between a doctor and his pupil, Apollinarus, on some of the practical problems involved in wearing spectacles :

APOLLINARUS : If everyone is like me, it is certain they can hardly profit from your advice, which is to put spectacles on the middle of the nose so that they will not be too close to the eyes, because that causes too much swelling of the nose.

DOCTOR : I will give you a solution to that problem, which is to wear the spectacles attached to a wing or paddle which can be inserted between the hat and the head, and with that the spectacles will remain in the air and you will be able to see, holding them suspended by this wing, without which they would touch your nose.

APOLLINARUS : This is only for kings, who hardly ever take off their hat to anyone ; but I, who am a poor man, cannot use that method, for at the first compliment the whole apparatus would fall to the ground ; but believe me that if it were not for that defect, I would have gone off already to draw the design.

DOCTOR : There are several who put their glasses so heavily on the end of the nose that they can neither speak freely nor let the humors flow from there, holding them with the hat instead of putting them in the place where it seems that nature has made a place for them alone. I have seen others better advised, who attached them to the ears by a cord in order to free the hands.

Although both the extension under the hat (Plate 7-F and Figure 29 in Chapter 5) and the cords around the ears (Figures 10 and 12) were extensively worn, they were clearly stop-gap solutions to be used only until something better was invented. The cords over the ears marked the end of the Spanish influence on the development of spectacles.

In most European countries, other than Spain, spectacles were not considered fashionable, as we have mentioned, and were not worn by elegant people, at least in public. We do, however, have the report of a lady who could not resist spying on Louis XIV and Madame de Maintenon one day as they were getting into their carriage. Madame, who was dressed in a faded-leaf coloured damask ornamented with a cross of four diamonds, was hardly settled in the carriage before she put on her spectacles and drew out some work from her bag.

Spectacles were sold both in shops (Figure 23) and by itinerant peddlers, who often promised improvements in health or welfare as a result of looking at the sun or moon through various colours of spectacles. Some of the peddlers sold only spectacles (Figure 24), whereas others had a variety of products (Figure 15).

It is curious to note once again a parallel between the Spanish and the Chinese,

Fig. 22 : Marqués de Velada y Astorga, Vice-
roy of Naples. Engraving after a
painting by De la Borde, 1668

among whom there existed a superstitious reverence for spectacles. Lebensohn
points out that 'tortoise shell comes from a sacred animal ; the lenses are made of
lucky stones, such as rock crystal, topaz, and amethyst, which are found among
the sacred mountains, and are ground with sand from the sacred rivers. Glasses
are worn not only for visual defects, but for good luck and for the relief of all sorts
of ocular ailments. Moreover, they serve as a badge of superior social status, and
accordingly frames are often worn without lenses.'

According to Rasmussen, the Chinese used tortoise shell, brass, and silver but
never gold for frames and mountings. In using shell, they first made it into flat
plates, then cut it out and finished it by hand filing. The brass they cast in moulds,
then finished by hand. They used silver only occasionally, as, for example, during
periods of mourning, when white was the traditional colour. The parts were
riveted together, never assembled with screws.

For the lenses the Chinese used crystals, not glass ; and Rasmussen believes
that, contrary to some reports, they did not use precious stones. The crystals
were of several types, such as water crystals (white), tea crystals (brown), and black
crystals (ink or smoke-coloured). And in each of these general categories there
were additional classifications—clear, clouded, streaked net, streaked wave, and

streaked fish scale. The value of these varied considerably, depending on clearness and lack of imperfections. The same materials continued to be used into the twentieth century.

Chinese spectacle cases were commonly made of wood, either carved and painted or covered with cloth, clay, embroidery, or shark's skin. The cloth and embroidery cases were usually decorated with floral designs. Tassels and beads were often added to the finished case. Most cases were more or less oval in shape and all of about the same size.

## THE GUILDS

Once again the spectacle makers banded together into guilds and were granted charters. The guilds consisted of masters, journeymen, and apprentices; and before becoming a master one had to have approved certain 'master-pieces' (see Plates 3-A-B-C and 4-G). Members were expected to maintain a certain standard of excellence in their work.

In England the Worshipful Company of Spectacle Makers was established in 1629 under Charles I. Regulations were strict, and even the Great Fire of London was evidently insufficient cause for any notable relaxation of the rules. The following is from the minutes of the Court of Assistants for April 20, 1668:

'Isaac Alt owing 40ˢ to this Company for Quarteridge due at La: day last and desiring some time to pay the same It is ordered That iff he paies Tenne shillings parte thereof to Mr. Warden Radford within 20 daies and gives bill to him for this Companies vse to pay 30ˢ more on the 28th day of October next in full of his quarteridge And then likewise payeing to Mr. Warden Radford 40ˢ for his fine for taking an Apprentice according to the ordinances he shall then take and bynde an Apprentice to him without further order, and after paies the 10ˢ downe in Court.

'It is thought fitt and soe ordered that William Spencer doe not furhher or longer ymploy Thomas Spencer his son at the Trade of Spectacle making or anything therevnto belonging ffor that the Thomas Spencer the son is not at this present an Apprentice neither hath he served Seaven yeares to the same Trade It being contrary to the ordinances & if he doth or shall ymploy him at this Trade any longer Then the said Wm Spencer to be sued at Comon Lawe for the same.

'It is ordered that William Spencer be arrested at Comon Lawe for 3ˡˡ he owes to this Company the same having bene due above these 7 yeares past.'

On the same day the following case was disposed of:

'Nicholas Sheild upon search by the Mr. and Wardens of this Company at his house in ffenchurch streete having found there and he on worke on them eighteene paire of Spectacles being looking glasse wrought only on the one side and not on the other side for wᶜʰ according to the ordinances he is fined 20ˢ for every paire w^ch is demaunded of him here in Court the w^ch he refuseth to pay. And he owing 5 for his quarteridge doth now pay the same to Warden Radford here in Court.'

Two months later his fine was reduced to six pounds, which he agreed to pay in two instalments, the second to be due on Christmas day. For September 30 however, we find the following entry:

'At this Court Nichas Sheild paies downe in Court three pounds parte of the six pounds fine ymposed on him last Court And did here earnestly entreate the Company to accept of the said three pounds in full paym^t and to remitt the residue And doth promise not to offend in the least hereafter in the making setting vp or fitting for himselfe or any others any Spectacles made of looking glasse wrought onely on one side or in that kind or any other made badd This Court taking his poore Condition into Consideration Doe accept of the said Three pounds in full payem^t and satisfaction of and for the said Six pounds And the said Nichas Sheild Is hereby fully discharged of the same.'

In the records of 1669 we find reports of the searching of haberdashers' shops for spectacles not made by members of the guild. The searchers were successful in four of the shops and proceeded to break the spectacles by consent of the owner. Following is the report on the search of the fourth shop:

Fig. 23 : DE BRILLEMAAKER.
Engraving by J. van
Luiken, *c.* 1695

Fig. 24 : SPECTACLE PEDDLERS. Early seventeenth-century etching

'At the house of Mr. Clarke a wholesale Haberdasher living against London Wall There was found in his shop 31 dozen of ffrench Spectacles The said Mr. Clarke desired that the Wardens would break both frames and glasse of them of his own voluntary and free will sayeing he would deale no more in them. But the Wardens did onely breake the glasse and lefte the whited Copper frames vndefaced. But upon his very much complayning of the greate losse he had susteyned by the late dreadful ffire and the losse in the defacing of these 31 dozen of Spectacles and promising never to deale more in them being fforque Spectacles The Wardens gave him freely Tenne shillings in money the w$^{ch}$ he tooke very thankfully.'

On 8th July 1669 came an order :

'That an Indictm$^t$ be preferred at the next Sessions for London against John Briggs of the parish of St. Brides London Gardner for that he doth vse the Trade of Spectaclemaking by making and grynding watch glasses Convexe and Concave he having not served yeares to the same Trade as an Apprentice.'

In August 1671 the wardens were still in pursuit of illegal spectacles :

'Mrs. Elizabeth Bagnall widow a wholesale Habre in her shop were found two and twenty dozen of English spectacles all very badd both in the glasse and frames not fitt to be put to sale she saith her husband and her man are both lately dead and she knowes not of whome they were bought being in the shop at their decease They are all Seized and taken away by the Mr and wardens by vertue of the Chre [Charter] of this Company and the Lo : Mayors warrant and carryed to Guildhall and there in the Mayors Court by a Jury were found bad and deceiptfull and by the Judgment of the Court Condemned to be broken defaced and spoyled both glasse and frames the w^{ch} Judgm^{t} was executed accordingly in Canning streete *on the remayning parte of London stone* where the same were with a hammer broken all in pieces.'

## THE PROSPECT GLASS

Perhaps the most significant development in the seventeenth century, at least in terms of fashion, came about as a result of the invention of the telescope, usually credited to Galileo. Galileo himself, however, gave credit to the Dutch for the

Fig. 25 : Soldier with case of spectacles. Early seventeenth-century engraving

Fig. 26 : MEDICO. Italian engraving by
G. M. Mitelli, 1675

discovery of the principle which made his telescope possible. In 1606 a spectacle
maker of Middelburg, named Lippershey, applied for a patent for a telescope. The
committee considered the request at the beginning of October ; but before reaching
a decision, they asked Lippershey to construct a double telescope with both tubes
united.

Two years later Lippershey's claims were disputed by another inventor named
Metius, who claimed priority because of his research. In 1609 the government
refused to patent Lippershey's telescope because he was not the only one to construct one. About the same time, a third contender, Zach Janssen, appeared.

The Janssens, father and son, spectacle makers of Middelburg, are known to
have made both telescopes and microscopes. William Boreel, a native of Middelburg and Ambassador to England in 1619, described a microscope made by the
Janssens as 'a tube eighteen inches in length and two inches in diameter, of gilt
brass, supported by three dolphins on a base of ebony. Objects placed on this base
were considerably magnified through the tube.'

It was not long before the principle of the telescope began to be applied to non-
astronomical devices of a more modest size, regular production of such devices
being undertaken in England about 1680. Although it was not until the eighteenth
century that these miniature telescopes competed, in a sense, with eyeglasses, they

were used, none the less, much as binoculars came to be used several centuries later. Various terms were coined to designate them. *Prospect glass* was used in England as early as 1617 and continued to be used throughout the eighteenth century. Later they were also called *spyglasses*. *Prospect glass*, unfortunately, is easily confused with *prospective* or *perspective* glass, which, as we have seen, was something quite different.

A good deal of confusion also arises from the fact that the French called them *lorgnettes*. The term seems to have first been used in the time of Louis XIV in the *Mémoires de Saint-Simon*. The French *Dictionnaire de l'Académie* defined it as a *petite lunette d'approche*—a small telescope. Although the term was used for more than a century in this way, its meaning did eventually change in France. And when it was taken over into English, it meant something still different. Therefore, to avoid some of the confusion, the French term, when used in its original sense, will be italicized.

Although these small telescopes had their practical uses, they were evidently irresistible as playthings. In a letter to Madame de Grignan, her daughter, Madame de Sévigné (1626–96) described her delight with an early *lorgnette*:

'By the way, have I told you about an admirable eyeglass which entertained us in the boat? It is a masterpiece; it is even more perfect than the one the abbot loaned to Grignan. . . . You can imagine the use we made of it on the banks of the Loire, but this is what I do with it here. You know that when reversed it puts things farther away, and I turn it on Mademoiselle du Plessis and I find her suddenly two leagues from me. . . . When one is oppressed by bad company, one has only to send for one's glass and turn it the wrong way.'

THE OCULISTS

In 1666, about the time Madame de Sévigné was putting people at a distance with her spyglass, there was published a curious volume entitled *The Compleat* BONE SETTER *Enlarged: Being the method of Curing Broken Bones, dislocated Joynts, and Ruptures, commonly called* BROKEN BELLIES. *To which is added, the Perfect Oculist, the Mirrour of Health, the Judgment of Urines. Treating of the* PESTILENCE, *And all other Diseases written originally by Frier Moulton, Englished and Enlarged by Robert Turner Med. The Second Edition. London, Printed for Nath. Crouch, at the Rose and Crown in Exchange Alley, near Lombard Street.*

*The Perfect Oculist*, which was not included in the first edition, was evidently Turner's work. Despite advances in ophthalmology, Turner freely prescribed medieval-sounding medicines requiring the use of celandine, fennel, endive, betany, rue, vervain, pimpernel, eyebright, maidenhair fern, ewe's milk, red snails, and hog's grease. There was also for the eyes a powder called Conaventure, made of sugar candy, tutty, and rose water.  This had to be fumigated with aloes and frankincense, dried and powdered, and kept in a box made of pewter or brass.  It was to be inserted into the eye only with a silver pencil.  For squint he recommended the blood of a tuttle (*sic*) or the head of a bat—powdered, of course.  And for strengthening weak sight he proposed hanging the eyes of a cow around the neck.

Fig. 27 : La Veve.  French engraving by Moncormet,
mid-seventeenth century

PLATE 4 : THE SEVENTEENTH
CENTURY 1600–1700

A  German.  Frame of heavy brass wire
   tied with binding thread to hold the
   lenses firmly in place.  This style
   continued in use throughout the
   eighteenth century.  (*Nordiska Museet, Stockholm*)

B  Rigid frames made of leather.

C  End of the century, Chinese.  Made
   of horn.  Small holes at either side
   of frame are for attaching cords.

D  End of the century.  Spring frames
   with attached spring bridge.

E  Perspective glass with silver mounting.  These were used by fashionable  gentlemen  throughout  the
   century.

F  Frames made of brass wire.  After
   the lenses were inserted, the frames
   were pulled tight and tied with binding  thread.  Not used before the
   seventeenth  century.

G  1687, German.  'Master-piece' (see
   Plate 3).

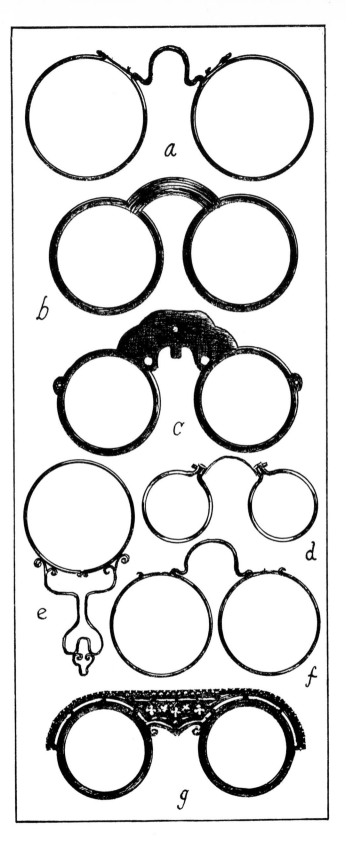

PLATE 5 : THE SEVENTEENTH
    CENTURY 1600–1700

A  *c.* 1700, German.  Spring frames with wire winding, tied with binding thread.  Made in Nürnberg.

B  Last quarter.  Brass magnifying glass, used in England.

C  End of the century, Swiss.  Prospect glass, used in England.  The outer body is of green shagreen, the single draw-tube is covered in green tooled vellum, and the mounts are of ivory, that for the object-glass bearing the inscription 'Giuseppe Moschino in Geneva'.  (*Science Museum, London*)

D  1677, French.  Pivoted eyeglasses. Also worn in England.

E  *c.* 1600, German.  However, they were probably known as early as 1550.  Double horn frames.  The bridge, made of curved strips of horn, gives enough flexibility to hold the glasses on the nose.

F  1675, English.  Slit frames to give slight flexibility.  (See also Figure 20.)

G  *c.* 1600, German.  Horn rims, side springs also of horn.

H  *c.* 1630, German.  Gilded silver. Made in Augsburg.

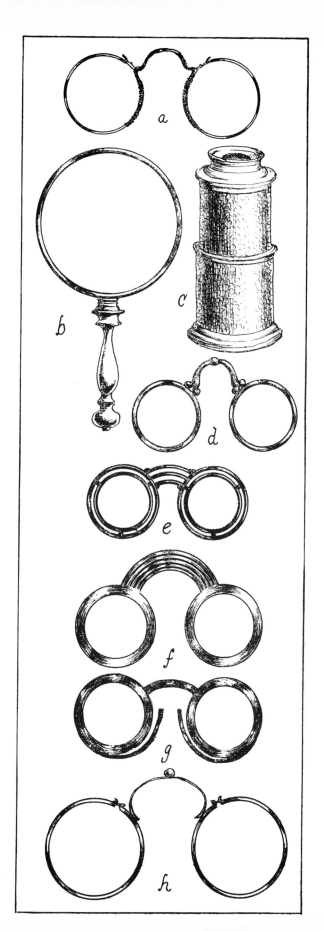

Fig. 28: THE SLEEPING CONGREGATION.  Engraving by Hogarth of 1736, retouched by Hogarth in 1762

# 5 · The Eighteenth Century

Everything was made for a purpose;
everything is necessary for the fulfilment
of that purpose. Observe that noses
have been made for spectacles; therefore
we have spectacles.

DR PANGLOSS 'CANDIDE'

The eighteenth century brought a number of striking developments in eyeglasses, the most significant being a practical means of keeping them on. Unfortunately, these glasses were evidently too utilitarian in appearance to be considered fashionable. The more decorative and stylish forms of glasses were mercilessly ridiculed by the satirists as affectations. As usual, those at whom the satire was directed paid no attention and continued to carry their fancy eyeglasses whether they needed them or not.

## THE EARLY YEARS

At the beginning of the century the style of glasses worn was much the same as it had been. Cuming describes a pair of spectacles dating probably from the time of Queen Anne: 'The frames are of light coloured tortoise-shell, united by a steel spring, which has a hinge at each extremity so that one may be folded over the other when placed in the case. The case is of wood, covered with fish-skin, and is in the form of a heraldic rose.' Perhaps these were something like the pair shown in Plate 6-D. Another pair he believes to date from early in the reign of George I (1714–27): 'The lenses are of Brazil pebble, mounted in black frames, with the steel spring jointed in the centre, so that one lens may slide over the other, the lower part of the circular case being elongated to receive the spring. The case is of wood covered with fish-skin.' These may well have been similar to those shown in Plate 6-E.

Diderot points out that for rigid, non-folding spectacles one must have a case with two circular compartments for the two lenses. Such a case is shown in Figure 21.

Although all-leather frames were evidently abandoned in England in the early part of the eighteenth century, the use of leather persisted in rims to which were attached steel springs (Plate 6-C). These looked very much like horn—so much so,

Fig. 29 : Un Trio Convaincu. Detail from an eighteenth-century gouache, showing spectacles with frontal bow

in fact, that a study of certain of these frames still in existence required microscopic examination to determine that they were actually made of leather instead of horn. Later, horn was used in the same way, replacing leather.

There was an attempt in the eighteenth century to revive for the use of women the sixteenth-century style of eyeglasses with a front bow which slid under the cap (Plate 7-F); but since this style interfered with the coiffure, it was soon abandoned.

In Swift's *Gulliver's Travels*, written 1720–25, Gulliver found an unexpectedly practical use for his spectacles:

'I walked down to the North-East Coast over against Blefuscu; where lying down behind a Hillock, I took out my small Pocket Perspective Glass and viewed the Enemy's Fleet at anchor, consisting of about fifty Men of War and a Great number of Transports. . . . While I was thus employed, the enemy discharged several Thousand Arrows, many of which stuck in my Hands and Face; and besides the Smart, gave me much disturbance in my work. My greatest apprehension was for my Eyes, which I should have infallibly lost, if I had not suddenly thought of an Expedient. I kept, among other little Necessaries, a Pair of Spectacles in a private Pocket which, as I observed before, had escaped the Emperor's Searchers. These I took out and fastened as strongly as I could upon my Nose; and thus armed went on boldly with my work in spite of the Enemy's Arrows, many of which struck against the Glasses of my Spectacles, but without any other Effect further than a little to discompose them.'

Spectacles, which were considered highly unfashionable, were worn in private even by the rich and the fashionable. On New Year's day in 1751 the duc de Luynes sent to Marie Lesczyñska a casket which contained, among other things, a pair of spectacles, with which she was delighted. On the following day she wrote to him: 'Do you know what I was doing when I received the letter from Monseigneur, Bishop of Bayeux? I was with—guess who?—the beautiful eyes of my casket. . . .'

The Queen's spectacles were undoubtedly beautifully made and very costly; but for the masses there were quantities of cheap spectacles, often badly made. In London in 1773 the cheapest English nose-glasses sold for a shilling, but imported German ones could be had for four pence. In an attempt to capitalize on their skill in mass production, the south German manufacturers, once noted for their fine workmanship, turned out shoddy spectacles as fast and as cheaply as possible. The greenish lenses were often poorly ground, and the metal frames were only brass thinly coated with silver, which soon wore off. It was these cheap German spectacles which figured prominently in one chapter of *The Vicar of Wakefield*:

'Moses came slowly on foot, and sweating under the deal box, which he had strapped round his shoulders like a peddler.

'"Welcome, welcome, Moses; well, my boy, what have you brought us from the Fair?"

Fig. 30 : A Spectacle Peddler. Etching
by Dietrich, 1741

"'I have brought you myself," cried Moses, with a sly look, and resting the box on the dresser.

"'Ah, Moses," cried my wife, "that we know, but where is the horse?"

"'I have sold him," cried Moses, "for three pounds five shillings and two pence."

"'Well done, my good boy," returned she, "I knew you would touch them off. Between ourselves, three pounds five shillings and two pence is no bad day's work. Come, let us have it then."

"'I have brought back no money," cried Moses again. "I have laid it all out in a bargain, and here it is," pulling out a bundle from his breast : "Here they are— a gross of green spectacles with silver rims and shagreen cases."

"'A gross of green spectacles !" repeated my wife in a faint voice. "And you have parted with the colt and brought us back nothing but a gross of green paltry spectacles !"

"'Dear Mother," cried the boy, "why won't you listen to reason ? I had them a dead bargain, or I should not have bought them. The silver rims alone will sell for double the money."

"'A fig for the silver rims,'' cried my wife, in a passion; "I dare swear they won't sell for above half the money at the rate of broken silver, five shillings an ounce.''

"'You need be under no uneasiness,'' cried I, "about selling the rims, for they are not worth sixpence, for I perceive they are only copper varnished over.''

"'What,'' cried my wife, "not silver, the rims not silver!''

"'No,'' cried I, "no more silver than your saucepan.''

"'And so,'' returned she, "we have parted with the colt and have only got a gross of green spectacles, with copper rims and shagreen cases! A murrain take such trumpery. The blockhead has been imposed upon and should have known his company better.''

"'There, my dear,'' cried I, "you are wrong. He should not have known them at all.''

Fig. 31 : La Lunetière. Late eighteenth-century engraving by Binet from *Contemporaines*

Fig. 32 : Spectacle Peddler.   Eighteenth-century etching, after a
painting by P. Cramer

'"Mary, hang the idiot," returned she, "to bring me such stuff.   If I had them,
I would throw them in the fire."

'"There again you are wrong, my dear," cried I; "for though they be copper,
we will keep them by us, as copper spectacles, you know, are better than nothing."'

In rural areas spectacles were sold by itinerant peddlers, as shown in the 1741
etching by Dietrich (Figure 30).   As always in such cases, they were selected
according to the age of the buyer or simply by trial and error.   But in the cities all
the latest forms of eyeglasses and telescopes were to be found in special shops.   In
1756 there appeared in the *Boston Evening Post* the following advertisement
illustrated with a pair of nose glasses, probably of horn or leather : 'Just imported
in the Scow Two Brothers, Cpt. Marsden, from London and to be sold by Hannah
Breitnall at the Sign of the Spectacles, in the Second-Street near Black-Horse-
Alley.   Variety of the finest chrystal spectacles, set in temple, steel, leather, and
other frames.   Likewise true Venetian green spectacles for weak or watery eyes,
of various sorts.   Also concave spectacles for short sighted persons, magnifying
and reading glasses, telescopes, perspectives, with multiplying glasses, and glasses
for Davis's quadrants &c. &c.'

Figure 31 shows a well-dressed young lady of this period polishing lenses in a
French spectacle maker's shop and surrounded by telescopes, spectacles, perspective
glasses, magnifying glasses, and spyglasses, as well as miscellaneous lenses, tools,
and a very attentive young man.

But no matter where the glasses were purchased, George Adams's *Essay on*

*Vision* makes it clear that even as late as 1789 the customer still had most of the responsibility for choosing the right glasses for himself :

'Though in the choice of spectacles every one must finally determine for himself which are the Glasses through which he obtains the most distinct Vision—yet some confidence should be placed in the judgment of the Artist of whom they are purchased, and some attention paid to his directions. By trying many Spectacles the Eye is fatigued as the Eye endeavours to accomodate itself to every change that is produced. Hence the purchaser often fixes upon a pair of Spectacles not the best adapted to his sight, but those which seem to relieve him most, while his Eyes are in a forced and unnatural state ; and consequently, when he gets home and they are returned to their natural state, he finds what he had chosen fatiguing and injurious to the sight.'

Spectacle cases were sometimes very ornate and very expensive. According to the *Mercure de France* for October 1775, an enamelled gold snuff box with a watch in the top and a pair of spectacles in the bottom could be had for 2400 *livres*. Some cases were designed to hold two pair of spectacles, one with tinted lenses to wear in the sunlight. Figure 21 shows a carved case for hinged spectacles. The general

Fig. 33 : THE GROSS OF GREEN SPECTACLES.
Etching by George Cruikshank for
*The Vicar of Wakefield,* 1832

acceptance and usefulness of spectacles was reflected in the increasing mention of them in works of fiction.

A few years later, in 1782, William Cowper made his contribution to the literature about spectacles in verse :

> Between Nose and Eyes a strange contest arose—
>     The spectacles set them unhappily wrong ;
> The point in dispute was, as all the world knows,
>     To which the said spectacles ought to belong.
>
> So Tongue was the lawyer, and argued the cause
>     With a great deal of skill, and a wig full of learning ;
> While chief baron Ear sat to balance the laws,
>     So famed for his talent in nicely discerning.
>
> In behalf of the Nose, it will quickly appear,
>     And your lordship, he said, will undoubtedly find
> That the Nose has had spectacles always in wear,
>     Which amounts to possession time out of mind.
>
> Then holding the spectacles up to the court—
>     Your lordship observes they are made with a straddle
> As wide as the ridge of the Nose is ; in short,
>     Designed to sit close to it, just like a saddle.
>
> Again, would your lordship a moment suppose
>     ('Tis a case that has happened, and may be again)
> That the visage or countenance had not a nose ;
>     Pray who would, or who could, wear spectacles then ?
>
> On the whole it appears—and my argument shows,
>     With a reasoning the court will never condemn,
> That the spectacles plainly were made for the Nose,
>     And the nose was as plainly intended for them.
>
> Then, shifting his side (as a lawyer knows how),
>     He pleaded again on behalf of the Eyes ;
> But what were his arguments few people know,
>     For the court did not think they were equally wise.
>
> So his lordship decreed with a grave solemn tone,
>     Decisive and clear, without one *if* or *but*—
> That whenever the Nose put his spectacles on,
>     By daylight or candlelight—Eyes should be shut.

Fig. 34 : Daniel Chodowiecki (1726–1801).
Portrait by Anton Graff

## TEMPLE SPECTACLES

At last, nearly 350 years after the invention of spectacles, a suitable means of keeping them on was found. It appears that in the Western world temple spectacles (that is, spectacles held in place with rigid side-pieces) were invented—or, at least, perfected and effectively promoted—by Edward Scarlett, a London optician, between 1727 and 1730. Von Rohr, however, believes that they appeared somewhat earlier, perhaps as early as 1702. It is true that Valdés mentions Spanish experimentation in this direction, but evidently it was not successful. Scarlett's invention spread to Germany, France, and Spain, where it was looked upon as an English style. Minguet's Spanish broadsheet of 1763 (Figure 36) shows temple spectacles along with other styles currently in use.

Early temple spectacles were probably made of steel, usually with round lenses

Fig. 35 : Jean Baptiste Chardin. Self-portrait dated 1775. Spectacles probably of tortoise shell

and hinged side-pieces terminating in large rings, which pressed against the head to hold the spectacles on (Plate 8-B). Although no examples of Scarlett's spectacles are known to exist, a shop print bearing a diagram of them gives a good idea of what they were like (see sketch in Plate 11-G). Surprisingly, the lenses are represented as being oval. Whether this is actually a representation of oval lenses or an attempt to represent round lenses in perspective is not clear. The French called these glasses *lunettes à tempes permettant de respirer à l'aise*—temple spectacles permitting one to breathe easily. They were thus described in 1746 by Monsieur Thomin, optician to the French Queen, who offered them *au plus juste prix*. Later there were hinged or sliding extensions, as shown in the plates. Gold, silver, brass, and horn were used as well as steel.

In 1752 James Ayscough advertised his latest invention—spectacles with double-hinged side-pieces (see Plates 8-10). These became extremely popular and appear more often than any other kind in paintings, prints, and caricatures of the period. As for lenses, which were made of tinted glass as well as clear, Ayscough wrote: 'It has been found that the common white glass gives an offensive glaring light, very prejudicial to the eyes, and on that account, green and blue Glasses have been advised though they make every object appear with their own hue. . . . I was induced to make trial of a new kind of glass and of a greenish cast. It is harder. Some . . . opposed it in public lest it should hurt the craft, giving as a reason that it would spoil the sale of spectacles made of Rock Crystal and Brazil Pebbles.'

In Spain in 1763 Pablo Minguet recommended turquoise, green, or light yellow lenses but not amber or red. Andrews tells of 'a man of olden times who fastened a pair of green-tinted spectacles before the eyes of his horse so that when it looked at some straw he had placed in its manger, the animal might be deluded into thinking it was grass'.

In 1760 an English optician named Benjamin Martin published a book entitled *An Essay on Visual Glasses, (vulgarly called* SPECTACLES) *Wherein it is shewn from the Principles of* OPTICS, *and the Nature of the* EYE, *that the common Structure of those Glasses is contrary to the Rules of Art, to the Nature of Things, &c. and very prejudicial to the* EYES. The book was 'Printed for the AUTHOR, and sold at his House, two Doors below Crane-Court, Fleet-Street'. And since this was the fifth edition, evidently it sold well. Martin begins by quoting a 'remarkable Passage' from Molyneux:

'Were there no other Use of DIOPTRICS than that of Spectacles for defective Eyes, I should think the Advantage that Mankind received thereby inferior to no other Benefit whatsoever, not absolutely requisite to the support of Life. For as the Sight is the most noble and extensive of all our senses, as we make the most frequent and constant Use of our Eyes in all the Actions and Concerns of human Life, surely that which relieves the Eyes when decayed, and supplies their Defects, rendering them useful when almost useless, must needs of all others be esteemed of the greatest advantage. How melancholy is the condition of him, who only enjoys the Sight of what is immediately about him? With what disadvantage is he engaged in most of the concerns of human Life? *Reading* is to him troublesome; War more than ordinary dangerous; Trade and Commerce toilsome and unpleasant. And so likewise on the other Hand, how forlorn would the *latter Part* of most Men's lives prove, unless Spectacles were at hand to help their Eyes, and a Little Piece of Glass supplied the Decays of Nature? The curious *Mechanic*, engaged in any Minute Work, could no longer follow his Trade than to the 50th or 60th Year of his Age. The Scholar could no longer converse with his Books, or with an absent Friend in a Letter. All after that would be melancholy Idleness, or he must content himself to use another Man's Eyes for every Line. Thus forlorn was the State of most old Men, and many young before this admirable Invention, which on this very Account cannot be praised too highly.'

Martin then lists a number of objections, from the optical point of view, to the spectacles currently in use and described how he has overcome these deficiencies in his own design, which he finds 'greatly approved of, and very well received, even beyond my Expectation'. The relatively few objections he considers 'scarce worth mentioning' but mentions them anyway:

'One has said, *he can't see how to read better in these, or find them easier to his*

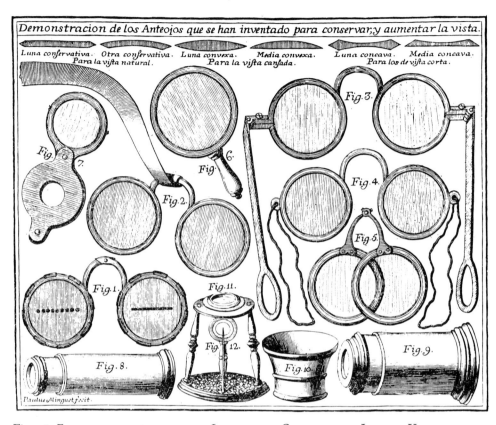

Fig. 36 : Eyeglasses which have been Invented to Conserve and Improve Vision.
Spanish broadsheet by Pablo Minguet, 1763

*Eyes, than common Spectacles.* That is undoubtedly true, and who would expect a sensible Difference immediately, if it be considered that the Eye is so admirably formed that it can view an Object tolerably well by Rays of Light refracted upon it in the worst Manner possible ? But can this be a Reason why Vision should not be performed in the best Manner ? But farther—*they do not find the Light hurt the Eye in one Glass more than in the other.* Very true ; nor do they see *the Stone grow hollow by the dripping of Water in Half an Hour* ; yet this will be the Case in Time ; and every wise Man looks to the Consequence in the Use of Things of so interesting a nature.

'Another has Objected—*that these visual Glasses have an uncouth Look, sit askew upon their Nose, &c.* To which, if any Answer be due, I can only say, that, to a judicious Person, whatever is best, has the best look ; and they sit most properly in that Position which Nature has directed. But Sir *Francis* —— has a numerous family, and when their Eyes require Assistance, 'tis natural to expect they should chuse *Spectacles*, rather than *Visual Glasses*, especially if they have the Privilege of paying a very great Price for them.

'I shall take no Notice of the low Arts that have been practiced to villify this Invention; they who pretend that I have stolen it from *some old Author*, would do well to produce that Author, lest their *Veracity* and *Honour* should be called in question; or, what perhaps they would have still less disputed, their *Wit*, in not securing to themselves what they think, in my Hands, will do them such mighty Harm.

'To those who charge me with *underselling them*, I answer, I know not their Prices; and as I have sufficient Profit on which I sell, it proves that they have taken *too much*; for which the Public must think themselves greatly obliged to their Candour and Gratitude.'

Despite Martin's enthusiasm, his reasonable prices, and the evident success of the book, his 'visual glasses' did not replace the more conventional spectacles.

Figure 36 shows a rare print of a broadsheet of 1763 illustrating types of eyeglasses in use in Spain. *Fig. 1* represents the conventional style of eyeglasses with pivoted bridge. The series of dots and the solid line represent, respectively, small holes and a narrow slit in a metal disk placed over the lines by means of tabs, as shown. These were explained rather vaguely as being useful for people in ill health to help sharpen the image. Presumably they were to correct astigmatism.

*Fig. 2* is perhaps the most interesting of all since it shows a metal strap welded to the nosepiece. This could be curved to the shape of the head and worn under the hat, thus suspending the glasses in front of the eyes and avoiding pressure on the nose. Evidently this was preferred by some people to temple spectacles (*Fig. 3*) and the old Spanish glasses with ear loops (*Fig. 4*). Minguet also mentions that some people preferred their glasses attached to a handle. *Fig. 5* shows collapsible spring glasses. Frames were made of leather, shell, and various kinds of metal.

*Fig. 6* represents a reading glass with wood or metal frames and *7* a perspective glass. The telescope and single opera glass (*Figs. 8* and *9*), Minguet suggests, can be made of either leather or cardboard. *Figs. 10-12* represent a microscope. Across the top of the print are cross sections of the types of lenses in use.

For testing eyeglasses, Minguet suggests that 'in order to find out if both lenses are identical, you open the balcony doors or the window in your room, and then find the darkest spot in the room, where you will attach a piece of white paper to the wall; and at a moderate distance, holding your glasses in your hand, you try to find the length of focus that you have, and on the piece of paper you will see if the transparency of both lenses is matched'.

Despite improvements in the construction and appearance of spectacles, they did not receive the sanction of fashion, at least outside Spain; and a gentleman frequently made some sort of apologetic remark when putting them on. George Washington, on one occasion, is reported to have said, 'Gentlemen, you will permit

Fig. 37 : Gentleman in an art gallery. From a Dutch painting by Adriaan de Lelie, 1794

me to put on my spectacles ; for, as you see, I have not only grown gray but almost blind in the service of my country'. A pair of Washington's spectacles is shown in Plate 10-F.

The early style of temple spectacles with large rings (sometimes covered in velvet) to press against the head were still being worn, as seen in the portrait of painter Daniel Chodowiecki, Figure 34. Chardin evidently wore a later model of tortoise shell (Figure 35). In 1794, in a Dutch painting of an art gallery by Adriaan de Lelie, we find a gentleman wearing spectacles with short temples with heart-shaped ends (Figure 37). At the same time eyeglasses without temples were still being worn by women (Figure 47) as well as men.

In 1770 the French spectacle makers became *opticians*, and in 1776 the French manufacturers of spectacles, mirrors, and toys were reunited with the upholsterers, furniture brokers, and leather workers. Figures 38 and 39 are reproductions of plates from Diderot's *Encyclopédie* pertaining to the manufacture of spectacles and mirrors. At the top of Figure 38 we see a workshop of the period. The young man on the left is holding a lens attached to a muller against the polishing plate, while the second young man is turning the polishing machine. The worker sitting at the table is polishing a lens by hand, and the one standing is operating a lathe.

Around the studio we can see various tools and finished products. The large machine on the right is used to cut lens mountings. Elsewhere there are mirrors, telescopes, spectacles, and tools, most of them shown more clearly in the bottom half of the plate and in the following one, Figure 39.

In Figure 38, *1-17* represent the various types of lenses used—plano-concave, plano-convex, and double convex—for spectacles, telescopes, and microscopes. The square piece in *18* is the crude lens ; in *19* it has been cut to the required size and shape ; in *20* it is seen mounted on the muller ; and in *21* it is placed on the plate, ready to be ground and polished.

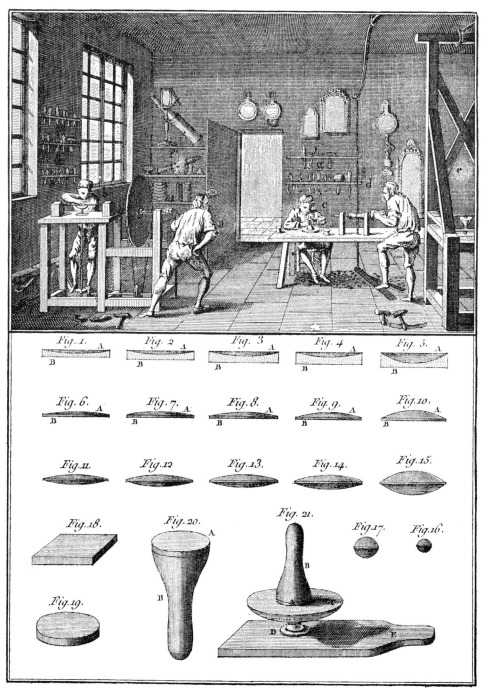

Fig. 38 : LUNETIER.  Spectacle-maker's workshop, lenses, and tools.  From Diderot's
*Encyclopédie,* 1772

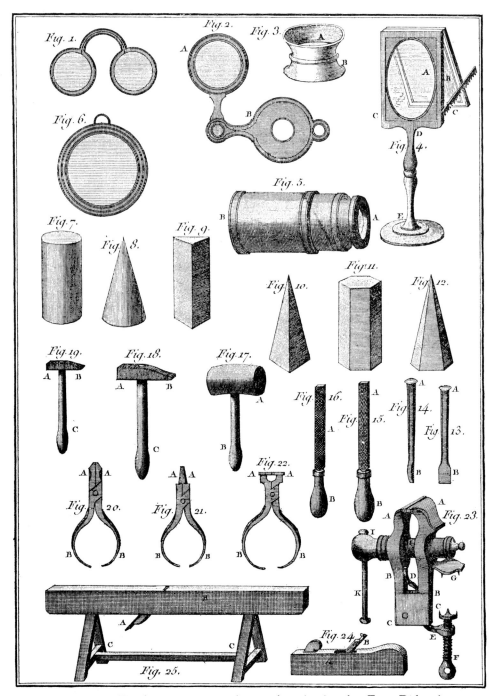

Fig. 39 : Lunetier. Eyeglasses, mirrors, and spectacle makers' tools. From Diderot's *Encyclopédie*, 1772

Figure 39 shows spectacles mounted in horn or tortoise shell (*1*), a single glass mounted in horn or shell with its protective sheath attached (*2*), a loupe (*3*), an optical glass with mirror (*4*), a single opera glass or perspective glass (*5*), a burning glass (*6*), and various cylinders, prisms, cones, and tools. These two plates give a reasonably good idea of what the manufacture of spectacles was like in the third quarter of the century.

In 1784 Benjamin Franklin (Figure 41) found himself much in the position of Samuel Pepys, who had written on the last day of June 1668 : 'My eyes are bad, but no worse . . . only weary with working. I am come that I am not able to read out a small letter, and yet my sight is good, for the little while I can read, as ever it was, I think.'

Unwilling to give in to his failing sight, Franklin improvised what later came to be known as bifocals, which he described in a letter to George Whately, a Philadelphia optician :

'I imagine it will be found pretty generally true, that the same convexity of glass, through which a man sees clearest and best at the distance proper for reading, is not the best for greater distances. I therefore had formerly two pairs of spectacles, which I shifted occasionally, as in traveling I sometimes read, and often wanted to regard the prospects. Finding this change troublesome, and not always sufficiently ready, I had the glasses cut and a half of each kind associated in the same circle. By this means, as I wear my own spectacles constantly, I have only to move my eyes up or down, as I want to see distinctly far or near, the proper glasses being always ready.

'This I find more particularly convenient since my being in France, the glasses that serve me best at table to see what I eat not being the best to see the faces of those on the other side of the table who speak to me ; and when one's ears are not well accustomed to the sounds of a language, a sight of the movements in the features of him that speaks helps to explain ; so that I understand French better by the help of my spectacles.'

Evidently the idea of bifocals had already been experimented with in London as early as 1760 (possibly by Franklin himself, who was there at the time), though never used extensively. Franklin's letter may possibly have been merely a report of an earlier experiment. It should be pointed out, however, that the idea of the split lens was suggested by Hertel in 1716 ; but there is no evidence that any practical application of the idea was made before 1760.

About this time (between 1781 and 1789) silver spectacles with sliding extension temples were being made in France ; a pair owned by Franklin is dated 1788. But it was not until the nineteenth century that they gained any widespread popularity. There are a number of examples in the nineteenth-century plates.

In 1783 A. Smith was making double spectacles ; and in 1797 I. Richardson, an English optician, invented and patented spectacles with four lenses, two of which could be swung away from the eye. Thus the two pair could be used together, or the stationary one could be used alone. The earliest ones had large round lenses in heavy brass frames with inside glasses of dark green (Plate 37-A in Chapter 6). Later they were somewhat more delicate, with hexagonal frames and azure blue glass. Dr Greeff states that, contrary to the opinion of Dunscombe, the coloured glass was purely protective, not optical. Later ones framed in horn did have secondary convex lenses. The Richardson glasses were popular during the first half of the nineteenth century.

In the same year Dudley Adams patented a curious form of spectacles in which the lenses were suspended in front of the eyes from a rod across the forehead (Plate 8-E). They were 'designed to relieve the temples and nose from pressure and also to provide several adjustments to the lens holders. The latter can be raised or lowered, rotated, and their separation varied, allowing thereby of suitable adjustment for any person.' It is hardly surprising that the populace did not rush to buy them. A pair can be seen in the Science Museum in London.

In 1799, according to von Rohr, 'the best double-jointed standard gold spectacles (gold case included) were sold at 16 guineas, and in 1813 the same optician still offered a pair at 12 guineas'.

Fig. 40 : David Levi.  Engraving by Bromley from
a painting by Drummond, *c.* 1799

Fig. 41 : Benjamin Franklin. Engraved
from a painting by Martin

## THE QUIZZING GLASS

In his dictionary, published in 1725, Furetière described a 'kind of eyeglass which consists of a simple lens, encased in a circle of horn or precious material, with a small handle by which it can be held. With the aid of this glass, which one holds up to one eye while closing the other, one observes all that happens ; one observes without seeming to do anything.' (See Plates 4, 7, 11, 12, 13, and 15.)

Although this single eyeglass with a handle was certainly nothing new, it achieved great popularity in the eighteenth century. Figure 43 is a French carica-ture of an English gentleman using his quizzing glass. But once again we are faced with a puzzle in terminology. Furetière calls his glass a *lanstier*, a term which seems not to have been widely used. The most popular English term was *quizzing glass* (or occasionally *quizzer*), a term still used by modern authors and museums to refer to these single eyeglasses.

But the *Dictionary of American English* defines *quizzing glass* as a monocle, a term which eventually came to mean a single glass worn in the eye. Evidently the quizzing glass was sometimes so used. In *Harper's Magazine* in 1886 we find a reference to 'a cockney . . . lighted pipe in mouth and quizzing glass screwed into one eye'. Other authors mention the *wearing* of a quizzing glass, but that could refer simply to carrying it on a cord or chain about the neck. McLean's caricatures

Fig. 42 : Jelderhuis, Dutch landscape painter.
From a late eighteenth-century
portrait

of around 1830 show dandies with a quizzing glass stuck in the eye in the manner of a monocle. The term is believed to have been used in the United States about 1802. Eventually it became old-fashioned and was replaced by *monocle*.

Richard Horne, an Englishman writing in *Frasers Magazine* in 1876, had quite a different idea about the quizzing glass of the late eighteenth century. Referring to a book entitled *The Art of Preserving the Sight Unimpaired to an Extreme Old Age*, published in 1821, he stated that the author 'alludes to, and of course denounces the impudent foppery of a "quizzing-glass", which he considers simply as a single glass of magnifying or other mischievous qualities ; whereas the real old "quizzing-glass" of the days of Beau Nash and the Bath-chair fops was not like any other eye-glass of the period, and there have been none of like kind since. How few living men have ever seen a "quizzing-glass" even in an old curiosity shop. I am a rare exception, having seen one in the possession of the late Samuel Drummond, A.R.A. . . . who kept it as a curious relic of Hogarth's period. It was a little looking-glass of just the size and appearance of an ordinary single eye-glass. You would never suppose that the person who was scrutinizing your face was the one whose back was turned to you, and who was carefully examining some object in front of him. And so he *was*. The insidious little mirror had, however, its compensating disadvantages ; for inasmuch as listeners seldom hear any good of themselves, so did those who possessed a little talisman for seeing what passed behind their backs often see gesticulations and other things that were neither complimentary or delightful.'

In all probability the term meant all of these things at different times. But for our purposes it would perhaps be best to use it to refer only to the single glass with a handle. Originally the quizzing glasses were round. As they became more fashionable, oval and rectangular shapes were also used (Plates 12 and 13). They were usually worn on a silk cord or ribbon around the neck.

In a letter written in March 1784, William Cowper referred to Mr Greenville, a political candidate: 'He has a pair of very good eyes in his head, which not being sufficient as it should seem, for the many nice and difficult purposes of a senator, he has a third also, which he wore suspended by a riband from his buttonhole'.

Fig. 43 : UNE SAGE RECOMMANDATION. French caricature of an Englishman with his quizzing glass, 1783

Fig. 44 : Ah, le Beau Jupon Court!
Eighteenth - century French
engraving

Magnifying glasses, still popular with the longsighted, became much more elegant in the eighteenth century and, during the reign of Louis XV, were frequently oval in shape (Plate 13-B). Oval or round, they were often encased in tortoise shell or mother-of-pearl laced with gold or silver so that when the glass was not in use it would look like a medallion. Often the case was richly enamelled or decorated with precious stones.

A curious form of large single glass, occasionally seen in portraits of women, was suspended in front of the eye by a strap (Figure 45). This, like all single eyeglasses, was denounced by the opticians. In *An Essay on Vision*, published in 1789, George Adams had some harsh words about the popularity of reading glasses :

'These puerile propensities give rise to a variety of artifices by which each individual endeavours to hide from himself and others what no artifice can conceal. Opticians have daily experience of the truth of this Observation, and in no instance more so than in the preference given by many to Reading Glasses merely because they think that the decay of their Sight and their advances in age are less conspicuous by using a Reading-Glass than Spectacles.

'But the Eyes in endeavouring to see with a Reading-Glass are considerably strained and in a short time much fatigued. And there is another objection to the use of Reading-Glasses, which arises from the unsteadiness of the hand and the motion of the head, which occasions a perpetual motion to the Glass, for the Eye endeavours to conform itself to each change, and this tender organ is thereby kept in continual agitation. To these evils we may add the dazzling glare and irregular reflexion from the surface of the Glass which so weakens the eyes that those who accustom themselves to a Reading Glass are in a short time obliged to take to Spectacles, and to use them much older than they otherwise would have done.'

Figure 46 shows a large Italian reading glass with only a vestigial handle. Utilitarian reading glasses with handles have been used with astonishingly little change since the thirteenth century; but since these are not suitable for carrying about in the pocket, a variety of more portable styles have been devised.

Fig. 45 : Anna Dorothea Therbusch.
Self-portrait, *c.* 1780

Fig. 46 : Il Primo Abboccamento : Marfisa welcomes her elegant suitor. From *Il matrimonio di Marfisa*.
Italian engraving in colour by Lasinio, *c.* 1795

### Scissors-Glasses

Another form of eyeglass became popular in the last half of the century—the double
eyeglass on a handle. One used by George Washington (Plate 13-A) shows a
strong resemblance to the Nürnberg drawings of 1600 and may conceivably have
been inspired by them. In the Directoire period in France they were extremely
popular with the dandies known as *les incroyables*. Since the two branches of the
handle came together under the nose and looked as if they were about to cut it off,
they were known as *binocles-ciseaux* or scissors-glasses (Plates 14 and 15). Often
they were extremely elegant. Plate 15-B shows a pair made of steel encrusted with
pearls. There was usually a ring in the end so that the glasses could be hung
around the neck by a silk ribbon or a gold or silver chain. The English version
was less elegant.

In *Push-pin* (Figure 47) we find 'Wicked Old Q' (for Queensberry), a notorious
reprobate, leering through his scissors-glasses as he plays at push-pin, a fashionable
intellectual game of the time. His companion is the equally notorious Mrs Windsor,

Fig. 47 : Push-Pin.  Caricature by Gillray of 'Wicked Old Q' (with scissors-glasses) and 'Mother Windsor' playing at push-pin, 1797

sometimes obliquely referred to as the 'lady abbess' whose novices were much admired, but more frequently known, especially by her customers, simply as Mother Windsor.

## The Prospect Glass

In the eighteenth century miniature telescopes, called 'prospect glasses' by the English and *lorgnettes* by the French, became enormously popular among men and women of fashion (Plates 16 and 17).  The lower classes usually wore spring glasses from Germany.  Figure 48 shows an English fop so absorbed with his prospect glass that he fails to notice that he is about to be served with a summons :

> Sir Fopling Flutter through his Glass,
> Inspects the ladies as they pass,
> Yet still the Coxcomb lacks the Wit
> To guard against the Bailiff's Writ.

Fig. 48 : The Arrest. English engraving,
1768

In 1745 Anne-Marie Lepage complained of the excessive use of prospect glasses at the theatre : 'I entered my box. Hardly was I seated when I noticed twenty glasses pointed toward me ; I had sometimes seen, at the Opéra or at the Comédie, this use of the *lorgnette*, but never with such effrontery. They used a fan or a hat in order not to be noticed ; but on this occasion they used not the slightest discretion.'

The fashionable *lorgnettes*, which artists and artisans made and decorated with gold, silver, wood, ivory, porcelain, wedgwood, leather, enamels, and precious stones, were treasured as works of art as well as for their practical value. In December 1756 a celebrated French merchant sold to Madame de Pompadour, for 180 *livres* (very approximately £900), a glass of Vincennes porcelain decorated with gold. On the same day he sold the comte de Lutzelbourg a similar one decorated with garlands and provided with a case. A year later the same merchant charged Madame la duchesse de Mazarin 312 *livres* for a glass decorated with gold.

Until 1760 the *lorgnette* or prospect glass was usually in the form of a single tube, with variations mainly in the covering and the decoration (Plate 16-A and Figure 49). Then the tube became larger at one end and smaller at the other (Plate 16-F and Figure 49). In France this was known as the pear-shaped glass (*lorgnette poire*). The next step was the division of the inner, sliding tube into a number of collapsible sections so that the glass could be closed into a more compact form for

Fig. 49 : French *lorgnettes*, late eighteenth century. From Heymann's *Lunettes et lorgnettes de jadis*

carrying (Plate 16-E). In Plate 18-B (Chapter 6) we see a glass which collapses into the size and shape of a pocket watch. The French called these vest-pocket *lorgnettes*.

According to a French publication of 1775, two enamelled gold *lorgnettes* had been sold, one for 900 *livres*, the other for 432; and in 1790 the French King offered the Grand-Vizir an English glass worth 540 *livres*.

There were still complaints about the excessive use of prospect glasses. In *Tableau de Paris*, published in Amsterdam between 1782 and 1788, Mercier added his: 'Paris is full of merciless oglers who place themselves in front of you and fix on your their bold, staring eyes. This custom is no longer considered indecent because it is so commonplace. Women don't take offence provided it happens at the theatre or along the promenades. . . . Excellent eyes pretend to be imperfect in order to use a useless instrument which is more often than not an affectation.'

There was in France a curious offshoot of the *lorgnette*, which is perhaps best described by Thomin, optician to the Queen, writing in 1749:

'It is still another kind of opera glass which is called *lunette de jalousie*, which has the same proportions as the first, but in which the difference consists of a plated mirror set at an angle in the tube, pierced with an oval opening on the side. It is sufficient to turn this opening in the direction of whatever one wishes to observe, and the curiosity is immediately satisfied. Its usefulness is confined to letting us observe surreptitiously a person we seem not to be looking at. This *lorgnette* might have been called a "decorum glass" because there is nothing more rude than to use an ordinary opera glass for looking at someone face to face.'

The *lorgnette de jalousie* was described by Chevalier in his *Conservateur de la vue* as 'an eyeglass which makes it possible for us to see a person on whom our gaze does not seem to rest and which permits us to follow all his actions while concealing the attention we are paying him. Such an eyeglass must frequently lead to dissension, and it is by extension thus called the "jealousy glass", for jealousy is not the most peaceful of passions. One can say that this glass satisfies the curiosity without impoliteness. From this point of view it is very convenient to use.' (See Plate 17-B.)

Both Madame de Pompadour and Madame Du Barry used these jealousy-glasses. The former had a red and gold enamelled one painted by Boucher. They were used extensively at the theatre for keeping track of who had arrived without turning round to look.

When the boldness of the ordinary prospect glass eventually began to pall and even the jealousy-glass seemed indiscreet, tiny lorgnettes were imbedded in fans, heads of canes, and other useful and ornamental objects (Plates 18-21 in Chapter 6). On the 23rd of May 1782, at a reception at Versailles, Marie-Antoinette discreetly presented such a fan, studded with diamonds, to the Grand Duchess of Herse-Darmstadt, wife of the future Paul I of Russia, saying: 'I know that, like me, you are shortsighted. Let me place at your disposal this small object, which I beg you to keep as a memento.'

Fig. 50 : THE OPTIC CURLS.   Caricature by Mary Darly, 1777

Sometimes there was a round hole at the end of each blade of the fan, worked into the design, with the two end holes each containing a lens. When the fan was closed, the holes in the blades formed a tube with a lens at each end. More often the miniature glass served as a fulcrum for the blades of the fan (Plates 18, 19, 20).

During the reign of Louis XVI prospect glasses were even mounted in the covers of elegantly decorated utility boxes (Plate 17-E), used to hold scissors, pencils, small rulers, knives, perfume, sweets, and so on. In using the glass, one would seem to be peering into the box. The length of canes with glasses in the handles (Plate 17-A) was so calculated that when the gentleman was seated, the glass would be at eye-level.

In the Directoire period *lorgnettes* became so small that they were sometimes even worn as charms (Plates 17, 18, 19, 21). They continued to be incorporated into various useful objects—fans, walking-sticks, snuff boxes, perfume bottles, watch fobs, and even toothpick holders. Their popularity continued into the nineteenth century.

PLATE 6 : THE EIGHTEENTH
CENTURY 1700–1800

A  Four-slit spectacles. Although this particular pair is believed to date from the eighteenth century, the style is more typical of the seventeenth.

B  Mid - century, probably English. Rims of leather with a steel spring riveted to the leather protrusions at the top.

C  Probably English. Leather rims with steel spring.

D  English. Folding eyeglasses of tortoise shell and silver.

E  German. Made in Nürnberg.
-G

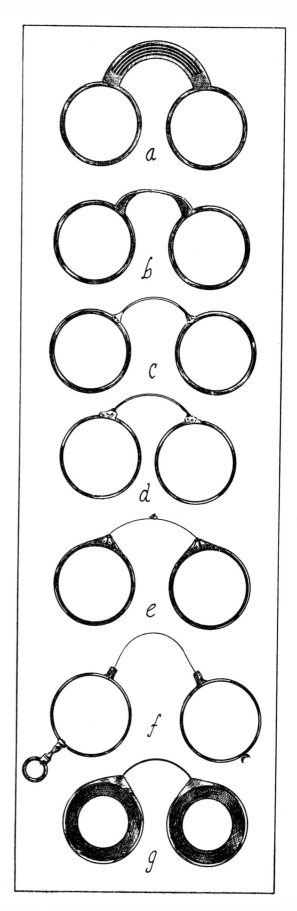

PLATE 7 : THE EIGHTEENTH
CENTURY 1700–1800

A   *c.* 1750.   Silver spectacles probably belonging to Swedish archbishop Troilius.

B   French.   Silver frames.

C   French.   Pivoted silver frames.

D   Mid-century, French.   Burning glass with steel frame. (*Nordiska Museet, Stockholm*)

E   Mid - century, German.   Reading glass.   Manufactured by Jonas Schwartz in Fürth. (*Nordiska Museet, Stockholm*)

F   Silver frames with hinged forehead piece.   The long extension was inserted under the hat to hold the glasses in place. (See also Figure 36.)

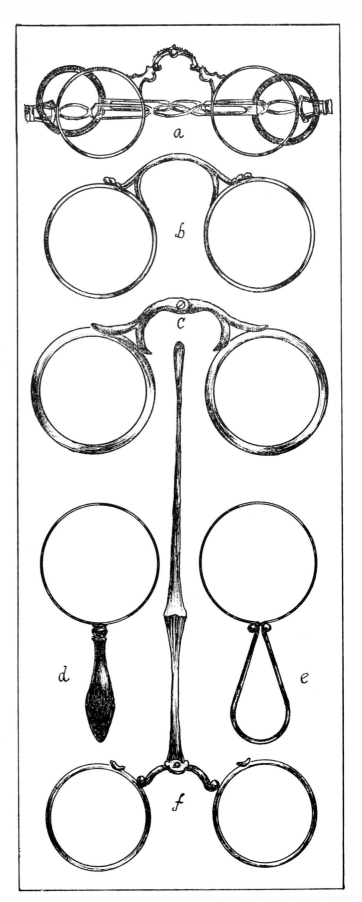

PLATE 8 : THE EIGHTEENTH
CENTURY 1725–1800

A  Iron frames with inner rims of horn. The wheel-like ends of the temples pressed against the head to hold the frames in place.

B  *c.* 1750. Steel frames with short temples and C-shaped nosepiece. Temple spectacles probably date from 1728. (*Science Museum, London*)

C  *c.* 1770. Iron frames with inner rims of wood. Turnpin temples. (*Science Museum, London*)

D  1770, English. Benjamin Martin's Visual Glasses. Steel frames with turnpin temples. (*Science Museum, London*)

E  1797, English. Dudley Adams's Patent Spectacles, 'designed to relieve the temples and nose from pressure and also to provide several adjustments to the lens holders. The latter can be raised or lowered, rotated, and their separation varied, allowing thereby of suitable adjustment for any person.' (*Science Museum, London*)

F  Silver frames with folding sidepieces.

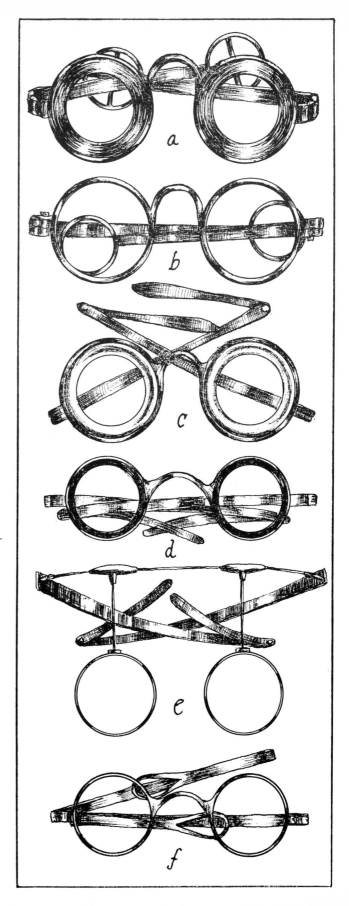

PLATE 9 : THE EIGHTEENTH CENTURY 1725–1800

A   End of the century.

B   End of the century.  Silver or gold.

C   Chinese.

D   Last quarter, Swedish.  Steel frames, C-nosepiece.  Possibly manufactured in Stockholm by Anders Wahlbohn.  (*Nordiska Museet, Stockholm*)

E   *c.* 1788, American.  Glasses worn by Benjamin Franklin, may have been made in France.  Early example of extension temples.  (*New York Historical Society*)

F   Chinese.  Frames of white metal.

G   Last quarter, French or possibly Italian.  Tortoise shell.  Believed to be not unlike the spectacles worn by Chardin in his self-portrait of 1775 (Figure 35).  (*Nordiska Museet, Stockholm*)

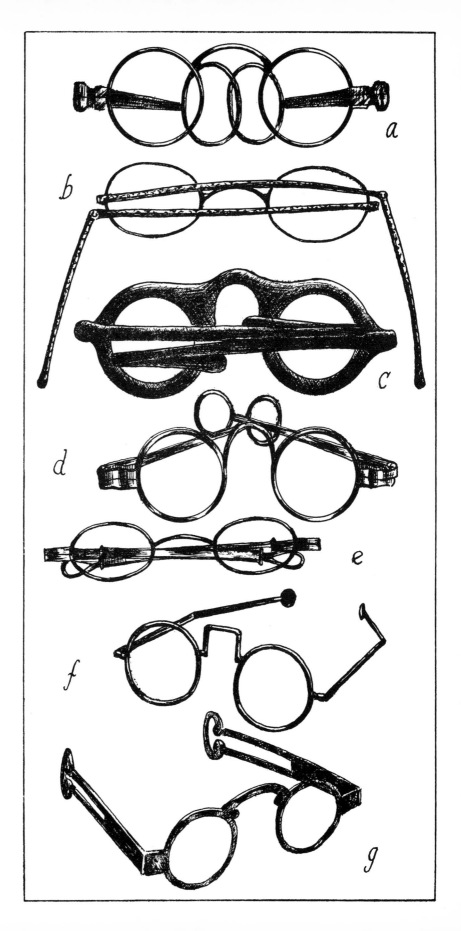

PLATE 10 : THE EIGHTEENTH CENTURY 1750–1800

A   Steel frames with inner rims of horn.

B   *c.* 1790, English.   Frames of heavy steel.

C   Steel frames with inner rims of horn.

D   Steel frames with inner rims of horn.

E   Swedish.   Steel frames manufactured 1790–1825 in Stockholm.   (*Nordiska Museet, Stockholm*)

F   American.   Worn by George Washington at his inauguration.

G   *c.* 1775, American.   Worn by Major-General Israel Putnam in the American Revolution.   (*New York Historical Society*)

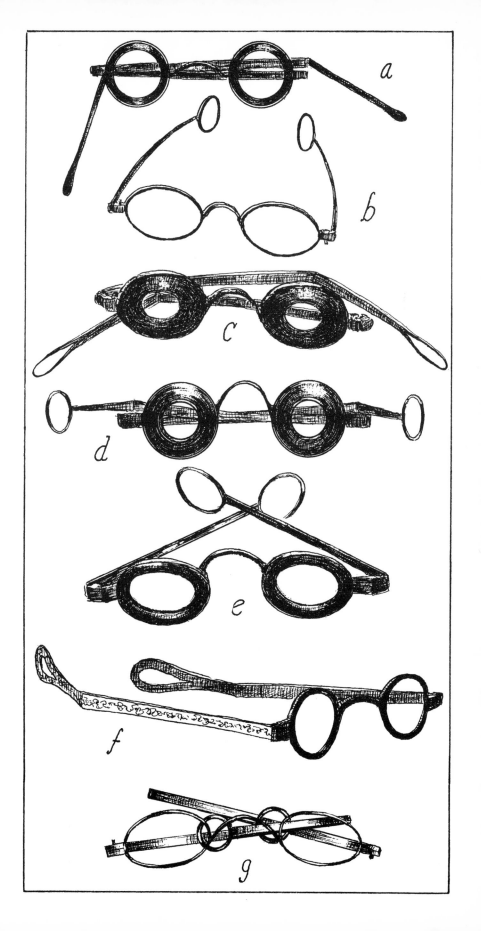

PLATE 11 : THE EIGHTEENTH
CENTURY 1700–1775

A  1758.  Silver spectacle case taken to Utah in 1852. (*Pioneer Museum, Salt Lake City*)

B  *c.* 1750, Swedish.  Case for reading glass. (*Nordiska Museet, Stockholm*)

C  *c.* 1700, French.  Reddish leather case with silk-tasselled cord for hanging.  Designed to hold collapsible eyeglasses.

D  *c.* 1700.  Single lens with frame, bound with wire.

E  Probably second quarter, English. Early temple spectacles.

F  Third quarter, American.  Prospect glass.

G  *c.* 1728, English.  Scarlett's temple spectacles.  These are believed to be the first spectacles with temples.

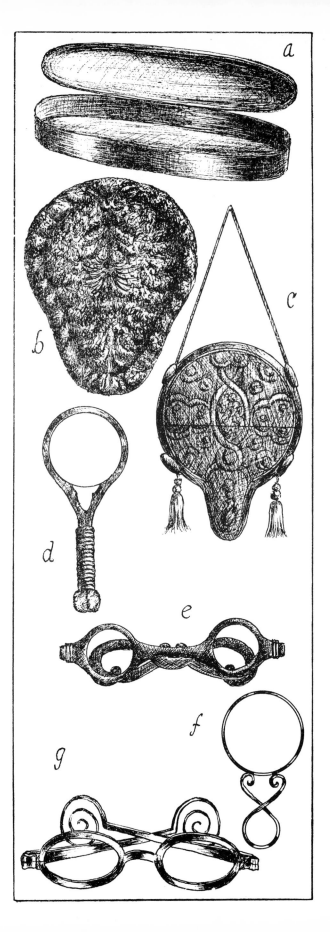

PLATE 12 : THE EIGHTEENTH
        CENTURY 1775–1800

A     Fashionable quizzing or perspective
-G    glasses.  These usually hung from a
      black silk cord or ribbon.

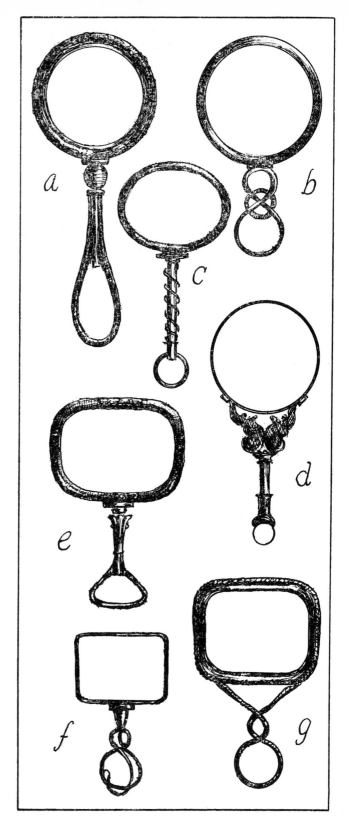

PLATE 13 : THE EIGHTEENTH
CENTURY 1700–1800

A  Last quarter. Scissors-glasses for reading, used by George Washington (1732–99). This type of eyeglass can be traced, in less ornate form, to the 1750s.

B  Second half. Reading glass in gold and enamel case, belonging to Stanislaus II (1732–98), last King of Poland.

C  Second half. Quizzing glass used in New York. (*Museum of the City of New York*)

D  Third quarter, French. Reading glass in enamel and silver case.

E  Probably first quarter, Dutch. Horn and silver. Temples, except for flat horn discs on the ends, and nosepiece are of silver. (*Rijks Museum, Amsterdam*)

F  Pivoted eyeglasses of heavy wire. Frames are tied with cords to hold lenses in place.

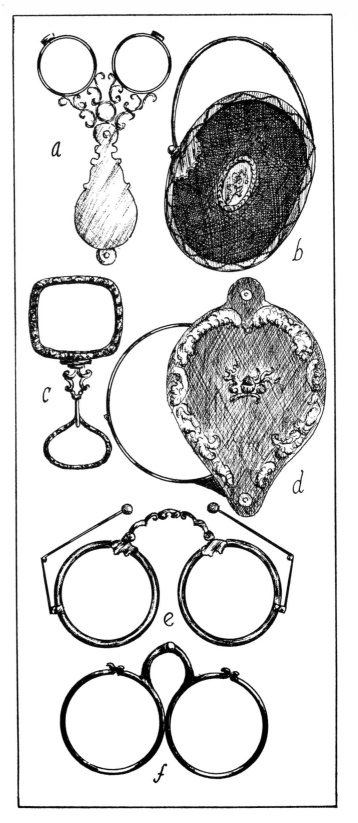

PLATE 14 : THE EIGHTEENTH
          CENTURY 1750–1800

A   Directoire period (1795–99), French.
     Double and single eyeglass com-
     bined.   Used by the *Incroyables*.

B   Directoire period, French.  Scissors-
     glasses used by the *Incroyables*.  This
     general form dates to the 1750s.

C   French.   Silver glasses on pivot.

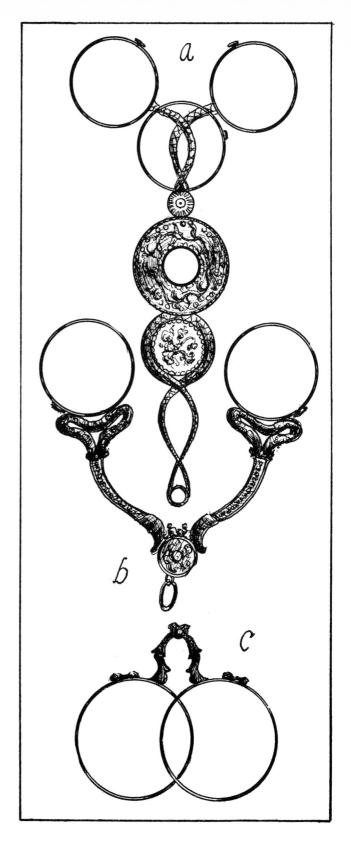

PLATE 15 : THE EIGHTEENTH CENTURY 1725–1800

A   *c.* 1800, French.   Perspective glass made of steel, decorated with pearls.   Used by fashionable and elegant young men.

B   *c.* 1800, French.   Scissors-glasses (*face-à-main, forme ciseau*).   An elegant design of steel decorated with pearls.   Popular with the *Incroyables.*

C   French.   Scissors-glasses of engraved and gilded copper.   Fashionable style used by men.   This form of scissors-glasses has not been traced earlier than the 1750s.

D-F   French.   Fashionable perspective glasses of chiselled steel.

G   *c.* 1725, French.   Miniature *lorgnette* or prospect glass with carved floral design.

H   French.   Single eyeglass of gold.

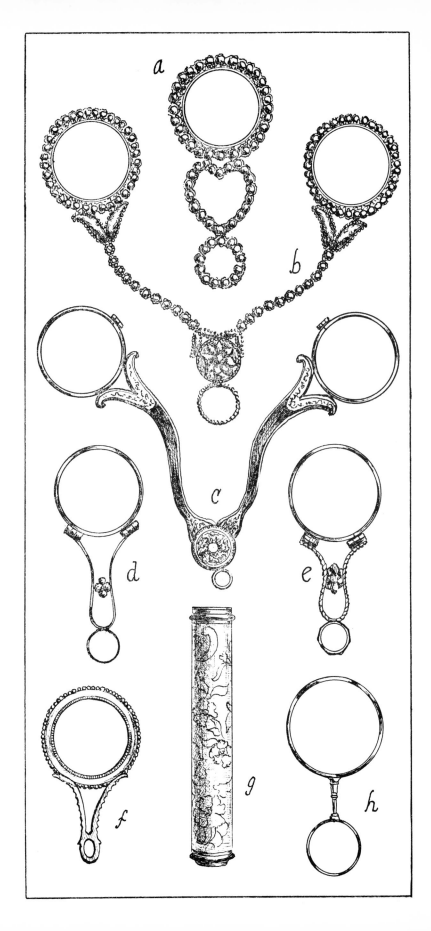

PLATE 16 : THE EIGHTEENTH
CENTURY 1740–1800

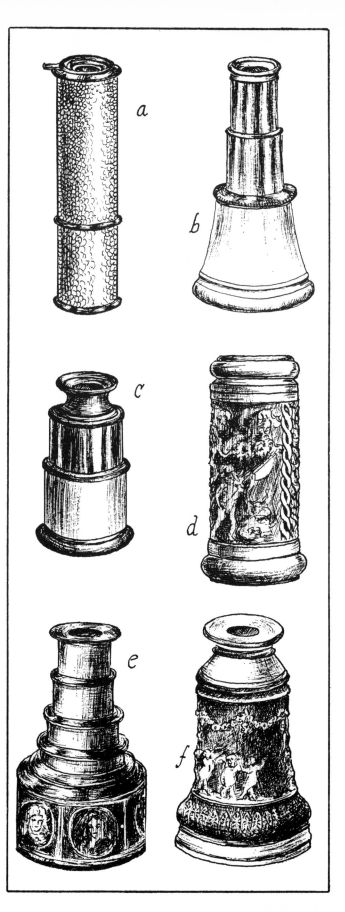

A  *c.* 1749, English. Prospect glass,
made in London by Thomas Rib-
right, who patented a method of
making 'small perspective glasses,
with mathematical and other instruments and twees in one and the same
case'. Body of brass, covered in
green shagreen, fitted with manicure
instruments. 'The eyeglass is fixed
to the sliding top of the case, and
the instruments are arranged inside
around the aperture of the eye-
stop.'—(*Science Museum, London*)

B  Second half, English. Prospect
glass, made in London by Adams.
Body-tube of ivory and draw-tube of
brass. (*Science Museum, London*)

C  *c.* 1790, English. Made by Rams-
den, London. Body-tube of ivory,
draw-tube of silver. (*Science Museum, London*)

D  French. Prospect glass or *lorgnette.*

E  After 1760, French. Collapsible
prospect glass or *lorgnette.*

F  End of the century, French. Prospect glass or *lorgnette.*

PLATE 17 : THE EIGHTEENTH
CENTURY 1700–1800

A  Louis XV period. Head of a
walking-stick containing a *lorgnette*
or small spyglass.

B  Louis XV period. Jealousy-glass
containing a pill box in one end and
a rear-vision mirror inside. The
mirror and the side opening permit
the viewer to see what is going on
behind him (see text).

C  Louis XVI period, French. Ivory
*lorgnette*.

D  Louis XIV period. Ivory telescope.

E  Louis XV period. Utility box in
agate and gold with small prospect
glass.

F  Directoire period (1795–99), French.
Cut-glass perfume bottle in the form
of a charm, containing a miniature
*lorgnette*. Such charms in various
forms were fashionable in this
period. The exact date of this particular example is uncertain. The
fashion continued into the nineteenth
century (see Plates 18, 20, and 21).

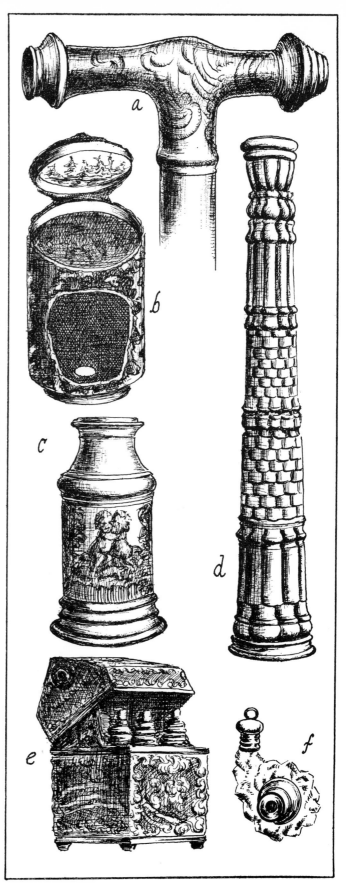

Fig. 51 : LES AMATEURS DE TABLEAUX. Lithograph by Boilly, *c.* 1824

# 6 · The Nineteenth Century

The nineteenth century brought an end to the fad for ornate and expensive eye-glasses in various elegant or eccentric disguises and a sort of grudging acceptance of more practical eyewear, at least for men. No fashionable woman could afford to be seen in public wearing spectacles, and, after the influence of the *Incroyables* had died out, no man could afford to be seen in public or anywhere else using a lorgnette. Eventually pince-nez became a sort of compromise for both sexes.

## Spyglasses

At the beginning of the century, however, the French *lorgnettes* or miniature spyglasses were still enormously popular. Joséphine, who loved baubles of all sorts, is said to have been passionately fond of them. Napoleon was frequently painted with a telescope or a *lorgnette* in his hand or within reach. One of his telescopes, manufactured by Dollond in London and left behind at Waterloo, was composed of two tubes of leather measuring 17 cm. when fully extended, 12 cm. when closed. Inside the tubes he kept a chamois for cleaning the lenses. The glass itself was kept in a velour case along with various medals and decorations.

In the Empire period pear-shaped spyglasses were still used in France, but cask-shaped ones, inspired by Napoleon's barrels of powder, were also popular (Plate 19-B). Decorations were much less elegant than in the eighteenth century, and colours were sharper. A single N was frequently the central element in the design. *Lorgnette* fans, still popular, became much smaller (Plate 19-F). Madame de Genlis attributed this to the fact that ladies didn't blush as much as they had formerly and had no desire to hide what few blushes there were. Some of these fans could be opened into a complete circle with a handle (Plate 18-F).

In 1818 Dr William Kitchiner, a London practitioner, published the third edition of his book on telescopes, opera glasses, and spectacles. Although most of the information is technical in nature, he made a few observations of more general interest:

'My favourite opera-glass is constructed with a single plano-convex object-glass, of an inch and three quarters focus, the diameter of about an inch, with which I use an eye-glass, about an inch double concave : the length, when in use, is about three inches : this magnifies full three times and a half, which is as much as can be used in a theatre, the vapour arising from the breath of a large assembly of persons, and the quantity of smoke from numerous lamps, candles, &c. prevent our employing higher powers. An opera-glass, on the scale I recommended, is very conveniently portable, and a delightful companion for those who frequent theatrical amusements. To the object-end of this opera-glass may be attached a plane mirror, placed at an angle of 45 degrees, like the small speculum of a Newtonian telescope. If this be well made, and the lateral aperture of the same diameter as the object-glass, very little light will be lost by the reflection, and the diagonal will be as sharp, and almost as bright, as the direct vision. The *diagonal eye-glass* is another very pretty contrivance for a bashful beauty to watch her sweetheart with ; and is an invaluable oracle for a fair lady to refer to, to repair her all-conquering charms, and adjust the irresistible artillery of her eyes and smiles.'

This latter seems to have served much the same purpose as the jealousy-glass, which was rarely found in the nineteenth century. Chevalier wrote as early as 1815 that it had been completely abandoned.

About 1820 the spyglasses in French fans were sometimes replaced by tiny kaleidoscopes, which had achieved great popularity. Figure 55 represents a travelling kaleidoscope-merchant in the early part of the century showing his wares. Monocles and miniature spyglasses were hung about the neck, often with chains of coral, steel, or gold. Plate 18-E shows a combination monocle and spyglass of English make. The monocle position is shown. In order for the spyglass to be used, the gadget would have to be held at a ninety-degree angle to the eye.

In the spring of 1823 a paragraph in the *Journal des Dames et de la Mode* indicated that the style in spyglasses or single opera glasses had changed : 'The enormous achromatic opera glasses with a single ivory tube, which were first seen in the hands of the fashionable in the balconies of large theatres, are today those which are carried by our *merveilleuses* in the first boxes ; of a dozen opera glasses, there are ten of this sort. Because of their weight, it is the escorts of these ladies who put them in their pockets when they leave for the theatre and again when they go home. A bunch of violets, an embroidered handkerchief, a large opera glass, and a bottle of smelling salts—those are the four things a lady of fashion must have at the theatre.'

In the early part of the century it finally occurred to someone to put two spyglasses together so that one could use both eyes at the same time. The resulting binoculars or double opera glasses required some experimentation in order to coordinate the operation of both glasses, but this was accomplished in Paris about 1823. Although the single glass continued to be made after this date, it was gradually superseded by the double one. Plates 19-A and 24-F show early examples.

Fig. 52 : THE KING OF BROBDINGNAG AND GULLIVER. Napoleon and George III. Etching by
Gillray, presumably from a design by Lieutenant-Colonel Bradyll of the Coldstream
Guards. Published 1803

By the end of the century opera glasses, especially those manufactured in Paris, had reached such a high degree of perfection that it became necessary to add gadgets to make one brand seem more desirable than another. One of these was a handle, which was considered smart by fashionable women, both handle and glasses frequently being decorated with mother-of-pearl or sometimes gold. Then improvements were made in the handle. In 1895, according to an advertisement in the *Optical Journal*, the latest novelty was an opera glass so constructed that its focus could be easily adjusted by turning the detachable handle (Plates 22-D-E and 23-B). Somehow this was considered more convenient than turning the adjustment wheel between the tubes, though both hands would certainly be required for the operation.

## THE LORGNETTE

Double eyeglasses, which Napoleon favoured over single ones, became fashionable for a while. In March 1812 the optician Lerrebours furnished Napoleon with 'a binocle of mother-of-pearl, the handle of gold, decorated with quartz crystals, at the price of 230 francs'. An English caricature of 1830 shows a bewigged schoolmaster holding a pair of sturdy scissors-glasses, which were by that time as much out of fashion as his wig. Nearly identical ones can be seen in the two Boilly caricatures in Figures 51 and 57.

When the era of the heavy scissors-glasses had passed, they grew smaller, changed their form, and became lorgnettes (in the English sense) for the use of the ladies. These were basically a pair of spectacles attached at one side to a handle (Plates 21-28) of mother-of-pearl, tortoise shell, or metal.

In October 1819 the *Journal des Dames et de la Mode* noted that the *lorgnons* preferred by fashionable young ladies were made of extra-fine steel and could be found at the optical shop of Monsieur Cauchois, the most fashionable optician in Paris. Prices ranged from 12 to 150 francs. The *Journal* praised not only the beauty of the mountings but the quality of the lenses. The term *lorgnon*, referring, in English usage, to a short-handled lorgnette, is believed to date from the beginning of the nineteenth century.

In 1825 R. Bretell Bate patented handled spectacles—a form of lorgnon—designed to be folded so that they looked like a single glass (Plate 24-A).

The lorgnette maintained its popularity with ladies of fashion, who would not, of course, wear spectacles but did occasionally have to see something with reasonable clarity. And since it was used by fashionable people, it became fashionable.

In 1870 Tomes's *Bazar Book of Decorum* spoke sharply to its readers on the use of eyeglasses :

'The functions of the natural eye and eyeglasses are much abused. It is quite clear that the whole world of fashion has not all of a sudden become so afflicted

Fig. 53 : AT THE OPERA.    Early nineteenth-century engraving by
          Springsguth

Opticien.

Fig. 54 : OPTICIEN.    Early nineteenth-century French engraving of an
          optical shop

Fig. 55 : Le Md de Kaléïdoscopes.  Early nineteenth-century French
engraving by Chassdat

with shortsightedness as to render the use of artificial means for its relief universally necessary. Nine tenths of the people, male and female, who are constantly eyeing the universe and each other through glass, require no other medium than the one provided by Nature. Nothing can be more ill bred, and we assert it in the face of assenting fashion, than ogling a stranger in the streets through an eyeglass—"with a stony British stare", or surveying an opposite neighbor at the theatre with a lorgnette.'

At the end of the century the lorgnette had lost none of its popularity. In September 1895 a New Jersey firm begged 'leave to call attention of the Optical Trade to their line of Lorgnettes, in Gold, Silver, and Tortoise Shell with 14 K Gold Eyeglass Frames and Mechanism'.

Fig. 56 : LA LORGNETTE. Lithograph by Gavarni, 1837

Fig. 57 : LES LUNETTES.   Lithograph by
Boilly, 1821

## THE MONOCLE

Professor von Rohr dates the introduction of the monocle, as differentiated from the
quizzing glass, at about 1806, though he admits the date is speculative.   In any
event, it appears to be of British origin and probably appeared at the beginning
of the century.   Pitt Herbert (in *An Eye on the Monocle*) suggests that it probably
originated on the stage and that through the attention thus attracted, it was gradually taken up by the British aristocracy.   Sometimes the monocle-addict carried
two, one for distance and one for reading.   In pre-bifocal days this was considerably
simpler than carrying two pairs of spectacles and alternating them.

Early monocle frames were often of solid gold, occasionally studded with
diamonds.   But with their spread in popularity came less expensive styles in silver
or gold plate, mass produced.   Although the first monocles were certainly used
for corrective purposes, later ones were often worn purely as a matter of fashion
in imitation of the aristocracy.   Whereas they were originally used largely by older
men, later they were adopted by young men to conform to the fashion.   'They
were worn with an air of conscious elegance', says Mr Herbert, 'and often one had

the feeling the wearer was being a trifle foolish, an attitude which resulted to some extent from the fact that monocles frequently did not fit and kept dropping out of place. The orbit of the eye was too small, too large, or too shallow; the eye bulged too much, or the lashes rubbed against the lens. Obviously, the mass production of monocles was anything but an encouragement to fitting precision.'

A portrait of the poet Thomas Moore, possibly dating from about 1810, shows him with a monocle (Figure 58). Beethoven had a silver monocle on a black cord and is said to have used it continually in the street. But he also owned several pairs of spectacles with bows. Victor Hugo, on the other hand, disdained glasses of any kind, even opera glasses, though eventually, in his old age, he was reluctantly forced to resort to them.

Fig. 58 : Thomas Moore (1779–1852), Irish poet, friend and biographer of Byron. Engraving after a painting by Shee, *c.* 1810

The fad for monocles subsided for a few years ; and, in general, only the people who really needed them wore them. But then about 1820 they were suddenly revived ; and monocles of various shapes and sizes (round, oval, octagonal, square, rectangular) and of various materials (gold, silver, gold-plate, horn, shell) were seen in profusion. Even rimless ones with a hole for the cord or ribbon were worn. English caricatures of the 1820s give a good idea of the variety of styles. Usually they were shown on foppish young men (Figure 59). Some had long handles, some short ; some were even shown attached to the handle of a riding whip. Occasionally they were shown being used by women.

In order to make it easier to hold the monocle in the eye socket and to keep it a little farther away from the eyeball, extensions called 'galleries' were added to the rim (Plate 28-D). The fad again subsided in a few years ; but by that time the monocle had become solidly entrenched in British life, and there remained a hard core of devotees who could not or would not give it up.

In *Little Dorrit*, which was intended to take place in 1826, Dickens mercilessly ridiculed the monocle, as used by the young Barnacle :

'The present Barnacle, holding Mr. Clennam's card in his hand, had a youthful aspect, and the fluffiest little whisker, perhaps that ever was seen. . . . He had a superior eye-glass dangling round his neck, but unfortunately had such flat orbits to his eyes and such limp little eyelids that it wouldn't stick in when he put it up, but kept tumbling out against his waistcoat buttons with a click that discomposed him very much.

'"Oh, I say. Look here ! My father's not in the way and won't be in the way today," said Barnacle Junior. "Is there anything that I can do ?"

'(Click ! Eye-glass down. Barnacle Junior quite frightened feeling all round himself, but not able to find it.)

'"You are very good," said Arthur Clennam. "I wish, however, to see Mr. Barnacle."

'"But I say. Look here ! You haven't got any appointment, you know," said Barnacle Junior.

'(By this time he had found the eye-glass and put it up again.)

'"No," said Arthur Clennam. "That is what I wish to have."

'"But I say. Look here ! Is this public business ?" asked Barnacle Junior.

'(Click ! Eye-glass down again. Barnacle Junior in that state of search after it, that Mr. Clennam felt it useless to reply at present.)

'"Is it," said Barnacle Junior, taking heed of his visitor's brown face, "anything about—Tonnage—or that sort of thing ?"

'(Pausing for a reply, he opened his right eye with his hand and stuck his glass in it, in that inflammatory manner that his eye began watering dreadfully.)

'"No," said Arthur, "it is nothing about tonnage."

'"Then look here. Is it private business ?"

'"I really am not sure. It relates to a Mr. Dorrit."

Fig. 59 : A REAL RUBBER! Engish caricature published by Thomas McLean, 1827

'"Look here, I tell you what ! You had better call at our house if you are going that way. Twenty-four, Mews Street, Grosvenor Square. My father's got a slight touch of the gout, and is kept at home by it."

'(The misguided young Barnacle evidently going blind on his eye-glass side, but ashamed to make any further alteration in his painful arrangements.)'

Young Barnacle's difficulties with his eyeglass seemed never to leave him but were heightened, if that is possible, at dinner :

'Conversationless at any time, he was now the victim of a weakness special to the occasion and solely referable to Clennam. He was under a continual necessity of looking at that gentleman, which occasioned his eye-glass to get into his soup,

Fig. 60 : Revolving Hat. *Which by a slight touch presents its Wearer with* Eye-Glass, Cegar, Scent-Box, Spectacles, Hearing-Trumpet, &c. &c. *without the intolerable trouble of holding them.* Published by Thomas McLean, London, 1830

into his wine-glass, into Mrs. Meagles's plate, to hang down his back like a bell-rope, and be several times disgracefully restored to his bosom by one of the dingy men. Weakened in mind by his frequent losses of his instrument, and its determination not to stick in his eye and more and more enfeebled in intellect every time he looked at the mysterious Clennam, he applied spoons to his eye, forks, and other foreign matters connected with the furniture of the dinner-table.'

The monocle, whenever it was fashionable, was always looked upon with disfavour by opticians. An anonymous German treatise on glasses, published in Leipzig in 1824, is no exception :

'The monocle, with which a single eye is used, must be avoided because it disturbs the balance of binocular vision. However, grown-up children of both sexes play with the monocle, hanging it on the chest like the triumph of their science, or wearing it attached to the hat in front of the face. . . . Numerous young people with normal vision use a monocle with a plain glass. It seems truly that they use this style of eyeglass to lend themselves an amiable air of impudence and to make themselves noticed. The style of our day does not tolerate healthy vision and demands that one appear or that one be half blind.'

In the same year in London Dr Kitchiner wrote that a 'Single Glass, set in a smart ring, is often used by Trinket-fanciers merely for fashion's sake, by folks who have not the least defect in their Sight, and are not aware of the mischievous consequences of such irritations. This pernicious plaything will most assuredly in a very few years bring on an imperfect vision in One or Both Eyes.'

In Paris in 1847 the monocle again came under attack, this time by Magne in a work entitled *Hygiène de la vue*:

'In our day the lorgnon has dethroned spectacles—that is to say, a grotesque custom has been replaced by an even more grotesque one. Of a hundred persons who use this little square piece of glass, which they hold in place only by making faces, ninety surely could do without it. The only result is that they make themselves vulnerable to myopia at the same time that they prematurely develop crow's-feet, the despair of so many women.'

It would appear from Magne's reference that square monocles as well as round were actually held in the eye and were, perhaps, more fashionable than round ones in Paris at mid-century.

Although the fashion for monocles declined, they were worn throughout the century by the Germans (Figure 61) and the British (upper-class, of course). The British monocle-wearers were typified, at least in the American mind, by Lord

Fig. 61 : OPERETTA IN POLITICS. Kikeriki's caricature of Bismarck (1815–98) and friend

Fig. 62 : E. A. Sothern as Lord Dundreary in *Our American Cousin*. After a photograph of 1881

Dundreary (Figure 62), a role created by E. A. Sothern in *Our American Cousin*. His monocle seemed as much a part of him as the whiskers, which ever since have borne his name. Whistler, too, seemed to be inseparable from his unadorned single lens.

In the latter part of the century monocles, when used, were worn in the eye, not held up to it with a long handle. And they were nearly always round. More often than not, for purely practical reasons, the monocle was attached to a cord or a ribbon, worn around the neck, as in the caricature of Bismarck (Figure 61). It was introduced into the United States about 1880 and was worn mostly by the fashionable set in the larger cities. But somehow it always had a foreign air about it.

SPECTACLES

In 1804 ordinary temple spectacles with bi-convex lenses cost 3s. 6d. Von Rohr mentions that the spectacle trade in England declined in the second quarter of the nineteenth century because of an increased interest on the part of the opticians in producing mirror telescopes. But the price of spectacles was high. Frequently the responsibility of choosing the correct lens lay, as it always had, with the customer. In 1833 Alexander Alexander wrote, in *A Treatise on the Nature of*

*Vision*: 'Oftentimes a number of spectacles are laid before the purchasers for the purpose of their selecting what may suit them, and who generally choose glasses much too powerful, elated at the idea of seeing objects very large. . . . Those spectacles should be preferred which show objects nearest their natural state, neither enlarged nor diminished, and at the same distance, and with the same ease as could be seen before the eyes were impaired.'

Even when the optician was asked to choose, it was often on a rather casual basis. C. S. Flick reports, in his *Gross of Green Spectacles*, that in 1852 Lord Buckinghamshire requested Mr Dixey of Bond Street 'to send him down to Sidmouth a pair of spectacles such as he thinks will suit a youth of 16 years of age, who has never worn any, but is so shortsighted as to be obliged to hold his face close to his plate when he takes his meals. They are wanted for one of Lord B's sons.'

Spectacles were still available from travelling salesmen; and in *Doctor Marigold's Prescriptions*, which appeared in *All the Year Round* in 1865, Dickens presented a cheapjack, a travelling salesman of the time, who sold spectacles among his other wares: 'Then we had the spectacles. It ain't a special profitable lot, but I put 'em on, and I see what the Chancellor of the Exchequer is going to take off the taxes, and I see what the sweetheart of the young woman in the shawl is doing at home, and I see what the Bishops has got for dinner, and a deal more that seldom fails to fetch 'em up in their spirits; and the better their spirits, the better their bids.'

J. C. Bloom, writing in 1940, described the method of fitting glasses in the Western part of the United States in 1889, when he first went into practice: 'When a person came in to get a pair of glasses, you would look him over, ask his age, and then reach into one of the boxes that had the mounted goods and you would reach from box to box until the patient said, "Well, that is pretty good. I guess I can see with them." He would ask what the price was, and it was anywhere from $1.50 to $5.' Evidently things hadn't really changed much since the Middle Ages.

The Reverend Patrick Brontë's report of his operation for cataracts in 1846 is also somewhat medieval-sounding, at least by modern standards:

'. . . Belladonna, a virulent poison, prepared from deadly nightshade, was first applied twice, in order to expand the pupil—this caused very acute pain, for only about five seconds. The feeling, under the operation, which lasted fifteen minutes, was of a burning nature, but not intolerable, as I have read is generally the case with surgical operations. My lens was extracted so that the cataract can never return, and I was confined on my back, in a dark room, for a month, with bandages over my eyes for the greater part. . . . I was bled with eight leeches at one time, and six on another (these caused but little pain) in order to prevent inflammation. Through Divine Mercy and the skill of the surgeon, as well as my dear Charlotte's assistance, and the attentions of the nurse, after a year of almost total blindness I was so far restored in sight as to be able to read and write. . . . The operation is critical, and ought not to be ventured without due precaution. Leeches must be put on the temples, and not on the eyelids. . . . Mr. Wilson [the surgeon] charged me only £10.

'For inflammation of the eyes do not bleed the arm, but apply immediately eight or ten leeches to the temples, also taking half a wine glass of sherry, a table-spoon or two of castor oil every other day. Darken the room, avoid animal foods —and bathe the eyes with lukewarm milk and water till the disease is subdued. All intoxicating liquors must be avoided.'

Early in the century lenses were large and round, then small and round, and later octagonal, rectangular, or oval. Both oval and rectangular glasses were patented by Dudley Adams in 1797. The oval shape had already been in use for some years. But rectangular glasses were probably not in general use much before 1819. Silver was most commonly used for the frames.

Like most innovations, the small, oval lenses were not accepted with universal enthusiasm, particularly by the Germans. In 1818 Beer wrote, in a work with the formidable title of *Das Auge oder Vesuch, das edelste Geschenk der Schöpfung vor den höchst verderblichen Einflüssen unseres Zeitalters zu sichern*: 'Nothing is so ridiculous as the little oval lenses actually in use. They . . . singularly limit the field of vision. They come to us, as I understand it, from England. Likewise, spectacles are playthings for people who want to appear half blind, as is required by fashion; the unhappy wearers of these lenses must look over their glasses or are liable to fall down or step on people.' But, as usual, criticism, even from experts in the field, had no effect where fashion was involved. Thirty years later J. Sichel, a French optician (a charlatan, according to Dr Pansier), wrote: 'Spectacles are usually manufactured of an oval form and small size to render them more elegant; but as regards their utility, it is infinitely preferable that they should be large and round, covering not only the globe of the eye, but also a part of its vicinity'.

In the late eighteenth and early nineteenth centuries it was not uncommon to use a wide inner rim of horn or tortoise shell in spectacle frames (Plates 8, 10, 35). This is carried even further in a pair displayed in the Science Museum in London in which there is only a tiny hole left to see through (Plate 31-B). These were intended to correct squint. These diaphragm-spectacles, as they were sometimes called, were dismissed by Adams as just another invention of the spectacle merchants to increase their business and their reputation; and he considered them a disservice to the science and to the public.

In the Orient there was no such effort to supply a flood of new designs. A series of Japanese prints by Utamaro, entitled *Moral Teachings as Seen Through Parents' Spectacles*, done in 1803–4, shows a style of spectacles in use for several hundred years. The print in Figure 64 portrays the 'girl commonly called uncontrollable' drinking sake and holding a crab in her left hand.

In discussing spectacles in 1818, Dr Kitchiner pointed out that the great advantage of pebble lenses over common glass was that as they could not be scratched by

Fig. 63 : MODERN SPECTACLES. American political caricature published by W. H. Charles, 1806

anything but a diamond, they could be safely carried in the pocket without a case. He recommended 'silver frames with double joints (the second joint of which turns down over the first, so that they may be used with a single joint occasionally), because they bring the glasses close to the eye, and the pressure on the head is more equal and agreeable than the single ones, which press on the temples; and tortoise-shell spectacles are very easily broken'.

What Dr Kitchiner called double-jointed frames (Plates 31-B-D and 32-B, for example) enjoyed considerable popularity. Temples with sliding extensions, invented in the eighteenth century, were also extensively worn (Plates 32-D-E and 35-B-C-F, among others). Caricatures of this period show a number of these spectacles worn by both sexes though never by persons of fashion (see Figures 57, 59, 69).

In 1833, judging from a bit of advice in a weekly called *The Doctor*, reluctance to face the need for glasses was much the same as it would be a century later: 'Set aside all prudery, honestly confess that age is creeping on, and without coquetry or apology ask the optician for a pair of spectacles'.

Dr Kitchiner had already expressed this same view, somewhat more sharply, in his *Economy of the Eyes*, published in 1824:

'When would-be-thought-young Persons first feel the necessity of giving their Eyes optical assistance, they are nevertheless shy of mounting Spectacles, which they seem to consider an inconvenient manner of advertising their Age, upon their Nose—not reflecting that they are worn by many persons who have not seen half their years, but, being short sighted, are obliged to walk about in spectacles or forego the sight of the Human Face Divine.

'However, they suppose that spectacles are such unequivocal evidence of Age and Infirmity that they desire to dispense with exhibiting them as long as possible.

'Therefore, they purchase a "Reading Glass" and habitually put it up to one and the same Eye, leaving the other involuntarily to wander. After a few years the sight of the Idle Eye becomes of a Different focus and is often irreperably impaired.'

Evidently not everyone was reluctant to submit to the tyranny of spectacles. Dr Kitchiner recounts the story of a lady of seventy-nine who requested a pair of spectacles. After trying several pairs, she told the doctor impatiently that she

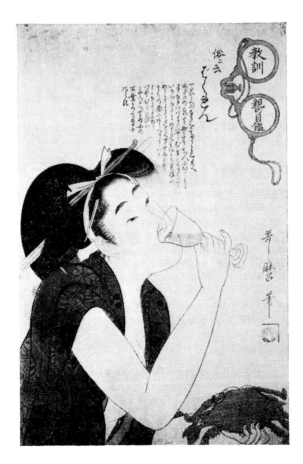

Fig. 64: THE GIRL COMMONLY CALLED UNCONTROLLABLE. Japanese print by Utamaro, from a series of *Moral Teachings as Seen Through Parents' Spectacles*, 1803–4

Fig. 65 : Joseph Prudhomme.  Drawing by
Henri Monnier, 1860

could see better with the naked eye.  When the doctor pointed out to her that she
was fortunate to be able to see as well as she did, even though she could not see to
read, the old lady assured him that she could see to read perfectly well ; but since
all her friends kept telling her how well they could see with glasses, she wanted to
enjoy the same advantage.

On the other hand, Goethe, according to contemporary biographer Johann
Peter Eckermann, had a strong personal prejudice against spectacles :

'It may be a mere whim of mine . . . but I cannot overcome it.  Whenever
a stranger steps up to me with spectacles on his nose, a discordant feeling comes
over me, which I cannot master.  It annoys me so much that on the very threshold
it takes away a great part of my benevolence, and so spoils my thoughts that an
unconstrained natural development of my own nature is altogether impossible.
It always makes on me the impression of the *désobligeant*, as if a stranger would say
something rude to me at the first greeting.  I feel this still stronger since it has been
impressed upon me for years how obnoxious spectacles are.  If a stranger now comes
with spectacles, I think immediately—he has not read my latest poems ! and that is
of itself a little to his disadvantage ;  or he has read them, knows their peculiarity
and sets them at nought, and that is still worse.  The only man with whom spectacles
do not annoy me is Zelter ; with all others they are horrible.  It always seems to
me as if I am to serve strangers as an object for strict examination, and as if with
their armed glances they would penetrate my most secret thoughts, and spy out

Fig. 66 : Madame Marie Tussaud (1760–1850).
Drawing attributed to Francis Tussaud

every wrinkle of my old face.  But whilst they thus endeavour to make my acquaintance, they destroy all fair equality between us, as they prevent me from compensating myself by making theirs.  For what do I gain from a man into whose eyes I cannot look when he is speaking, and the mirror of whose soul is veiled to me by a pair of glasses which dazzle me ?'

In his diary for June 1831 Goethe wrote : 'Mr Hippolyte Oloquet presented a good appearance, and I should have liked him if he had not had a pair of spectacles on his nose'.

In 1847 Heinrich Hoffman pointed out in verse one disadvantage of being without spectacles :

> He finds it hard without a pair
> Of spectacles to shoot a hare.
> The hare sits snug in leaves and grass,
> And laughs to see the green man pass.

Dr Kitchiner sometimes combined social consciousness with his concern for health—and possibly his eye for business :

'There could not be a more useful charity than that of providing proper Spectacles for the Poor.

'The best glasses set in Single-Jointed steel Frames, may be purchased wholesale at the rate of 18s. per dozen Pairs.  If a Single-Jointed Frame is fastened round the head with a Riband it may be kept on almost as steadily and comfortable as a Double-Jointed Frame.

'For the small sum of 18 pence the Benevolent may enjoy the gratifying reflection of giving an industrious workman the power of long continuing his labour with undiminished Ability, and of earning a subsistence till extreme Old Age.

'In no way can so much Good be done with so little money !

'Qui Visum, Vitam dat.'

'The greatest part of the Disorders of the Eyes of Poor People who are upwards of 45 years of Age are occasioned by their straining their sight for want of Spectacles, or by looking through Bad Glasses, or those of a Focus not suitable to their Eyes.

'I hope when this is considered by the Overseers of the Poor, the District Societies for Bettering the Condition of the Poor, and the Patrons of the Eye Infirmaries, that they will make the distribution a part of their Bounty.'

In another of Dr Kitchiner's publications the casual references to labour conditions in 1824 are perhaps more interesting than the information about the eyes :

'Forcing the Eyes to Work at Night, even for a few moments after they are

Fig. 67 : EMMA . . . JE VOUS AIME!  Lithograph by Daumier, 1840s

Fig. 68 : Henri Monnier.  Caricature by Carjat, 1862

Fig. 69 : THE POET AND THE MAN OF THE WORLD. German caricature by Voltz, 1811

tired, will often put them out of humour for the whole of the following Day, and is of all Eye-spoiling Acts the most mischievous.  Want of Mercy in this respect has prematurely ruined the Eyes of Thousands !

'Several young ladies, of only about 25 years of Age, have complained to me that they could not work without spectacles of 30 inches focus—who, I found on enquiry, very justly attributed this premature failure of their sight to having been obliged frequently to sit up at needle-work half the night during the time they were with Dress-Makers.

'Those who have any regard for the Eyes of their Children will make it part of the agreement, when they article them to any Business requiring the earnest exertion of their Eyes, that they shall never be required, on any pretence, to use them at latest after nine o'clock at night. . . .

'Mending Pens, and all operations requiring the Sight to be in its best condition, should be attended to early in the Day while the Nerves are brisk, and before the Eyes are fatigued.'

Also in 1824, a busy year for Dr Kitchiner, he invented a new kind of double spectacles : 'I think the best thing would be spectacles with glasses to see in the distance and another pair fastened to them and movable through hinges.  When the latter are dropped down, the glasses combine and the pair is set for near ; when it is wished to see in the distance, the latter are thrown up and lie on the forehead.'

Later in the century Bourgeois constructed spectacles very much like this (Plate 50-A). A late eighteenth-century portrait of the Dutch landscape painter, Jelderhuis, shows him wearing double spectacles (Figure 42) in which all four lenses were stationary. In 1839 C. H. Smith patented spectacles with three pair of lenses, one hinged pair in front of and one behind the stationary lenses.

Various ingenious methods were devised for making double spectacles which could be shifted quickly and easily. In 1854 van Münden arranged the second pair of lenses so that the release of a spring would send them flying upward, presumably hitting the forehead.

A version by Gradenigo was more complex, involving a hollow spring filled with mercury. When the head was inclined, the upper lenses were automatically drawn out of the line of vision, allowing one to look through a single pair. Figure 71 shows Peter Cooper wearing the more usual style, in which the auxiliary lenses were hinged on the side, requiring removal of the spectacles in shifting them.

In 1861 J. Braham of Bristol patented a pair of auxiliary spectacles which could

Fig. 70 : La Fille de Madame Angot.
Caricature by Gill, 1873

Fig. 71 : Peter Cooper (1791–1883), American inventor, industrialist, philanthropist. Engraving

be attached to the main pair by means of a spiral spring. This is the earliest evidence we have of what were called 'front-hangers'. However, Braham's glasses, if they were manufactured at all, evidently achieved no great popularity. But in 1870 front-hangers with single clips instead of springs were in use. Unfortunately, since they were not securely fastened, they tended to fall off when the head was inclined. Later improvements eliminated the problem, but the heaviness of the extra lenses caused more discomfort than many people felt was justified by the added convenience.

At about the same time that Dr Kitchiner invented his double spectacles, the first rimless spectacles were produced. A pair of these can be seen in the Science Museum in London (Plate 31-F). Von Rohr maintains that they were invented by Johann Friedrich Voigtländer (1779–1859); Lebensohn, on the other hand, believes the credit should go to Waldenstein in Vienna. In any event, they were in general use by mid-century.

In 1876 Richard Horne, writing in *Frasers Magazine*, recommended frames of blue steel, 'which is much better than the injurious dazzle of gold, silver, or any shining substance'. Before listing some of the styles of eyeglasses worn between 1816 and 1876, Mr Horne performed 'an act of duty . . . namely, that of scornfully expelling from our consideration the single glass, stuck by means of a grim grimace under one eyelid, for mere fashion's sake, in the Lord Dundreary style, and far rather let us think of the admirable surgical glass, whereby we are now enabled to look into the interior chambers of life'. Mr Horne then proceeded with his list:

Fig. 72 : Edwin M. Stanton (1814–69), U.S.
Secretary of State under Lincoln.
Engraving

'There are the ordinary shapes of spectacles—rounds, ovals, oblongs—and of different sizes, up to the grotesquely-large circles worn by the Chinese. There are the half-eye spectacles, the upper half being cut off; but these have been superseded by the pantascopic, or farsighted glasses, the frames of which are so arranged that the lenses are thrown obliquely under or before the eye. There are the K-shaped or French spectacles, with no comfortable bridge for the nose-bridge, which some people prefer and all the rest detest. There are the double-focus or split spectacles, the lenses in the upper halves being of a weak focus for distant objects, and the lower halves of a stronger focus for reading, &c., invented by Benjamin Franklin.

'I once knew an old Royal Academician who, being a great theorist in eye-glasses, sometimes wore, while painting a· portrait, three pairs of spectacles, one above the other, at the same time. One pair of glassed eyes were to bring you nearer, the other two pairs were for clearing or magnifying his work. The effect of these three sets of glassed eyes upon the sitter . . . as they continually rose and fell . . . was anything but conducive to a placid "expression".'

Evidently the use of three pair of spectacles at once was more commonly practised than one might suspect. Dr Greeff, in discussing the problem of securing clear vision at varying distances, describes the method used by a teacher of his:

'He wore for general use thick spectacles. When he read with them, he almost rested his nose on the book. If he wanted to look at the class, he put a pair of eye-glasses over the spectacles, and if he wished to cast his eye on some special pupil,

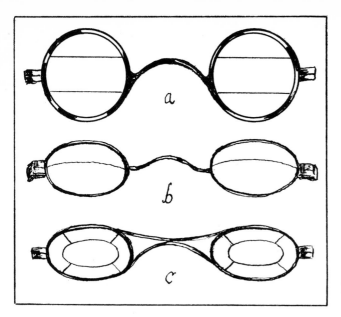

Fig. 73 : Early bifocals and trifocals, 1827–1840

he placed a pair of eyeglasses in front of the other one ; thus he wore three pairs of glasses at once. Aside from the fact that that was truly hideous, marking his defect, it is not advisable. The three glasses in front of one another, set, perhaps, obliquely in each plane, the whole system is decentralized, and there arises not only strong astigmatism of the oblique bundles but also prismatic diversion. We see this phenomenon rarely now.'

It was not until the beginning of the nineteenth century that astigmatism was understood, and in 1827 the first glasses to correct it were made by an optician named Fuller at Ipswich. In 1828 McAllister of Philadelphia also ground cylindrical glasses, as did Suscipi of Rome in 1844.

In 1824 bifocals had evidently not progressed much beyond Franklin's style, for Kitchiner wrote that he had 'known several Painters and other Artists who have, in their natural anxiety to see as well as possible, irremediably injured their Sight, so that when they become 60 or 70 years of age they were obliged to use two half glasses of different foci fixed in the rings of a spectacle frame—the upper half to help them to observe a distant picture or sketch, etc. and the lower half to transmit it to canvas. With such divided Glasses it requires considerable attention to raise or depress the Eyes sufficiently so as only to look through one half ; and that the rays from the other half may not confuse the Eye and distress its adjustment, which would be extremely perplexing and detrimental to the Eyes, as it would be to the Ears to have two Barrel Organs at the same moment—one playing "Sally in Our Alley" and the other "Ally Crooker".'

The terms *bifocal* and *trifocal* were introduced in London by John Isaac Hawkins, whose trifocals (Figure 73-A) were patented in 1827. According to Dr Greeff,

Fig. 74 : Reverend Timothy Dwight.
American engraving, 1817

they had 'stepped up strengths of the horizontally divided glasses from above down; the separate parts of the spectacle have a certain inclination to one another, turning towards the main directions of center of motion'.

In 1836 Schnaitmann of Philadelphia mentioned bifocal lenses made in one piece. The division between the two lenses was slightly curved (Figure 73-B). Four years later Pergens described bifocals with an oval lens in the centre for far vision, surrounded by four pieces of lens for near (Figure 73-C). In 1866 Samuel Gregg of Boston made improvements in bifocals, followed by fairly regular improvements by other opticians, many of them American.

According to Bugbee, the 'modern era of bifocal development begins in 1884, when B. M. Hanna was granted patents on two forms of bifocals which afterward became famous. One type was made by cementing a small wafer to the back of the distance lens, the other by inserting a plug-like reading lens into a round hole in a distance lens. . . . Hanna's two bifocals were given larger crescent-shaped segments by subsequent inventors, and by the end of the century they had become commercially standardized as the "Cemented" and "Perfection" bifocals. Both had the serious faults of ugly appearance, fragility, and dirt-collection at the dividing line, hence the stage was set for a better bifocal.'

Although John L. Borsch did develop a cemented countersunk lens in 1899, it was not until after the turn of the century that significant advances were made in bifocals.

In the 1890s there was a considerable increase in the use of bifocals in both England and America. At the end of the century the two sections of the lens were fused instead of cemented, an idea originated by L. de Wecker in Paris in 1897 but not patented until 1908 by John L. Borsch, Jr.

Fig. 75 : THE PERPENDICULAR PURPLE POLLY who Read the Newspaper and Ate Parsnip Pie with his Spectacles. Drawing by Edward Lear for *More Nonsense*, 1872

There is no evidence that smoked lenses were used in protective glasses before 1820 in England. Figure 74 shows an American engraving of 1817 in which the Reverend Timothy Dwight is wearing tinted lenses. In France at the beginning of the century blue and green were used for coloured lenses. In *Le Conservateur de la vue*, published in 1820, Chevalier wrote : 'Pale blue is a favourable colour. It is that reflected by a beautiful sky, the silent light the moon gives the entire horizon in the absence of the sun. . . . But it is above all green which by its nature seems the most friendly to vision ; it is the colour in which nature is bathed on beautiful days and on which the eye rests with the greatest pleasure ; also, green lenses are the most used.'

But in 1824 Kitchiner stated that 'Green or any Coloured Glasses veil objects with a gloomy obscurity and can never be recommended'. As for other forms of protective glasses, he found 'Gogglers, or black cups glassed with plain glasses and mounted in double-jointed frames formed to the shape of the face . . . preferable to those which are fixed in Leather and Silk and tied on with riband. The latter come so close to the face that they soon become a Vapour Bath for the Eye ; but the former are occasionally found very serviceable to travellers to protect their Eyes from Wind and Dust, and to shield them from a strong reflected light. Blue or Green glass may be fixed in them, but it must be of a very light colour.

'Some more nice than wise folks, among other ridiculous refinements, have recommended thin green gauze or Crape instead of green Glass—under the pretence that while it moderates the Light it still admits the Air, and is therefore cooler to the Eyes.

Fig. 76 : Spectacle cleaner, 1869

'All Coloured Glasses increase the labour of the Eyes, and soon bring them into such an irritable state as unfits them for all the ordinary purposes of life.'

In 1828, in *Der Ratgeber für Erhaltung der Augen*, Petitpierre was more permissive : 'For persons to whom, on account of photopsia, are prescribed by their physicians coloured glasses, the compiler has prepared several spectacles. If coloured glasses of short focus are desired, the spectacles must be furnished with double glasses, for the concave glasses are thinnest in the middle and the convex on the edges, so in these places their colour is paler and there appears in one and the same glass two kinds of colour. In order to overcome this defect, white glasses of the desired focus are covered with a coloured plane glass.' Petitpierre objected to green glass and recommended azure blue instead.

In 1858 blue was perhaps the favourite colour for lenses. Boehm expressed the view that it should be thought of not as a means of decreasing the intensity of light but more in the nature of an effective medication. Yet only six years later one could read that 'light blue spectacles, which have been sometimes recommended as "conservative spectacles", are, under ordinary circumstances, objectionable for a healthy visual organ'.

In *Good Society*, an English book on etiquette, published in 1860, the author, an unidentified countess, wrote : 'If spectacles are necessary they should be of the best and lightest make and mounted in gold or blue steel. For weak sight, blue or smoke-coloured glasses are the best ; green glasses are detestable.' Seven years later Richard Horne described various types of protective glasses in use at the time :

Fig. 77 : Professor Wilhelm Klinkerfues,
Director of the Observatory in
Göttingen. News engraving, 1881

'Of what may be termed the protective glasses, there are several—such as goggles, which are made like little cups of different forms, with gauze or very fine wire to keep off flies, dust, &c., glare of light, and cold draughts of wind. For this purpose there are also four-glass spectacles, having semi-opaque or coloured glass sides ; as also the coquilles, or shell-spectacles, covering the eyes as with a neutral-tinted cup. These latter I should have considered likely to be too much heating, but Mr. Alden [who wrote on spectacles in 1866] says they have perfect ventilation. For my own part, I recommend simply a strip of brown crape. Of those spectacles which are for special purposes, such as Donders' stenopaid spectacles ; and those which Mr. Cooper devised for the Polar and other expeditions likely to cause snow-blindness ; of decentred convex lenses, and orthoscopic spectacles, &c., this is not the place to speak, our business being to deal only with broad generalities.'

The year 1885 marks the development, in Philadelphia, of the first sunglasses made of glass instead of amber or mica. The window glass used, it is reported, was tinted by being left in the summer sun for a number of months.

Spectacle making was hardly big business in mid-century, but it was a growing one. In 1849 in the United States, according to Hugh G. Foster, a Mr Bausch sold a Mr Lomb half-interest in a tray of optical blanks and some miscellaneous horn

Fig. 78 : William Makepeace Thackeray (1811–63). Engraved from his last photograph

frames for $66 in cash. In 1961 the firm of Bausch and Lomb grossed $68,200,000 (more than 24 million pounds).

It was in the mid-nineteenth century that Bausch, using a piece of hard rubber he had picked up in the street, made his first pair of rubber eyeglass frames. The company started making vulcanite frames in 1866. Cheaper and lighter in weight than horn, it was purchased in large sheets, which had to be heated in a cookstove, then punched out on a hand press.

When William Beecher, a Massachusetts jeweller, founded what was later to become the American Optical Company in the mid-nineteenth century, imported English frames cost $75 (£27) a pair. He managed to reduce the wholesale price of frames to about a dollar. And by 1868 the United States was the centre for production of all-glass spectacles.

American Henry Kirstein recalled the early days of his father's optical business, founded in 1864: 'It was small and unpretentious—an office in his home, from which he traveled throughout the entire Eastern part of the country, engaged solely in the sale of frames and mountings. There were no eyewear styles as we know them today. Spectacles were of thin blue steel wire, or with heavy solid rims of steel or silver. Eye shapes were elliptical and in small sizes only. The saddle and ribbon bridge was the style of the day.'

Until rolled gold frames were developed in the last quarter of the century, spectacles were mostly of either gold or blue steel. The rolled gold frames provided the advantages of gold without its disadvantages, including a price within reach of the average wearer. Later an alloy of platinum and gold made possible further improvements in workmanship and lower cost.

An article in *Chambers' Journal* for 1891 discussed the difference between natural crystal and artificial glass for spectacles. Although it had been generally assumed that the crystal (still referred to as pebble) was far superior, the writer, having worn both kinds of lenses for a period of years, was of the opinion that there was no noticeable difference and that the glass had a great advantage in price. For protection against the sun he recommended blue rather than green, and he commented on the progress which was being made in the manufacture of smoky or grey glass for the same purpose.

Five years later in the same journal, an unidentified writer (possibly the same one) listed the variety of lenses in current use—'the non-focal coloured glasses, the plano-convex, the plano-concave, the double convex, and double concave, and the double focus or Franklin lens that appears cracked across the centre, but is in reality two pair of lenses in one frame, to suit eyes of different focus'.

It was reported that 'the lenses for spectacles are usually made from crown-glass, the cheapest of any; but convex glasses, which from their shape are peculiarly liable to injury from scratches, are nearly always constructed from either rock-crystal or flint-glass, both extremely hard substances. . . . The cheaper kind of spectacles sent over from Germany and elsewhere, are seldom free from blemishes, and as the slightest flaw is injurious to the eye, care should be taken not to use any that have tiny air-bubbles or minute specks on their surface.' The article went on to praise the contemporary development in frames:

'Like everything else in this progressive age, spectacles have been rapidly perfected, not only in the quality of the lenses, but more especially in their mounting. The heavy framework of bone, horn, and tortoise-shell, worn by our grandfathers, are a contrast indeed to the dainty light setting of modern glasses, the aim of the good spectacle makers of today. A frame of the slightest fine steel, or the lightest of gold, compatible with the safe holding of the lens, makes the wearing of glasses much less irksome than they must formerly have been. Pince-nez have frequently no setting at all beyond the necessary bridge; and the heavy double gold eyeglass, once such a favorite with young-old belles and antique beaux at Spas and fashionable watering-places, is now quite obsolete. Another craze too is gone, when everyone who wished to be thought smart, was bound to carry an eyeglass in order that they might properly recognize friends and effectually avoid detrimentals. There is a survival of this fashion on the Continent, in the constant use of the long-handled lorgnette.'

In the mid-twentieth century Charles H. Sullivan reminisced about this same period. In 1891, he recalled, frames in 'small sizes were used for the eyes and the

Fig. 79 : SHALL MAN BE MAN ? Illustration by Arthur
B. Frost for Lewis Carroll's *The Three Voices*,
1869

Fig. 80 : TO PURSUE IT WITH FORKS AND HOPE.
Illustration by Henry Holiday for Lewis
Carroll's *The Hunting of the Snark*, 1876

difference was made up in the bridge, which was of the "C" or curl type. The
materials were mostly of blue, bronzed, or nickel steel frames, mostly straight
temples.' Then he added :

'From 1892 on a decided change was noticed. Improvements in styles, sizes,
and materials came along, and shortly after that date gold-filled [rolled gold] frames
were on the market. One odd combination used greatly was the gold-filled bridge
with the solid silver frame. This was popular and sold at a popular price. The bad
feature of the silver, however, was that its softness kept the temples constantly out
of shape ; the filled bridge took care of the front.

'Rimless mountings were still new, and finger piece mountings were not yet
born. The old rubber eyeglasses, which were born in Rochester, N.Y., shortly
before the Civil War, were legion, and they were in great demand by those who
"just wanted a pair of reading glasses". . . . One Philadelphia house advertised
them for years for 10 cents a pair.'

In the United States in the nineties 10K riding bow frames sold for $5, blue,
bronze, or nickel frames for $12.50, and silver riding bow frames with rolled gold

bridges for $3. In 1893 Ernest Hart wrote in the *Atlantic Monthly* on the prevalence of eyeglasses among the general population : 'Ordinary people are in the habit of regarding with some misgivings the constantly increasing use of spectacles. In earlier days, these rather unsightly lenses were reserved mainly for old age ; and it is not without sadness that the uninitiated see innocent schoolgirls and sturdy schoolboys disfigured with these appendages. . . . But we must learn to correct these old-world notions.' Mr Hart added that Mr Williamson, president of the ophthalmological section of the British Medical Association, was looking forward 'with hopeful satisfaction to a time when, as an evidence of increasing knowledge among the people and advancing civilization, we may ultimately reach a position in which "a man who goes about with his eyes naked will be so rare that the sight of him will almost raise a blush". The prejudice against glasses is still so strong that in some cases and in some public services a man may not wear them at work, even when they give him perfect sight. But this prejudice is lessening.'

In 1898 the Empire Bible and Spectacle Institution of Tiverton, reports C. S. Flick, was offering to send out a 'Philanthropist's Parcel' containing '1 dozen good spectacles, ages assorted, 1 dozen cases, 1 dozen Gospel books, and 3 copies of the Gospel in 3 dozen foreign languages, all post paid in wooden case, for 36 penny stamps to any address in the United Kingdom'.

PINCE-NEZ

Pince-nez are believed to have appeared in the 1840s. Plate 45-A shows an early version ; Figure 82 represents French styles worn in 1859. T. Haines Moore, an American optician, tells of breaking a lens of a pair of rimless pince-nez in Berlin about 1850 and being unable to have it repaired because the glasses were of a more delicate construction than that used in Germany—the German customers wanted something more durable. Dr Moore would, perhaps, have had better luck in Italy. Plate 47-G shows an interesting Italian version of the early rimless pince-nez. A few years later, the delicately constructed, rimless pince-nez could be found all over Europe. Plate 47-E shows a very sturdy pair of German eyeglasses.

During the latter part of the century there was a great upsurge in the popularity of the pince-nez for both men and women. The plates at the end of the chapter give an idea of the enormous variety in styles. There were heavy rims, light rims, and no rims at all ; there were ribbons, chains, and unanchored glasses which the wearer hoped would not fall off and smash ; there were round lenses, oval lenses, half-moon lenses, and rectangular lenses ; and above all there was a wide variety of nosepieces for holding the glasses on.

Figure 83 shows various styles of pince-nez being worn by men from a variety of professions—diplomacy (c, g), music (e, p), theatrical producing (f), sports (h),

Fig. 81 : HANSARD.   Caricature by Ape (Pellegrini) for *Vanity Fair*, 1884

Fig. 82 : Champfleury. French caricature
by Nadar, 1859

law (i, j, q, t), banking (k), ministry (m), brokerage (n, t), merchandizing (o), and art (r). Although all are to some degree distinguished (a—Louis Pasteur, e—John Philip Sousa), they are of various ages. It is interesting to note that the one who appears to be the youngest (i) is wearing the heaviest frames. Observe also that only a quarter of them have their glasses anchored to chains or cords. It is also significant that in the *Fashions in Hair* plates for the last quarter of the century there were many more pince-nez than spectacles. It is probably safe to assume that had it not been for the socially approved pince-nez, a good many of these men would have removed their glasses before being photographed.

Unlike the monocle, the pince-nez did not seem to settle in one or two countries but was universally used in the Western world. It was, of course, not practical for flat-bridged Oriental noses. Figures 84 and 85 give us two contrasting British examples, whereas Figure 86 shows two German fops with their matching pince-nez. Although it was never truly elegant when worn by women (only the lorgnette had that distinction, and it was held, not worn), the pince-nez was tolerated on informal occasions by fashionable ladies, though its popularity was hardly in its favour. It was essentially a middle-class eyeglass.

Fig. 83 : Men wearing pince-nez, 1870–1900. From *Fashions in Hair*

Fig. 84 : MILITARY ADVICE.   Caricature by Ape (Pellegrini) for *Vanity Fair*,
1874

Fig. 85 : ACTIVE.  Caricature by Ape (Pellegrini) for *Vanity Fair*, 1878

Fig. 86 : Max und Jaromir.   Caricature by Oberländer, 1881

Fig. 87 : And the Dablet Pays Long Ceremonious Calls.   Illustration
by Harry Furniss for Lewis Carroll's *The Little Man That Had a
Little Gun*, 1893

Gentlemen wore any style which suited them—heavy or delicate, round or oval, straight or drooping—usually on a ribbon, cord, or chain about the neck or attached to the lapel. Ladies more often than not wore the oval rimless style on a fine gold chain which could be reeled automatically into a button-size eyeglass-holder pinned to the dress. Whatever the disadvantages of the pince-nez, it was convenient; and if it was not exactly becoming, it seemed a good deal less dreary than spectacles.

In 1898 a reader wrote to the English magazine called *Answers* on some advantages, beyond the obvious ones, of wearing eyeglasses, meaning pince-nez:

'Apart from the fact that certain faces are improved by glasses, a pair can be made to render their wearer real service. I find them of most use during discussions, either at home or at the debating club. While I am fumbling with them I gain several valuable seconds in which to collect my thoughts, and no one notices the pause. If I need longer grace, I dextrously allow the obstinate things to fall from my nose. Nervous people should certainly take to eye-glasses; they cover a good deal of bashfulness. Although they are only plain glass, and anyone can see through them, they act as a kind of shield. You feel something like the man who, from the interior of his house, is conducting a controversy with a man on the pavement. Through glasses you can look a man full in the face, when without them you would from pure nervousness avoid his glance.'

## Contact Lenses

As early as 1845 Sir John Herschel suggested the idea of contact lenses, though he evidently did nothing about it: 'Should any very bad cases of irregular cornea be found, it is worthy of consideration whether at least a temporary distinct vision could not be procured by applying in contact with the surface of the eye some transparent animal jelly contained in a spherical capsule of glass; or whether an actual mould of the cornea might not be taken, and impressed on some transparent medium'. Even this was not the first time the basic principle involved had been thought of, but it was perhaps the earliest specific suggestion leading directly to experimentation with contact lenses.

Evidently the practical application of a lens to the eyeball did not occur until late in the century, when F. E. Müller, a German maker of glass eyes, blew a protective lens to place over the eyeball of a man whose lid had been destroyed by cancer. The patient wore the lens until his death, twenty years later, without losing his vision. Other patients made use of Müller's lenses, but only for protective purposes.

The term *contact lens* originated with Dr A. Eugen Fick, a Swiss physician, who

Fig. 88 : THE IMPERIAL INSTITUTE.  Lithograph by Spy for *Vanity Fair*, 1893

in 1887 published the results of independent experiments with contact lenses. He worked first with rabbits' eyes, then experimented on his own with encouraging results.

In 1889, in a doctoral dissertation, August Müller, a German medical student, described his own experimentation with contact lenses. Although his attempts to use ground lenses were not successful, he did help lay the groundwork for further experimentation.

In 1892 other doctors and optical firms in Germany, Switzerland, and France co-operated in developing practical contact lenses; and before long several firms began specializing in manufacturing them. But the contact lens was not destined to gain much acceptance before the middle of the next century, and even then it was far from being perfected.

Fig. 89 : Woman with pince-nez, 1890s

PLATE 18 : THE NINETEENTH
CENTURY 1800–1825

A  1821, French. Miniature gold *lorgnette* charm.

B  1821, French. Collapsible *lorgnette* in the form of a watch with gold and pearls.

C  Probably 1820s, French. Collapsible ivory *lorgnette*.

D  Early years, French. Miniature *lorgnette* charms.

E  1810, English. Combination prospect glass and monocle. Gold decorated with turquoises.

F  First Empire, French. *Lorgnette* fan.

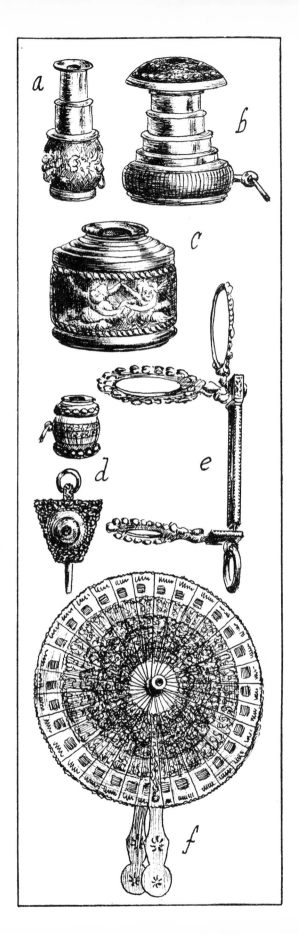

PLATE 19 : THE NINETEENTH CENTURY 1800–1850

A  1844, French.  Opera glasses in gold and blue enamel.

B  *c.* 1810, French.  Ivory *lorgnette*.

C  1823, English.  Spyglass with a watch in one end.  The watch is hinged and swings outward to permit the glass to be used.

D  Early years, French.  Miniature *lorgnette*.

E  Early years.  Folding eyeglasses or quizzing glass in case.

F  First Empire, French.  *Lorgnette* fan.

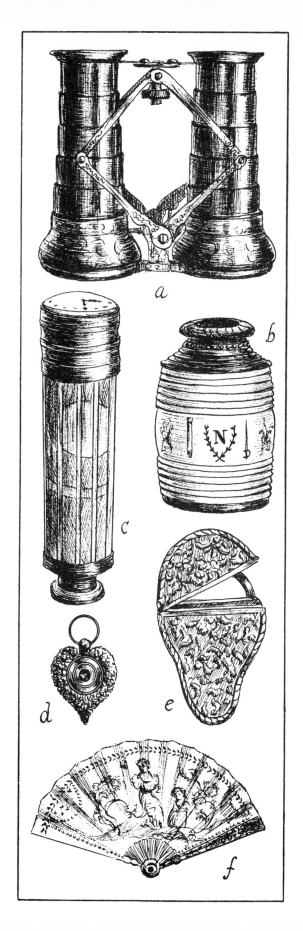

*a*

*b*

*c*

*d*

*e*

*f*

PLATE 20 : THE NINETEENTH CENTURY 1800–1840

A Empire period, French. *Lorgnette* fan. Very fashionable in the late eighteenth century and used by Marie-Antoinette.

B *c.* 1840, Austrian. Opera glass, made in Vienna by J. F. Voigtländer. Belonged to Andrew Pritchard (1804–82), noted English optician. 'The main body-tube is of ivory, and the single draw-tube and mounts are of brass. Both the object-glass and the eye-glass are achromatic and the magnification is about 3 diameters.' (*Science Museum, London*)

C French. Opera glass.

D English. Opera glass made by Thomas Blunt. Body-tube of leather-covered cardboard, draw-tube of silver plate, and mounts of ivory. Magnification is 2 diameters. (*Science Museum, London*)

E French. Prospect glass. Decorated with mother-of-pearl.

F French. Opera glass made by Chevalier, Paris. Tortoise shell and gilt brass. Magnification is 3 diameters. (*Science Museum, London*)

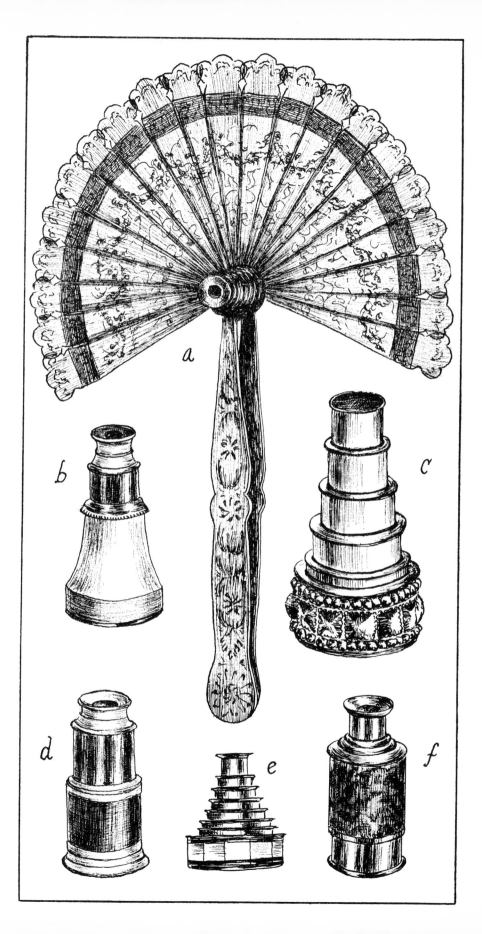

PLATE 21 : THE NINETEENTH
CENTURY 1800–1865

A  French. Folding *face-à-main* or lorgnette.

B  *c.* 1850, English. Pivoted eyeglasses of tortoise shell. (*Science Museum, London*)

C  Possibly *c.* 1830, French. Folding spring-lorgnette. This is the earliest use of this style.

D  *c.* 1840, English. Patented by R. B. Bate in 1825. Frames of silver. 'Bridge is at one end hinged to the glass, which is fitted with a handle, and at the other end the second glass is hinged so that the whole can be folded to form a single eyeglass.' (*Science Museum, London*)

E,  *c.* 1800, French. Miniature *lorgnettes*

F  used as charms. Very fashionable in the Directoire period. Exact date of these examples is uncertain.

G  1862, English. Pivoted eyeglasses of silver. (*Science Museum, London*)

H  English. Eyeglass for shooting. Mounted so that it can be screwed to the cap for shooting, hunting, etc. (*Science Museum, London*)

I  *c.* 1800, French. *Lorgnette* used as a charm. Also fashionable in the Directoire period. Exact date of this example is uncertain.

J  Empire period, French. Single eyeglass of gilded copper.

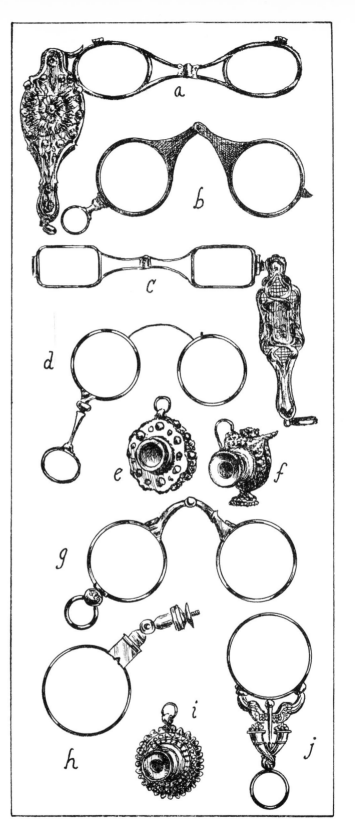

Plate 22 : The Nineteenth
        Century 1890–1900

A   Hand-carved tortoise-shell folding
    lorgnette for ladies.

B   1895, American.  Folding lorgnette
    for ladies in gold or silver.

C   1897, American.   Automatic eye-
    glass reel.  Made by Ketcham and
    McDougall, New York.

D   1895.   Opera glasses for ladies.
    Automatic focussing handle.

E   1897, French.   Sold in New York.
    Opera glasses for ladies.

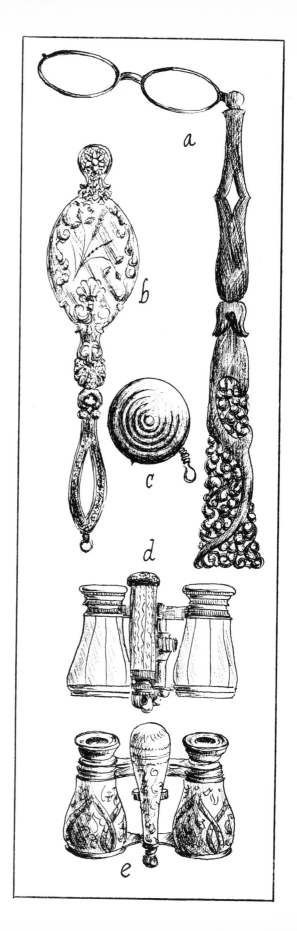

PLATE 23 : THE NINETEENTH
CENTURY 1890–1900

A  1897, American.  Folding lorgnette
made in Philadelphia.

B  1897, French.  Opera glasses with
focussing handle.  Available in
leather, mother-of-pearl, or limoges.
Sold in New York.

C,  American.  Leather eyeglass cases.
D

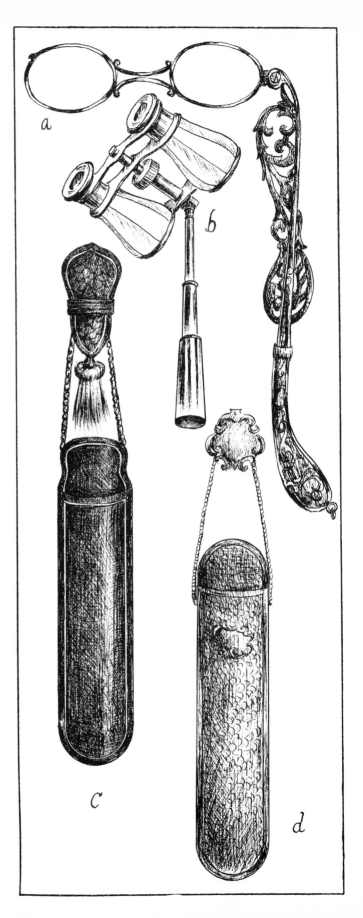

Plate 24 : The Nineteenth
Century 1800–1850

A English. R. Bretell Bate's spring
lorgnette, patented 1825.

B French. Scissors-glasses, pivoted
for folding.

C Quizzing glasses.
-E

F Opera glasses, patented 1825 by J. P.
Lemière.

G English. Hand magnifying glass
with quartz lens. (*Science Museum,
London*)

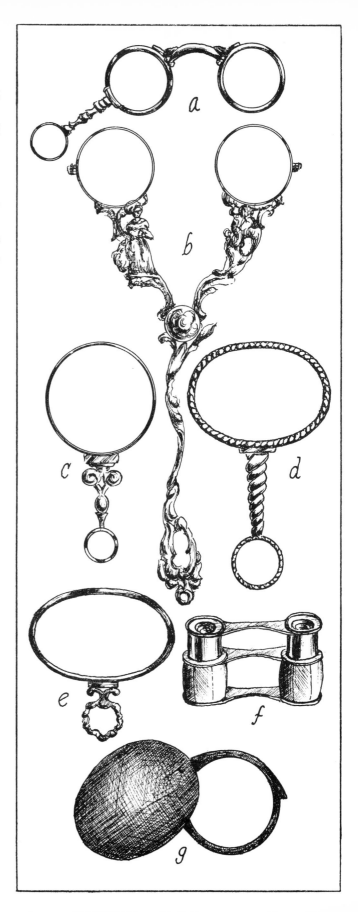

PLATE 25 : THE NINETEENTH CENTURY 1800–1875

A   1850, French.   Spring lorgnon in umbrella handle.

B   French.   *Face-à-main* or lorgnette.

C   *c.* 1872, Swedish.   Spring lorgnette belonging to a member of the Royal family. (*Nordiska Museet, Stockholm*)

D   Not later than 1837, Swedish.   Spring lorgnette made by Johan Erik Sundström, Stockholm. (*Nordiska Museet, Stockholm*)

E   First quarter, English.   Probably of horn.

F   Probably English.   This type of lorgnette dates to the 1780s.

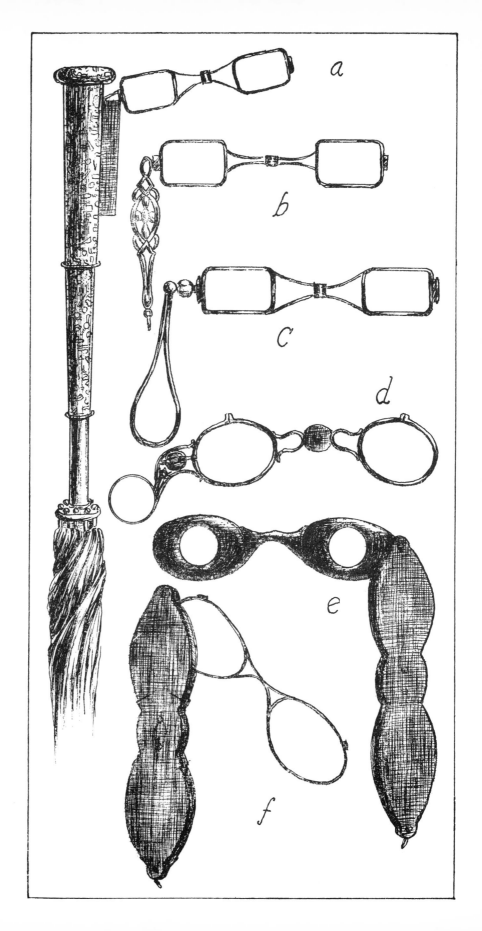

*a*

*b*

*c*

*d*

*e*

*f*

PLATE 26 : THE NINETEENTH CENTURY 1800–1850

A  *c.* 1830.  Hinged-bridge lorgnette of tortoise shell and gold.  This is the earliest use of this style.

B  Early years of the nineteenth, also the eighteenth.

C  Possibly *c.* 1825.  This is the earliest use of this style.

D  1809–19, French.  Gilded silver.  Used by Esais Tegnér, Swedish bishop and poet. (*Nordiska Museet, Stockholm*)

E  Mid-century.  Quizzing glass.  Owner's watch key is part of the frame.

F  First quarter.  Scissors-glasses of steel and horn.  Used in Sweden.  This style can be traced to the 1760s.  (*Nordiska Museet, Stockholm*)

G  *c.* 1848.  Folding lorgnette with pivot bridge.

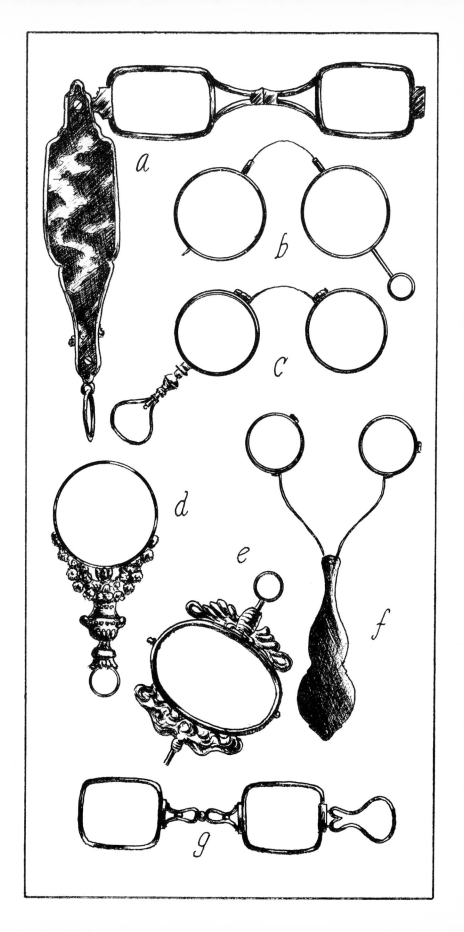

PLATE 27 : THE NINETEENTH
CENTURY 1840–1900

A   *c.* 1880–90.   Gold lorgnette on chain.
Used in Salt Lake City by Hattie
Jones Morris.   Lenses fold together.
(*Pioneer Museum, Salt Lake City*)

B   *c.* 1880–90.   Tortoise-shell lor-
gnette.   Used in Salt Lake City by
Mary Hooper Jennings.   (*Pioneer
Museum, Salt Lake City*)

C   Lenses to study eclipses.   Taken to
Utah from England in 1863.   Made
of tortoise shell with coloured glasses
of amber, blue, green, red, and
purple.   The sixth glass is missing.
(*Pioneer Museum, Salt Lake City*)

D   *c.* 1850, American.   Tan leather
glasses case.  (*Pioneer Museum, Salt
Lake City*)

E   1840s, American.   Silver glasses case
belonging to Joseph Smith.  (*Pioneer
Museum, Salt Lake City*)

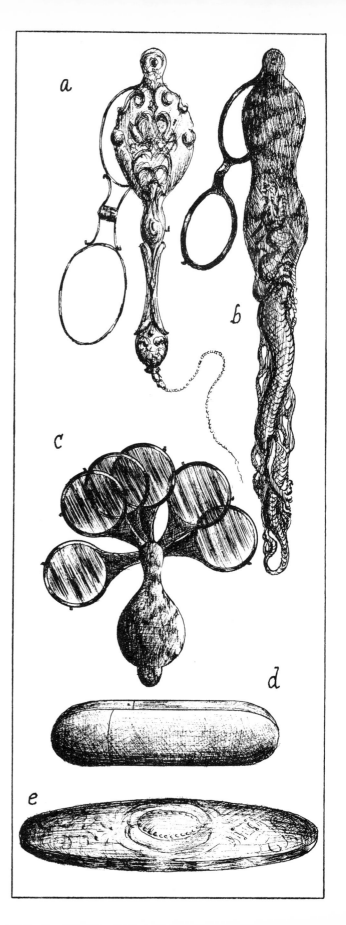

PLATE 28 : THE NINETEENTH
CENTURY 1800–1830

A  *c.* 1800.   Folding lorgnette.

B  *c.* 1800.   Scissors-glasses.

C  1825, English.   Magnifying glass.

D  English.   Monocle with 'galleries'.

E  English.   Monocle.

F  1826–27, English.   Monocles with
-K  handles.   Gold and silver.

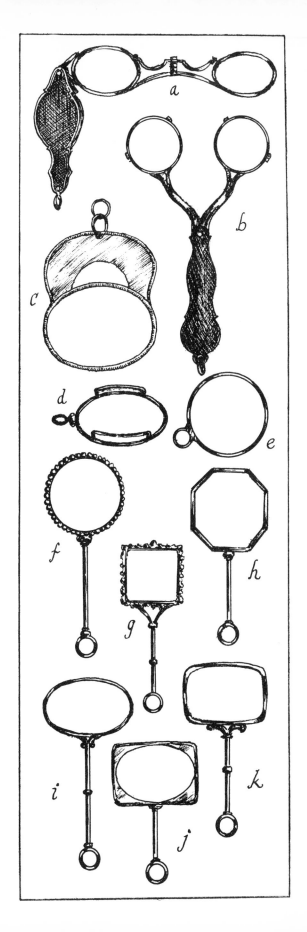

PLATE 29 : THE NINETEENTH
CENTURY 1800–1850

A  French.  Silver magnifying glass. Used in Sweden by Anders Adolph Retzius (1796–1860), anthropologist and professor of anatomy. (*Nordiska Museet, Stockholm*)

B  Magnifying glass of wood and black lacquered brass.  Used in Sweden by Professor Johan Spångberg (1800–1888). (*Nordiska Museet, Stockholm*)

C  French.  Magnifying glass of metal.

D  French.  Magnifying glass of metal and mother - of - pearl. (*Nordiska Museet, Stockholm*)

E  Magnifying glass of horn.  Used in Sweden by Samuel Grubbe (1786–1853), philosopher and cabinet minister. (*Nordiska Museet, Stockholm*)

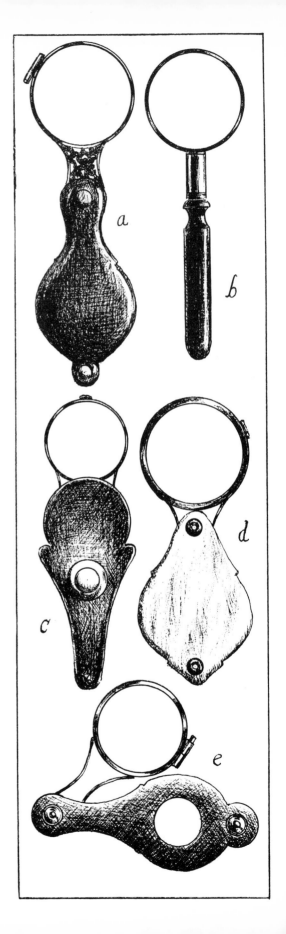

PLATE 30 : THE NINETEENTH
CENTURY 1800–1900

A   French.   Mother-of-pearl quizzing glass.

B   French.   Quizzing glass.

C   Not later than 1876.   Handle and ring of black horn. (*Nordiska Museet, Stockholm*)

D   Reading glass, used by Per Afzelius (1760–1843), professor of medicine at Uppsala, Sweden. (*Nordiska Museet, Stockholm*) (See also Figure 54)

E   Silver reading glass suitable for wearing on a cord or ribbon.   Used by Johan Olof Wallin (1779–1839), Swedish archbishop, poet. (*Nordiska Museet, Stockholm*)

F   *c.* 1800, German.   Made in Nürnberg.   Evidently widely used since examples are still to be found in both Sweden and the United States.   One in New England has a somewhat larger handle. (*Nordiska Museet, Stockholm*)

G   Frame and case of dark horn.   Used by Vilhelm Erik Svedelius (1816–1889), historical writer and professor at Uppsala, Sweden. (*Nordiska Museet, Stockholm*)

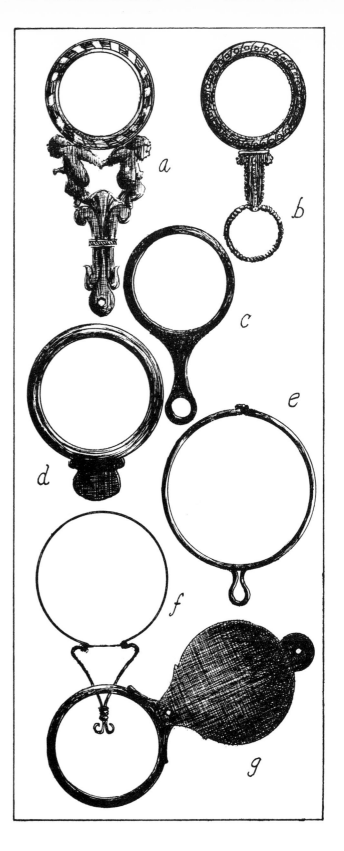

PLATE 31 : THE NINETEENTH
CENTURY 1800–1830

A  *c.* 1800, English.  Tortoise-shell frames.  (*Science Museum, London*)

B  *c.* 1800, English.  Spectacles for squint.  Steel frames with turnpin sides, fitted with tortoise-shell disks mounted in horn.  (*Science Museum, London*)

C  *c.* 1800, English.  Protective spectacles.  Steel frame with hinged, folding sides.  Viridian green glass. (*Science Museum, London*)

D  1820, English.  Silver frames with turnpin sides.  (*Science Museum, London*)

E  Early years, English.  Tortoise-shell frame with velvet-padded Japanese ends.  (*Science Museum, London*)

F  *c.* 1825, Austrian.  Early rimless spectacles made by Voigtländer and Son, Vienna.  Turnpin sides of rolled gold.  (*Science Museum, London*)

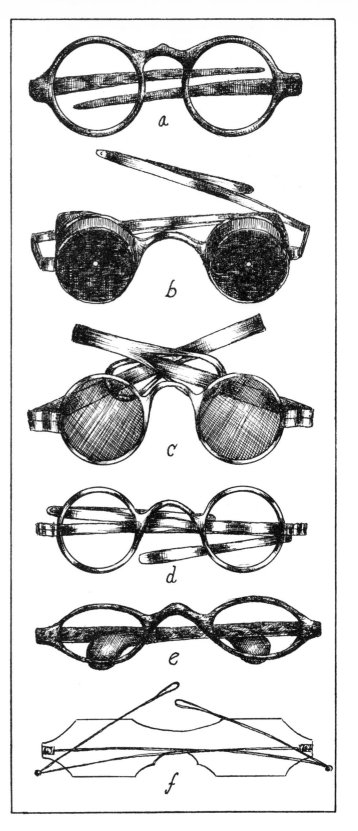

PLATE 32 : THE NINETEENTH
CENTURY 1800–1850

A  Swedish.  Peasant spectacles made of birch and tied on with cords. (*Nordiska Museet, Stockholm*)

B  Swedish.  Peasant spectacles of brass. (*Nordiska Museet, Stockholm*)

C  *c.* 1800, Swedish.  Possibly earlier, though probably not before 1750. Peasant spectacles of brass.  Nosepiece covered with tin. (*Nordiska Museet, Stockholm*)

D  *c.* 1825, American.  Silver spectacles with extension temples and C-shaped nosepiece, made by Charles Poole between 1819 and 1835.  Belonged to John Jay (1745–1829). (*Museum of the City of New York*)

E  *c.* 1840, American.  Made in New York by W. V. Brady between 1835 and 1847.  Belonged to William Whittingham (1771–1847). (*Museum of the City of New York*)

F  Mid-century, American.  Used in New York. (*Museum of the City of New York*)

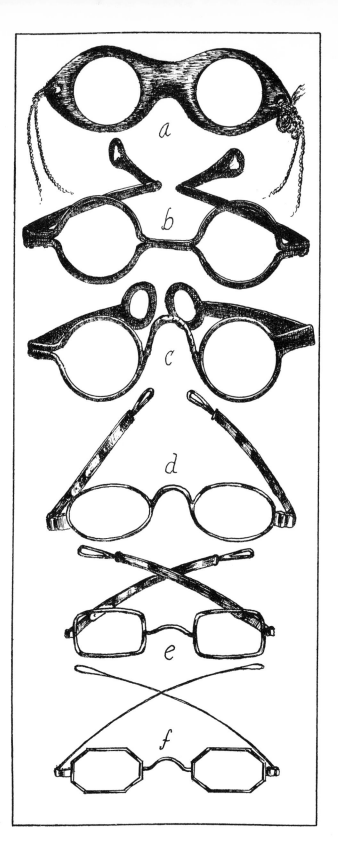

Plate 33 : The Nineteenth Century 1800–1850

A  1837, Swedish.  Gold frames with K-shaped nosepiece.  Manufactured by Johan Erik Sundström, Stockholm.  (*Nordiska Museet, Stockholm*)

B  *c.* 1800, English.  Worn by Pehr Henrik Ling (1776–1839), Swedish poet and gymnast.  Hinged bows.  Green silk ruffle was used to protect the eyes from excessive light.

C  Swedish.  Steel frames with X-shaped nosepiece.  Worn by Samuel Grubbe (1786–1853), philosopher and cabinet minister.  (*Nordiska Museet, Stockholm*)

D  Swedish.  Silver frames with hinged temples and X-nosepiece.  Worn by Lars Georg Rabenius (1771–1846), professor of law.  (*Nordiska Museet, Stockholm*)

E  Mid-century, French.  Frames of horn and steel.  Worn by Henrik Reuterdahl (1795–1870), Swedish archbishop.  (*Nordiska Museet, Stockholm*)

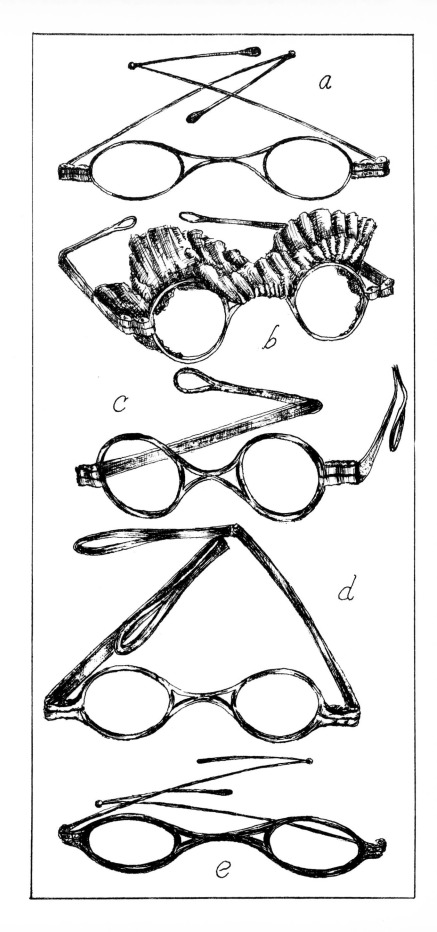

PLATE 34 : THE NINETEENTH CENTURY 1800–1850

A    Probably made not later than 1851, French.  Steel rims.  Worn by Carl Jonas Love Almquist (1793–1866), Swedish writer.  (*Nordiska Museet, Stockholm*)

B    French.  Steel rims.  Worn by Anders Erick Afzelius (1779–1850), Swedish professor of law.  (*Nordiska Museet, Stockholm*)

C    French.  Tortoise-shell and silver frames with X-nosepiece.  Worn by Christian Didrik Forsell (1777–1852), Swedish engraver.  (*Nordiska Museet, Stockholm*)

D    German.  Made of horn and silver.  Worn by Georg Adlersparre (1760–1835), Swedish general and statesman.  (*Nordiska Museet, Stockholm*)

E    French.  Made of horn.  Worn by Olaf Johan Södermark (1790–1848), Swedish portrait painter.  (*Nordiska Museet, Stockholm*)

F    Probably English.  Worn by Fredrik Dahlgren (1791–1844), Swedish poet.  A similar style was worn in the United States in 1825.  (*Nordiska Museet, Stockholm*)

G    Swedish.  Steel frames.  Worn by Samuel Owen (1774–1854), English-born industrialist and mechanic.  (*Nordiska Museet, Stockholm*)

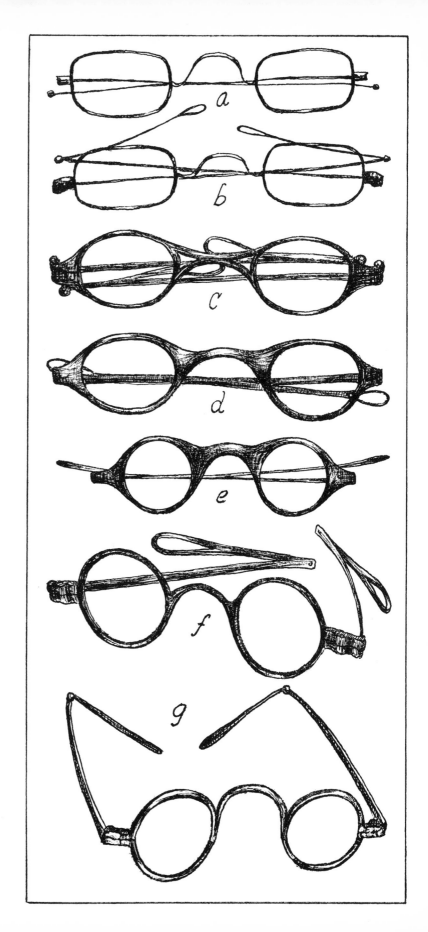

PLATE 35 : THE NINETEENTH CENTURY 1800–1850

A   Early years. Metal frames with inner rims of horn. C-nosepiece.

B   *c.* 1800. Metal frames with sliding temples and English-style nosepiece.

C   Early years. Gold or silver frames with extension temples. The sliding extension temple was known in France as early as the 1780s.

D   Early years. Temple rings are covered with cloth.

E   *c.* 1820, American. Silver frames with tie-on extensions.

F   *c.* 1840, probably Swedish. Metal frames with sliding extension temples, C-nosepiece. (*Nordiska Museet, Stockholm*)

G   French. Made of horn. Worn by Jöns Jacob Berzelius (1779–1848), Swedish chemist and professor. (*Nordiska Museet, Stockholm*)

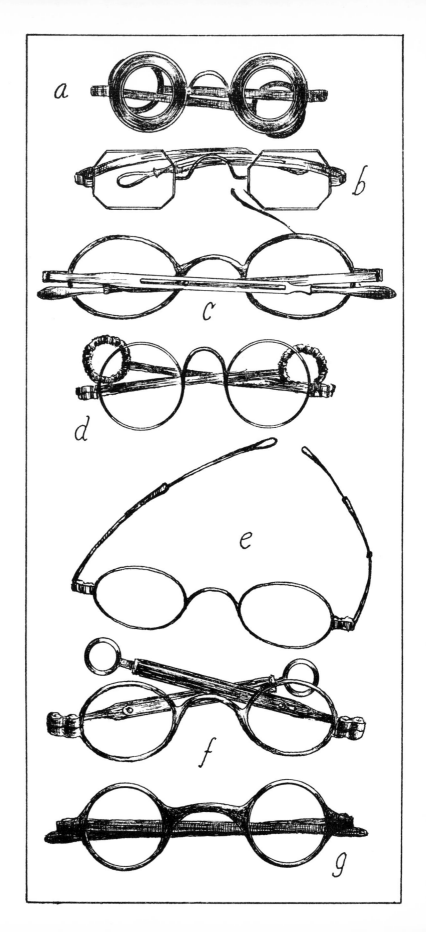

PLATE 36 : THE NINETEENTH CENTURY 1800–1850

A    Probably English.

B, C, D    1823, English.  Pivoted temples.

E    Probably English.

F    English.  Silver frames.  Worn by Nils Henrik Sjöborg (1767–1838), Swedish archaeologist and professor of history.  (*Nordiska Museet, Stockholm*)

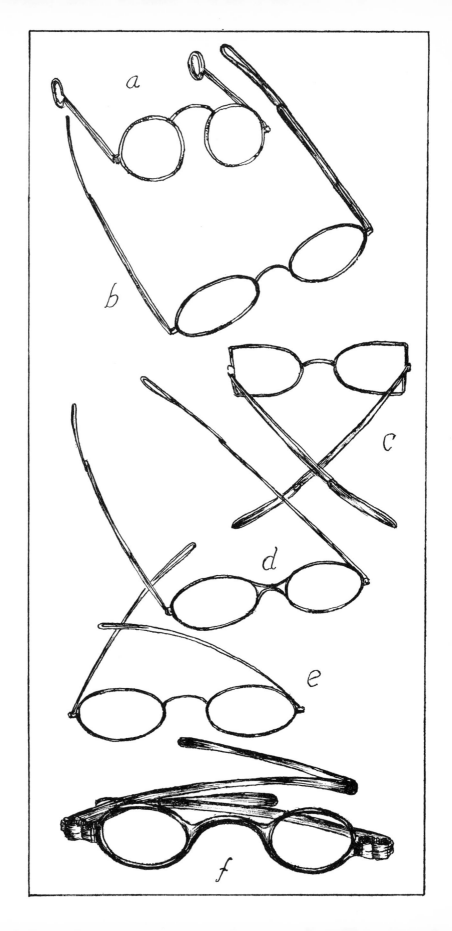

PLATE 37 : THE NINETEENTH CENTURY 1800–1875

A   Double glasses with hinged protective lenses. Manufactured in Sweden in 1860. English patent by I. Richardson, 1797. (*Nordiska Museet, Stockholm*)

B   Mid-century, French. Railway glasses, white metal frames. (*Nordiska Museet, Stockholm*)

C   Mid-century, French. Railway glasses with K-nosepiece. Worn by Anders Adolf Retzius (1796–1860), Swedish anthropologist and professor of anatomy. (*Nordiska Museet, Stockholm*)

D   French. Manufactured in Paris, 1819–38, of tortoise shell and silver. Worn in Stockholm. (*Nordiska Museet, Stockholm*)

E   Probably second quarter. Double glasses with hinged protective lenses and English-style nosepiece.

F   Double lenses with hinged bows.

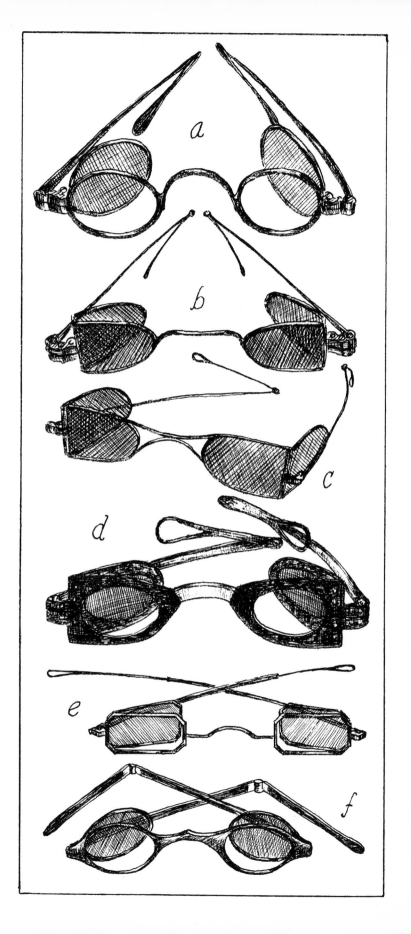

PLATE 38 : THE NINETEENTH CENTURY 1825–1900

A    French. Made of horn. Worn by Johan Fredrik Fåhræus (1796–1865), Swedish government minister. (*Nordiska Museet, Stockholm*)

B    Silver spectacles with folding temples, manufactured in Sweden not later than 1829. Worn by C. A. Wockatz (1795–1870), a Swedish agricultural administrator. (*Nordiska Museet, Stockholm*)

C    French. Steel rims. Worn by Swedish Princess Eugenie (1820–89). (*Nordiska Museet, Stockholm*)

D    1895, probably French. Made of nickel. W-shaped nosepiece. Worn by Alarik Frithiof Holmgren (1831–97), Swedish professor of philosophy. (*Nordiska Museet, Stockholm*)

E    French. Steel rims with W-nosepiece. Worn by August Strindberg (1849–1912), Swedish playwright. (*Nordiska Museet, Stockholm*)

F    French. Steel rims with K-nosepiece. Worn by Johan Vilhelm Beckman (1792–1873), Swedish curate. (*Nordiska Museet, Stockholm*)

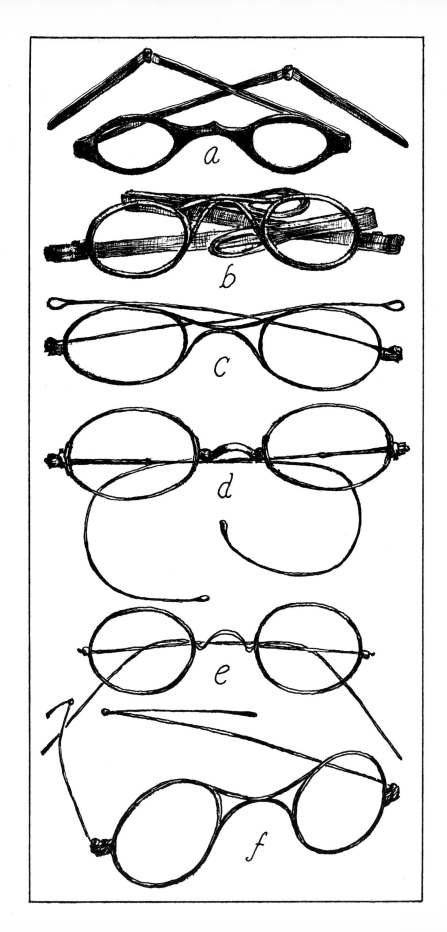

Plate 39 : The Nineteenth Century 1840–1880

A   Gold-rimmed pince-nez worn by Brigham Young (1801–77). (*Pioneer Museum, Salt Lake City*)

B   *c.* 1852, American.   Gold-rimmed spectacles with English nosepiece.

C   *c.* 1850–60, American.   Possibly brass. (*Pioneer Museum, Salt Lake City*)

D   1857.   Taken to Utah from England. (*Pioneer Museum, Salt Lake City*)

E   1844, American.   Steel-rimmed spectacles with C-nosepiece, worn by John Taylor in the Carthage jail when Joseph and Hyrum Smith were incarcerated before being murdered. (*Pioneer Museum, Salt Lake City*)

F   *c.* 1850, American.   Silver frames with plain viridian green glass. (*Pioneer Museum, Salt Lake City*)

G   1869, American.   Protective goggles with plain viridian glass, worn on the first trans-continental train.   Glass is surrounded by wire screen.

All of these glasses were worn by early Mormon pioneers.

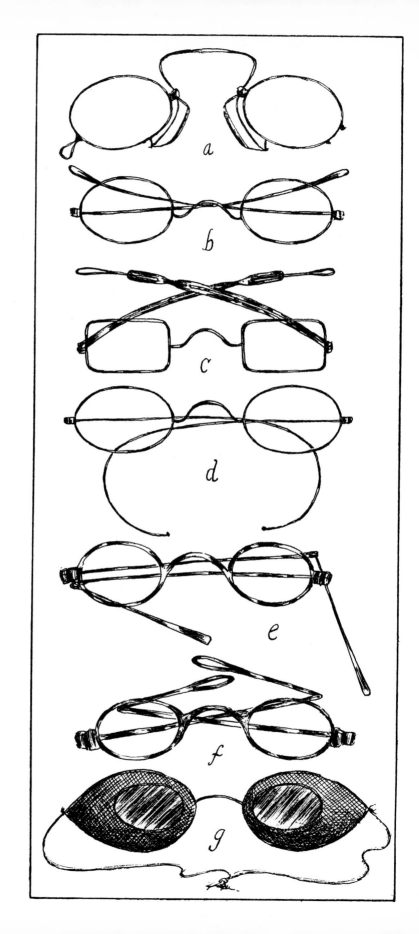

PLATE 40 : THE NINETEENTH
CENTURY 1850–1900

A  1853, American.  English nosepiece, extension temples.

B  1860.  Frame of fine blue steel wire, English nosepiece.

C  c. 1860, English.  Frame of yellow metal, English nosepiece.

D  c. 1860, American.  Gold frame with English nosepiece.

E  c. 1890, American.  Frame of white metal with extension temples.

F  c. 1890, American.  Pulpit-eyes for reading.  Steel frames with hooks for attaching to regular glasses.  Similar ones were used in France at the same time.

G  French.  Steel rims, X-nosepiece.  Worn by Swedish novelist Emilie Flygare-Carlén (1807–92).  (*Nordiska Museet, Stockholm*)

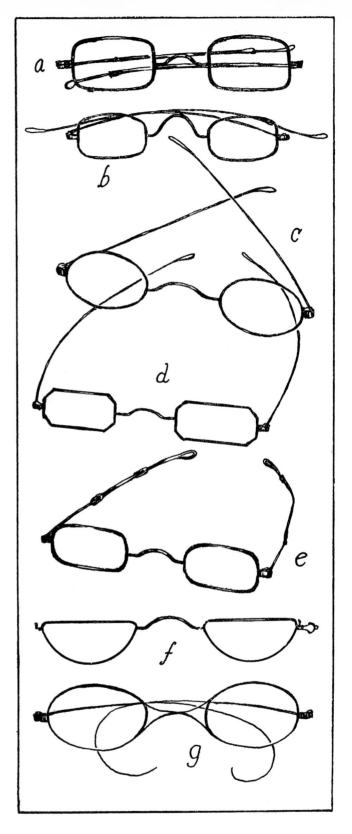

PLATE 41 : THE NINETEENTH
        CENTURY 1875–1900

A   Folding lorgnette of tortoise shell.
    Used in New York. (*Brooklyn
    Museum*)

B   1895, American.  Bicycle and driv-
    ing spectacles.  Sold for $1.45 a
    dozen, wholesale, including lenses.

C   *c.* 1889, American.  Pince-nez.

D   *c.* 1875, Venetian.  Sunglasses.

E   1894.  Tortoise-shell lorgnette.

F   1895, American.  Opera glasses with
    detachable handle.

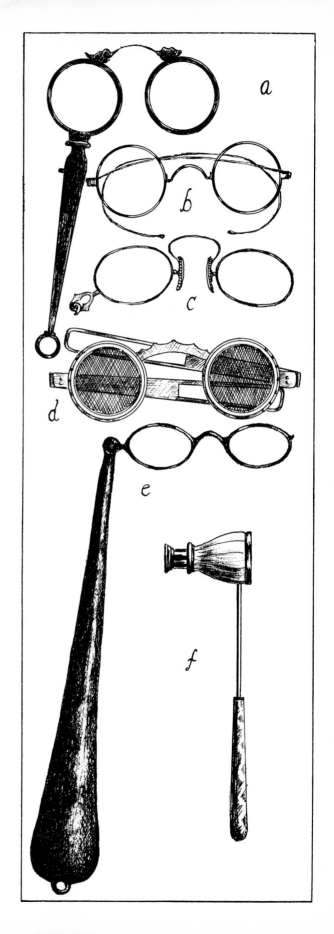

PLATE 42 : THE NINETEENTH CENTURY 1850–1900

A  French. Steel frames with K-nosepiece. Worn by Egron Lundgren (1815–75), Swedish painter and writer (see also E below). (*Nordiska Museet, Stockholm*)

B  French. Steel frames with X-nosepiece. Worn by Erik Edlund (1819–88), Swedish professor. (*Nordiska Museet, Stockholm*)

C  French. Steel frames with K-nosepiece. Worn by Anders Fryxell (1795–1881), Swedish physics professor. (*Nordiska Museet, Stockholm*)

D  French. Steel frames. Worn by Fredrik Achates Dalman (1801–81), Swedish publisher, politician.

E  Mid-century, English. Worn by Egron Lundgren (see also A above).

F  Probably end of the century, French. Rimless lenses with silver W-nosepiece and temples.

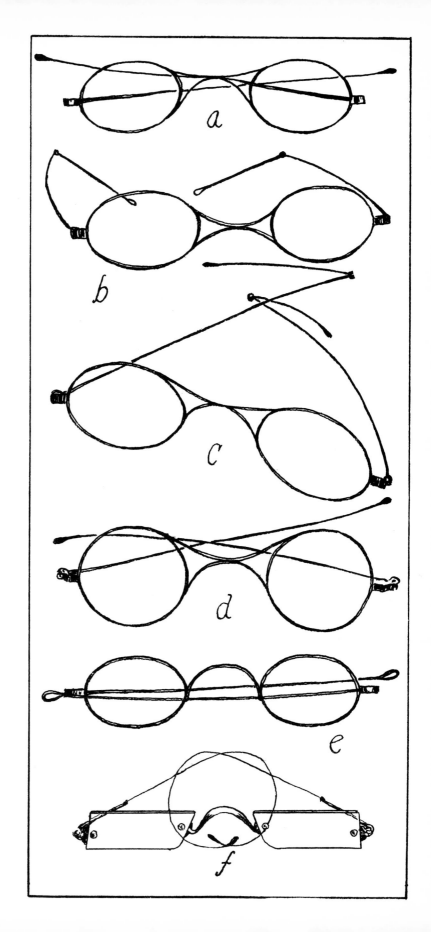

PLATE 43 : THE NINETEENTH CENTURY 1840–1900

A   1860, American.   Collapsible frame, tortoise-shell ring.   Manufactured by Bausch and Lomb.

B   Last quarter, American.   Manufactured by Bausch and Lomb.

C   *c.* 1840, English.   Shell frames, metal temples with loops for cord or ribbon.   (*Science Museum, London*)

D   *c.* 1850, English.  Blue steel frames, hinged at one side.   Turnpin bows and X-nosepiece.   For viewing both near and distant objects.   (*Science Museum, London*)

E   *c.* 1870, English.   Pale blue tinted glass, eye-shade of moss green velvet.   Loops in bows for ribbon or cord.   (*Science Museum, London*)

F   *c.* 1900, English.   Pantascopic spectacles, allowing reader to look over or under.   Silver frames, C-nosepiece.   Made by Aitchison, London.   (*Science Museum, London*)

G   English.   Pantascopic spectacles.   Light steel frame with short bow sides and W-nosepiece.   (*Science Museum, London*)

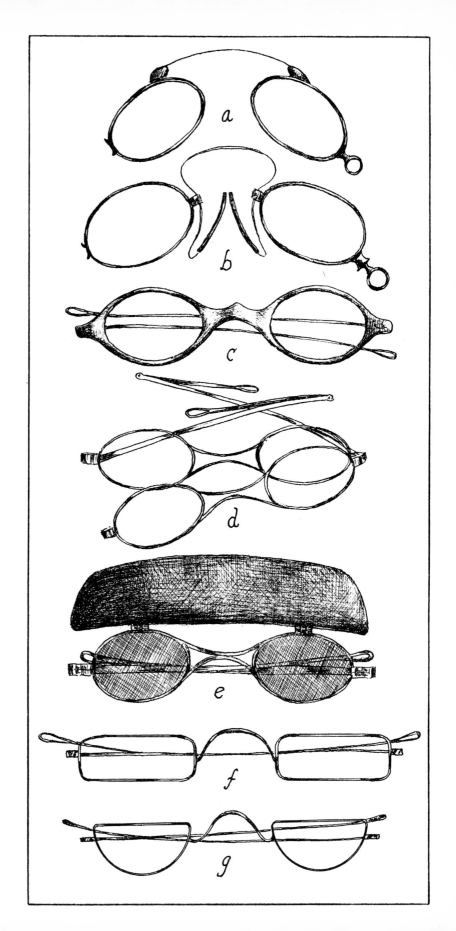

PLATE 44 : THE NINETEENTH CENTURY 1840–1900

A    Mid-century. Worn by Anders Jonas Ångström (1814–74), Swedish professor of physics. (*Nordiska Museet, Stockholm*)

B    *c.* 1870, Swedish. Worn by Lars Fredrik Svanberg (1805–78), professor of chemistry. (*Nordiska Museet, Stockholm*)

C    *c.* 1846, French. Pince-nez.

D    Eyeglasses with handle.

E    Steel-rimmed pince-nez.

F    Rimless pince-nez.

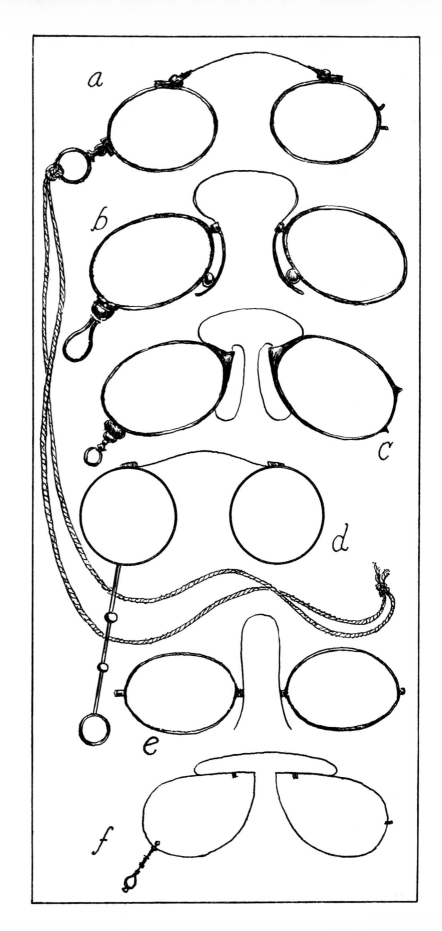

Plate 45 : The Nineteenth
Century 1840–1900

A   Mid-century, American. Pince-nez with adjustable steel bar spring.

B   French. Pince-nez with silver rims, cork nose-guards, spring bridge.

C   Pince-nez with cork-faced nose-guards.

D   Probably French. Made of steel and horn. Worn by Artur Hazelius (1833–1901) of the Nordiska Museet, Stockholm. This style was being worn in France in 1889.

E   Mid-century. Steel rims. Worn by Johan Edvard Bäckström (1841–86), Swedish poet. (*Nordiska Museet, Stockholm*)

F   1876, American. Patented by P. Hannays.

G   Probably fourth quarter. Pince-nez.

H   1893, American. Rimless pince-nez with hole for chain or cord.

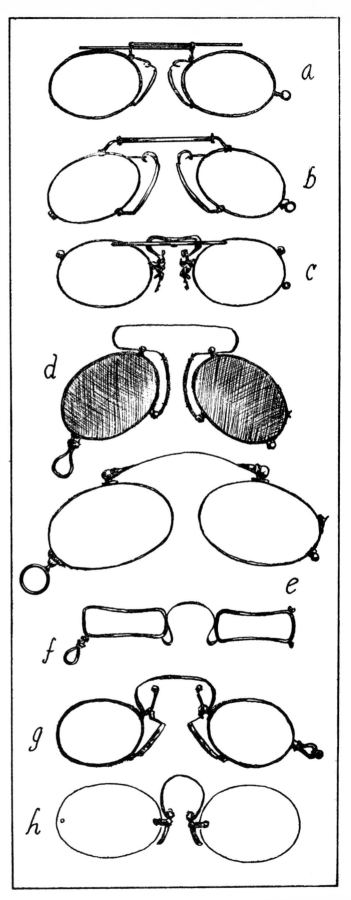

PLATE 46 : THE NINETEENTH
CENTURY 1850–1900

A  1870, American.  Folding eyeglasses.

B  *c.* 1870.  Hard rubber frame with
stationary guards.

C  1867, American.  Thin shell rims,
bridge of flat blue steel.  Folding
frames.

D  *c.* 1880, French.  Lightweight steel
frames.

E  *c.* 1875.  Folding, hard-rubber frame
with adjustable spring guards and
steel spring.

F  1880, American.

G  1875.  Folding frames of thin blue
steel, flat blue steel nose-spring.

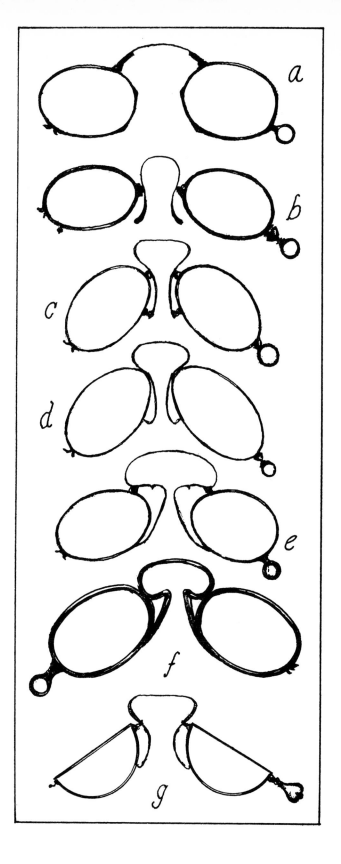

Plate 47 : The Nineteenth Century 1850–1900

A   1895, American. Pince-nez, made by Levy, Dreyfus and Company, New York, and advertised as the 'Improved Imperial Guard. The best and easiest adjustable eye-glass guard in the market.'

B   1897, American. Aluminium and steel pince-nez.

C   1897, American. Pince-nez with adjustable guard. Made by J. M. and A. C. Johnston, Chicago.

D   1895, American. Made by the Globe Optical Company, Boston, and advertised as 'the latest and best bar spring made, combining neatness, durability, and low price, the 3 requisites for a popular bar spring. Made in gold and steel.' A sample pair could be had by dealers for 75 cents.

E   1861, German and English. 'Beam' spring eyeglasses with screw spring.

F   1895, American. Eyeglass or lorgnette chain for ladies. Attached to sturdy hairpin.

G   c. 1850, Italian. Folding pince-nez with the catch made as part of the lens. Made by Oliva, Milan.

H   Third quarter, Italian. Folding pince-nez with metal catch attached. Made by Oliva, Milan.

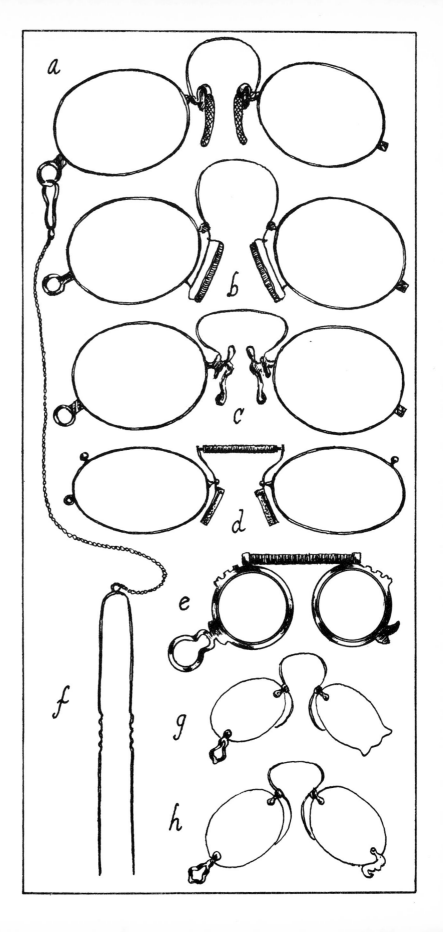

A   Folding pince-nez worn by Henry Amy, New York banker.

B   Rimless, drop-eye pince-nez worn by James Michael Fitzsimons, New York City judge.

C   Rimless pince-nez worn by Abram Lesse Dittenhoefer, New York lawyer.

D   Steel or silver rims. Worn by Henry Sayre Van Duzer, New York lawyer.

E   Folding pince-nez worn by Edward Mitchell, New York lawyer.

F   Rimless pince-nez worn by Thomas Fortune Ryan, New York financier.

G   Pince-nez worn by Reverend Richard Heber Newton, New York.

H   Folding pince-nez worn by William Montgomery St John, New York executive.

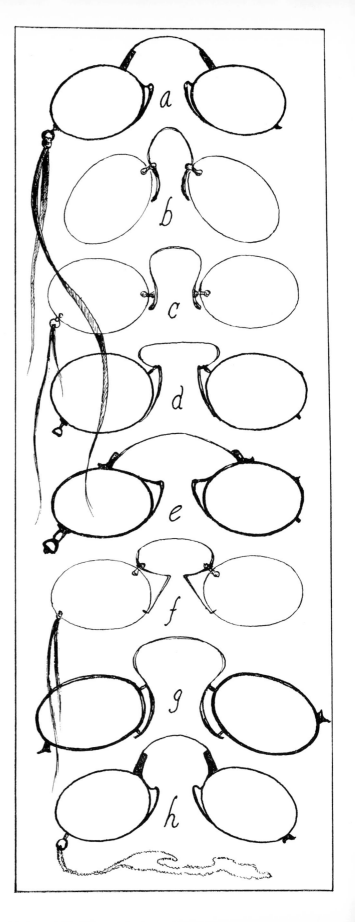

PLATE 49 : THE NINETEENTH
CENTURY 1880–1900

A   French.   *Face-à-main* or lorgnette,
open.   Long - handled lorgnettes
were not used before this time.

B   French.   Reading glass.

C   French.   Lorgnette, closed.

D   French.   Lorgnette or binoculars.

E   French.   Rimless pince-nez with
bridge tilting forward so that lenses
will remain vertical.

F   French.   Pince-nez with movable
nosepieces.

G   French.   Pince-nez with spring
bridge adjustable to any size of nose.

H   French.   Spectacles with metal rims
and W-nosepiece.

I   French.   Supplementary half-moon
lenses to be hung on distance glasses
to make them suitable for reading.
(See also Plate 40-F.)

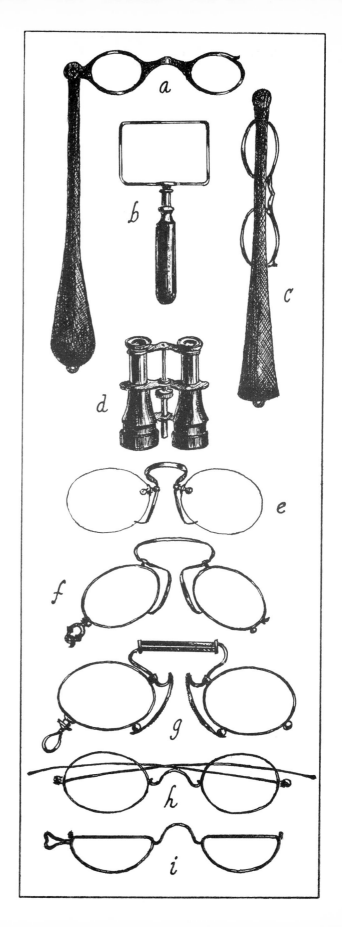

PLATE 50 : THE NINETEENTH CENTURY 1889–1900

A    1894, French.   Hinged double spectacles by Bourgeois.

B    1890s.   Bar spring pince-nez.   Still being worn in 1908.

C    1890s.   Bar spring pince-nez.   Still being worn in 1908.

D    1900, American.   Bar spring pince-nez.

E    1889, French.   Folding pince-nez.

F    1889, French.   Rimless spectacles with gold nosepiece and temples.

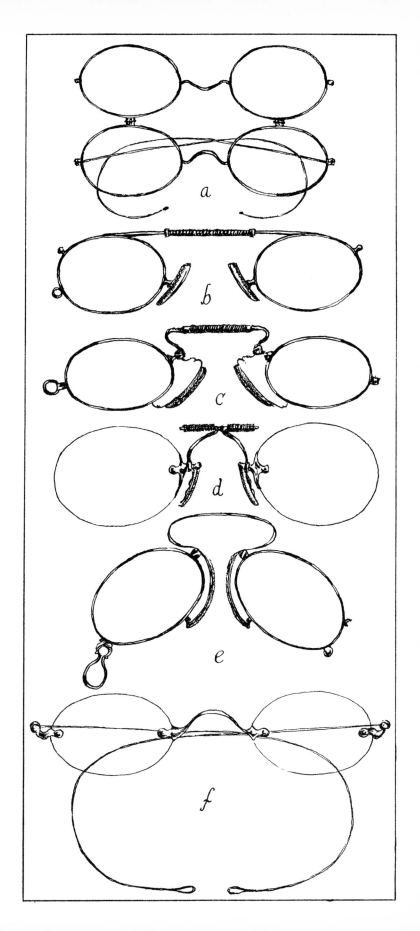

Fig. 90 : BOX AT THE METROPOLITAN OPERA. Etching and engraving by Reginald Marsh, 1934

# 7 · The Twentieth Century

It used to be that glasses were
Tho' needed, gruesome things to wear,
But now a wardrobe's not complete
Without a gaily matching pair.

ELSIE MURIEL FARR, 1947

The twentieth century brought greater developments in eyeglasses than there had been in their entire six-century history. Bifocals, trifocals, even quadrifocals were perfected; and contact lenses seemed to reduce the size and inconvenience of lenses to an absolute minimum. Eyeglasses, since they obviously could not be eliminated, were at last universally accepted, due in large part to the efforts of the designers to reduce their functional look with a veneer of style. The designers were helped enormously by the development of plastics suitable for frames. Though the entrance of eyeglasses into the world of fashion led occasionally to extremes of eccentricity, it made possible the wearing of glasses on any occasion without embarrassment. Thus, fashionable people were at last able to see clearly at all times if they really wanted to.

## THE EARLY YEARS (1900–20)

At the beginning of the century this revolution had not yet begun. In the autumn of 1900 Dr Norburne B. Jenkins wrote in the *Optical Journal*: 'Wearing spectacles or eyeglasses out of doors is always a disfigurement, often an injury, seldom a necessity. . . . Glasses are very disfiguring to women and girls. Most tolerate them because they are told that wearing them all the time is the only way to keep from having serious eye trouble. If glasses are all right, they will seldom or never have to be worn in public.'

Even though spectacles were still not considered quite suitable for wearing in public if it could be avoided, there was a variety of glasses and accessories available. In 1900 a wholesale optical dealer in Chicago listed among his products solid gold spectacles and eyeglasses, rolled gold spectacles and eyeglasses, gold and rolled gold eyeglass chains and hooks, chatelaine and spectacle cases, lorgnettes, opera glasses, field and marine glasses, spyglasses and telescopes, microscopes, reading and magnifying glasses.

The following year a New England optical firm announced that they were making a hairpin to be used with an eyeglass chain, the ring being formed from the pin itself rather than being soldered on. 'The great increase in the use of hair pin chains', the advertisement proclaimed, 'makes this pin particularly desirable for the trade at this time. We make them also of gold and they are better in every respect than any other pin now in use.'

It appears from a short paragraph in the *Optical Journal* of 1901 that itinerant peddlers were as troublesome as ever : 'If you value your eyesight, you will place no confidence in the statements of tramps who go from house to house selling spectacles. They will tell you your eyes are "diseased" and nothing but their "electric" or "magnetised" glasses will save you from blindness. Such talk is an insult to your intelligence.' Insulting or not, the peddlers evidently succeeded in selling their wares, as they had for centuries.

A drawing in the *Optical Journal* for November 1903 (Figure 91) shows a pair of goggles devised for high-bred, pugnacious show chickens to prevent their damaging each other's eyes. The frames were filled with glass or mica.

In 1908 Dr Richard Jones Phillips, writing about frames and materials currently in use, designated spectacle frames as the most useful form of glasses, though he conceded that pince-nez had an advantage in the ease with which they could be put on and taken off, as well as in general appearance. The appearance, he felt, was important since the glasses would be more likely to be worn if they were attractive than if they were not. Lorgnettes and quizzing glasses he dismissed as 'little more than playthings'.

The materials most in use at the time, according to Dr Phillips, were gold, silver, steel, gold-plated brass, and alloys containing nickel and tin. Horn, tortoise shell, and celluloid were used much less frequently. He recommended 10-14 carat gold. Silver and brass he considered too soft and flexible. For reading or close work Dr Phillips favoured the semi-oval shape, which allowed the line of sight to pass over their upper, straight edge in viewing distant objects. These were known as *half*, *pulpit*, or *clerical* glasses (Plate 53-F-H) and were worn off and on for a number of years.

Manufacturers advertised regularly in optical journals, playing up new designs or manufacturing processes and frequently making extravagant claims. On April 22, 1910, the Wheway Optical Company in Birmingham used the pages of *The Optician* to strike back at a competitor :

'We cannot allow the statement made by the Michigan Optical Co., in their advertisement in last week's "Optician" to pass unchallenged. In reference to the manufacture of Gold-Filled Cable Spect. Temples, they definitely state that "No other manufacturer uses Gold-Filled Cores." We are not in a position to say what is the custom with American manufacturers in this respect, but for ourselves we positively state that, having made thousands of dozens yearly of these goods during the past five years, we have always used Gold-Filled Cores.'

Fig. 91 : Chicken with protective glasses, 1903

Fig. 92 : Woman with pince-nez, 1901. From an advertisement

An advertisement in the October 28 issue showed an optician's seven-foot sign 'beautifully enamelled and glazed, with our largest size translucent eyes on each side (4 eyes in all), whilst between them are placed the flashing lights flashing in unison. . . . The whole effect, both by day and night, is remarkably fine ; and whenever a sign of this size can be used the results obtained will repay the costs many times over.'

In September of the same year there appeared among readers' letters in *The Optician* a plea for help from India :

'Sir,—Kindly publish the following complaint in your valuable journal. I shall be much obliged if any of your readers will suggest any remedy through your journal.

'One of my customers complains as follows. He sees mosquitoes and fly-like spots before his eyes. These are accompanied with slight pains in temple or in forehead. . . . He has also some complaint of constipation.' The letter was signed by Chatar Bhuj Bhargava & Co., Shahalmi Gate, Lahore.

In December 1909 a reader wrote in to enquire if anyone knew how he could fit his glass eye in properly without it turning round while he was wearing it and if there was any reading matter on the subject. He signed himself 'A Beginner'. The following week there was an answer of sorts by 'Abacus' :

'Sir,—In reply to "A Beginner" the *Traité de l'œil artificiel* by Dr. P. Pansier,

Fig. 93 : Gilbert Keith Chesterton. Drawing
by Paul Henry, 1904

published by M. A. Maloine, Place de l'école de Médecine, Paris, is possibly such a book as he requires. I take this reference from my notebook, which is as much as I can say, for I am not interested in artificial eyes.'

In 1903 the *New York Herald* commented on a passing fad among American women :

'The single eyeglass is no longer the sign of the Englishman of fashion, for the belles of New York and Chicago Society have claimed it for their own. It is the latest craze of the American smart girl, and it has caught on. . . .

'Generally speaking, the monocle is not stuck in her eye but is held there by a dainty little handle, doing away with the unsightly contraction of muscles. Many styles have a delicate little handle of filigree gold, studded with jewels, and sometimes tiny jewels set in the rim which frames the glass.

'The round glass which you stick in the eye and hold there by contracting the muscles is the monocle favored by some women. But it takes a daring woman to use it, not only because it is a detriment rather than an aid to beauty. The New York Society belle may look interesting when she gazes at you through her monocle, but she doesn't look any the lovelier because she has this odd little glass fixed in her eye. Hence the preference for the monocle with the handle. She wishes to be original and a bit English and eccentric too, but not for a minute does she wish to look less charming.'

Fig. 94 : Joseph Chamberlain (1836–1914).  Drawing by Scotson-Clark

Fig. 95 : ANTIGONOUS THE ONE-EYED : Inventor
of the monocle.  American caricature by
Paul Reilly, 1917

Instead of the black silk cord usually worn with monocles, the American girl
favoured the monocle chain.  Some of these—of black teakwood, for example—
were so long and heavy that they had to be tied in loose knots ; others, more
delicate, were fashioned of small jewels rimmed in gold or of crystals and jewels.

In November 1901 a New England firm (the same one which had earlier expressed
the conviction that its hairpins for eyeglass chains were better than anybody else's)
announced another new development—black silk eyeglass cords with gold and
plated trimmings, which, they boasted, enabled them 'to show the first attractive
chain of this description'.

In 1913 monocles became fashionable in New York and then in other large cities
of the United States.  Frames were made of gold, silver, rolled gold materials,
celluloid, and hard rubber.  The cheaper models could be bought for as little as
25¢ (1s. 10d.) and were used by men, women, and children more as toys than
anything else.  Then the fad died out.  But a small residue of monocle wearers
remained among the social set, appearing with marked frequency a few years later
in E. Foster Lincoln's satiric series of 'Great Americans', which ran in *Life* (Figure

96). In American caricatures it was used for Englishmen, Germans, or affected Americans. It was seldom portrayed, especially on Americans, in a favourable light. Honest, brave, upright, lovable men could on rare occasions be portrayed with spectacles but never with a monocle.

Even the lorgnette, which was widely used by elegant and fashionable women, did not escape criticism. Madame Heymann, writing in 1911, deplored the current fad for the long-handled lorgnette, known to the French as the *face à main*, which, she said, 'rages in all its horror. It is not only a fad, it is a necessity which the defect of feminine views imposes. Happily, women, always the coquettes, know how to use this trinket to their advantage, playing with it like a fan. One must, then, be reconciled to the *face à main*, which spares us the spectacle of gracious faces made ugly by a pince-nez or, what would be even worse, by unaesthetic spectacles.'

Fig. 96 : Great Americans : S. Lothario Looseways. Defendant in three different suits to recover alimony. Illustration by E. Foster Lincoln, 1917

The oxford eyeglass (a folding style with high, sweeping bridge) was reportedly first made in 1910 in New York. Although it was intended originally to be worn with a heavy ribbon by men only, the possibilities of doubling the sales soon became apparent, and it was promoted with great success for both men and women (Plates 54, 55, 56, 59, 60). The first oxfords were made only in 14 car. gold and sold for $18 (about £6), a very high price at that time. In 1914 shell oxfords were made and later white gold. Special frames were made in platinum and diamonds and sold for as much as $800 (£285). The dressier styles were worn on chains rather than ribbons. The plates show a variety of styles, some of them with handles. Those with very short handles were often known as 'shopping oxfords' (Plate 56-D).

In the autumn of 1913 the Kansas City *Star* reported that spectacles with large round lenses and tortoise-shell frames were very much in fashion for both men and women and had, in fact, been popular in the United States since their introduction five years earlier. A European style, the first ones, according to the *Star*, were imported from Vienna. They had not reached Kansas City until about 1910, when they were looked upon as an affectation and ridiculed in public.

But in time the fashion caught on to such a degree that the factories had trouble keeping up with the demand, which was given considerable impetus, the *Star* reported, by a young society man who returned from Boston, where he had attended an ultra-fashionable ball at which 'three-fourths of the men at the ball had the pince-nez style of tortoise shell nose-glasses, which were worn when not dancing and were allowed to hang from a braid around the neck when dancing'.

The article went on to point out that there was a time when it didn't matter too much what spectacle frames were made of so long as the lenses were properly placed. Then came the rimless spectacles, which were intended to be as inconspicuous as possible.

'And now comes an age of glorying in infirmity. The average human person, instead of being ashamed that his eyes are on the blink, actually seems to be proud of it. He gets his prescription done up in owl-like round lenses the size of twin motor lamps. And he has these framed in bulky tortoise shell, imitated in celluloid.

'Wearing them, he looks as wise as a tree full of owls and as conspicuous as a red-headed man at an Italian picnic. He is perfectly shameless about it and likes the idea so well (if he be really substantial) he has more glasses put up in heavy gold mountings with a spring capable of sustaining one corner of a motor truck. . . .

'Nearly all the lenses are perfectly round, but there is a variety, known as the "drop eye", in which the lens is finished straight across the top. This is made for the man or woman who has prominent eyebrows, which would prevent the wearing of a perfectly round glass. The straight top permits the spectacles to go under the beetling brows.

'The pince-nez is the correct style for evening wear. It is hung to a black moire or plain silk braid. The width of this braid is essential. It must be one-quarter

**L. K. LEON & CO.**

## OPTICIANS

TO THE

### PRINCIPAL OPHTHALMIC HOSPITALS

### 167, Piccadilly, London

(Opposite Old Bond Street).

### IMPROVED

# LADIES' EYE-GLASSES.

### Can be worn under veil.
### Do not slip or mark the most
### delicate skin.

---

**READING, DISTANCE,
SHOOTING, DRIVING, FISHING,
AND BILLIARD SPECTACLES.**

**Speciality Frames & Lenses
to Oculist's Prescriptions.**

Set of Test Lenses and Samples of Pince-
Nez or Spectacles for Self-fitting sent
Post Free.

**CATALOGUE POST FREE.**

Fig. 97 : Advertisement of a London optician, 1900

Fig. 98 : Jacob Smits (1855–1928).
Self-portrait

to five-sixteenths of an inch wide and be fitted with either a gold or black slide. The braid goes around the neck and the pince-nez hangs at about the middle waistcoat button.

'The first to wear the large·spectacles here were professional men, especially physicians and lawyers. An optician of this city . . . says they were taken up by the doctors and lawyers because the large lenses, mounted with stout tortoise-shell frames, gave an air of distinction or profundity. A lawyer who bought a pair said to the optician : "When I put these spectacles on, it will cost $5 more to talk to me".'

An optician said they were growing in popularity all the time and that he had 'sold as many as five pairs to one man, and hundreds have two and three pairs. They are very popular with women for use in sewing. I am told that in Vassar College all the girls wear them, and in Harvard nearly all the students wear them.'

In the spring of 1916 an article on current fashions in eyeglasses in the *Literary Digest* indicated that the heavy glasses were still very much in fashion :

'We are becoming reconciled to the individuals who disregard the wisdom of nature in giving them a nose, eyes, and a mouth of more or less comeliness, artistically disposed about their expanse of face, and who distort and conceal the same with the aid of tortoise-shell or imitation tortoise-shell spectacles. But even yet we have not all of us learned to pass without shying an individual adorned with a black ribbon flowing from his eye-glasses. Somehow we miss his long hair. And yet, it is quite true that this form of ornament is being even more widely affected.'

The *Digest* then quoted a correspondent to the *New York Sun* who defended the ribbon for the sense of security it gave and added a few notes on ways of wearing it:

'It is a curious fact, worthy of note, that the manner in which the ribbon is worn makes a vast difference in the appearance of the wearer. Because of this difference, the wearer of the glasses-ribbon has a sort of Protean equipment. With the ribbon behind his ear he looks neat and business-like; with the ribbon hanging down he at once takes on a learned and distinguished air and his nose is accentuated. When I am looking at pictures or listening to music I do not understand, or asking for credit, or serving on the jury, I always wear my ribbon down.

'The wearing of the ribbon hanging down is not without its drawbacks. At first it tickles you and makes you want to laugh on the right side of your face. Then, too, when the wind is blowing athwart your face it has a way of getting in your mouth, and thus interfering with your conversation.

'At first, when partaking of a highball, I had to put the ribbon up behind my ear, and for that reason wore it so most of the time, but now I can drink anything, except water and milk, without regard to the ribbon, and even without my glasses, for that matter.

'If the ribbon is free to fly about, care must be used when smoking a cigar. I once burned off a ribbon in a second when it chanced to light on the burning end of a cigar. At first the beginner will find that he often will catch the ribbon on the buttons of his right coat-sleeve. Then his glasses will be jerked off, and he will lose his dignity and his temper at the same time, to the unholy joy of those who chance to see him.

'Notwithstanding all these disadvantages I have pointed out, I believe the man who once wears a glasses-ribbon will continue to do so, except, perhaps, if he buys a pair of those so-called library-glasses and goes about looking like Horace Walpole.'

Presumably he meant Hugh Walpole, who did wear library frames (meaning any heavy, dark, round spectacle frames) and later (Figure 110) switched to pince-nez.

Despite the problems, aesthetic and practical, posed by eyeglasses, they were worn increasingly. In 1907 Dr Charles William Super wrote in *Popular Science Monthly* that there was hardly a person over fifty who did not use 'some sort of artificial aid to sight. In the German universities', he said, 'the situation is still worse. There, apparently, almost one half of the students wear eyeglasses. England furnishes a marked contrast; spectacles on the eyes of young men and young women are far less common. The chief reason doubtless is the fondness of both sexes for outdoor life.'

Although nothing much was being done about making spectacles less offensive to look at, technical advances were being made. It was in the first decade of the

Fig. 99 : GRANDMA STIFLING A YAWN WITH HER READING GLASS. American cartoon by R. B. Fuller, 1918

twentieth century, for example, that a significant improvement was made in the manufacture of bifocals. In 1908 John L. Borsch, Jr, was granted a patent on a fused bifocal lens, which overcame the disadvantages of the cemented bifocal but did not solve the problem of rainbow colours around the edges of objects seen through the reading part of the lens. This was not overcome for nearly twenty years. Following this, other technical advances were made in the construction of bifocals.

*Holiday* quotes Robert Shaw on the problem of getting adjusted to bifocals: 'You look down the stairs in your own house and see what ? An abandoned mine shaft down which you crawl, whimpering all the way, with both hands clutching the rail. Outdoors, the street heaves and bulges, and great fissures open at your feet. The idea of driving is suicidal, so you walk. And as you step off the curb, you want to shout "Geronimo !" But after a day or so you learn to look through the upper half of the lens, and the earth is back on an even keel.'

In 1912 A. Wolff, a German optician, devised auxiliary lenses which could be placed behind rather than in front of the spectacles. Additional forms were subsequently invented by Zeiss and others.   About this same time research on contact lenses began to move ahead but then was virtually abandoned until after the war.

On the other side of the world progress was more leisurely.   Rasmussen, writing in 1915, provides us with an intriguing description of the purchase of spectacles in contemporary China :

'Prospective buyers select their own spectacles accompanied by various encouraging remarks from the Optician to help out the process of progressive elimination. The rules and conditions of purchase are very rigid, for the Optician is quite independent of the customer's patronage and will not cater to arbitrary likes and dislikes in order to make a sale.   The spectacles are made up in a very fixed manner and unless the customer is willing to pay considerably more, there will be no interchanging of frames and lenses.   Very often a customer goes through a considerable portion of the stock before being satisfied.   At times during this process an altercation will arise, invariably due to the exacting tastes of the customer and the weariness and independence of the Optician, which breaks off peaceful negotiations and charges the atmosphere with much illuminating remarks and slamming of drawers, etc.   Occasionally peace is re-established and a sale effected to the satisfaction of both persons. . . . The hard and fast rules of purchase are very much in evidence when a customer desires to exchange an unsuitable pair of spectacles.   The demand is met with a flat refusal based on arguments that the

Fig. 100 : Boyle's spectacles, patented 1913 in the United
   States.   A U-shaped wire support, resting on the
   bridge of the nose, holds the spectacles on the forehead when they are not in use

Fig. 101 : I Shall Take my Children (if any) to Washington. Pen and ink illustration by Rea Irvin for *Letter of a Japanese Schoolboy,* 1918

purchaser made his own selection and is responsible for his own errors, miscalculations, etc., ad infinitum, with illustrations. The purchasing price is arbitrary, and the spectacles are quoted at a higher figure than that at which they are eventually sold. There is no clear reason for this bargaining method, which is in vogue in all forms of exchange in China, but it seems to be an attempt to hold in retention a final effort to effect a sale. It also seems to keep the buyer's mind more on the price than on the quality, as well as to make it appear that the margin of profit is small.'

Most Chinese lenses were at that time and had probably always been large and circular. They were worn at about a 45-degree angle (Figure 102), and the temples were always straight with a joint for folding. They were usually carried in a case attached to the clothing or hanging over the arm.

It was considered proper to remove the spectacles when talking with a friend and always in the presence of superiors—often even of inferiors. 'It is considered', says Rasmussen, 'a grave sign of disrespect to the presiding Judge to wear spectacles in his presence. Often when a man in giving evidence desires to read something from a paper he will make numerous apologies and remarks that he is poor of vision, and even when told to wear them he hesitates and sometimes will not put them on, much to the general embarrassment of the court. . . . When passing a friend on the street, it is also courteous to remove one's spectacles immediately before the greeting.'

In the Western world, where the wearing of glasses was considered a mark of advancing age, or at least infirmity, the need for them was usually ignored as long as possible. William Hemmingway, writing in 1913, described his own moment of truth :

'One evening when I was visiting down in the country, Mrs. Harding, the hostess, suddenly said, "Mr. Hemmingway, you need glasses !"'

'I jumped as if I had been accused of picking pockets or trying to burn the house—at least, I felt that way, though I hope I did nothing worse than change color and gasp and gurgle and do a few little things like that to cover my confusion as I replied : "Oh, no, it's just the angle at which the light strikes the page. There's a glare that confuses me a little. . . ."'

'That evening the optician handed me a pocketful of cute little spectacle cases. First I tried on a pince-nez, from which depended two lenses shaped like long sections of a glass pear. . . . I clamped them on the bony part of the bridge of the nose.

'"No, no," cried the optician, "that won't do at all ! About five thousand people out of five thousand put on their glasses wrong. Observe—I place the glasses above the bridge and as close to the eyes as possible. I spread the grips

Fig. 102 : Twentieth-century Chinese spectacles. After Rasmussen

Fig. 103 : Woman wearing pince-nez, 1913

Fig. 104 : ALADDIN AND HIS WONDERFUL LAMP. American
caricature by Ellison Hoover, 1918

wide apart and settle them in the flesh well up at the very top of the nose. There
you are, sir ! Now, you try it.''

'He pushed toward me a small oval mirror that stood on a rod. I sat before it
and faithfully worked at eyeglass drill. When at last I got the glasses high enough,
I had the top part canted too far forward. Again and again the optician had to
push out the lower part of the glasses.

'"Now you have it," he said, after half a dozen trials of my skill. "Please
remember : fix the glasses always parallel with the face and close to the eyes as
possible.''

'"Oh-ow !" I exclaimed. "They'll give me cramps in the eyelids : the
eyelashes are brushing them.''

'"Oh, well," he advised patiently, as one who had traversed the ground a
thousand times before. . . . "take a pair of scissors and trim your eyelashes
short.''

'. . . The best things were the automobile lamps. The moment I put them on
I was filled with a wild desire to dash abroad at a mad rate of speed, blowing a
devil horn and smashing people to death as I fled with roars of laughter. Once
that desire was throttled, I settled down to appreciation of the comforts of the
enormous round spectacles in their light but strong frame of black rubber.'

At the end of the decade pince-nez were still popular with women and with
older men. Women usually wore the oval rimless style on a fine gold chain, which
could be attached to an automatic reel pinned to the dress, to a hairpin which could
be anchored in the hair (Figure 103), or to a curved earpiece. Men also wore the

oval rimless, occasionally with a chain and earpiece; but other styles, as shown in Plates 52 and 53, were also popular. The drooping, dark-rimmed, oval lenses on a black ribbon were usually assigned in caricatures to doctors and politicians (Figure 104). Round lenses, rimless or with delicate light or dark shell rims, were also worn.


## THE TWENTIES

Although the enormous round spectacles, and to a lesser extent the pince-nez, continued to be worn, developments in styling continued. In 1921 T. Haines Moore wrote in the *Optical Journal*:

'Then came another change, the library frame, followed by the zylonite hook, side variety. The first of the former that I saw was worn by a smart-looking individual in a drawing room car on one of our Philadelphia–New York trains. His glasses excited unfavorable comment by the other occupants of the car. . . . During a visit to a Carolina resort patronized by society leaders, I counted more rimless glasses than other kinds. Is there a trend back to the era of frameless spectacle and eyeglass mountings? Or, will changes continue the great progress in shell products? As a matter of looks, I believe that the rimless is in advance of any other. It is cool, light, inconspicuous, and does not strongly call attention to the fact that one has defective vision. . . . On the other hand, shell and zylonite will undoubtedly continue to be popular for the library, golf, and other sports, for hunting, fishing, and a comfortable evening with a book or paper before the open fireplace.'

In the same year Dr George M. Gould, according to a report in the *Literary Digest*, warned against all eyeglasses, by which he meant any glasses without temples:

'One rule should . . . be unexceptional: Abolish eyeglasses and order only spectacles. All useful lenses have optical centers, and it is only by means of the temple-pieces of spectacles, curved behind the ears, that accurate and constant adjustments are possible. . . . The worst of the fashions is that of the sillies who dangle a long black ribbon from one side of their eyeglasses, which displaces the axes of the astigmatism of the lenses from 20 to 30 degrees, according to several quickly changing conditions, the movements of the head, the weight of ribbon, the slipping of the springs, etc.—an optical farce! . . . The prescription or sale of such tools should be adjudged as malpractice and subject to heavy penalty.'

But older people who had become attached to their pince-nez tended to stick with them. Lloyd George's, which he was seldom without, were thoroughly disliked by a white pigeon he was given in 1923. According to A. J. Sylvester, the pigeon would grasp the steel rims in her beak, then with a toss of her head, would flick them off his nose before settling down, cooing contentedly, to caress his eyebrows or his eyelids.

Even though the designers of glasses available in 1921 had still not managed to incorporate any real aesthetic appeal, there were those who were at least beginning to think in terms of trying to make the best of a bad thing. The *Literary Digest* quoted from Dr Frank G. Murphy's pamphlet entitled *Be Beautiful in Glasses*:

'To those whose glasses become them there is a comfort which to some extent is shared by their friends and all who look upon them. . . . Frames when once purchased practically become a part of the facial anatomy, thereby altering the personality, as they are usually worn for several years—sometimes to the end of life. We seek the knowledge of artists to beautify our gardens, houses, and barns but do not seek expert advice on the ornamentation of our own physiognomies. A comely face surely contributes to the happiness of a community quite as much as does a mansion with all its architectural beauty.

'A distinct line drawn through one object always makes that object appear longer and longer in the direction of the line. This is why spectacles with temples over the

Fig. 105 : David Lloyd George. Caricature by Massaguer, 1932

Fig. 106 : Austen Chamberlain (1863–1937).
Drawing

ears and low nosepieces make a face look broader. Light-rimmed or rimless glasses make the face look wider and those with dark rims make it appear narrower than it is. There is no face so nearly perfect that its weakest lines can not be emphasized by the caricaturist and but few are so handsome that artistically selected glasses will not improve their appearance.' Dr Murphy then suggests gold or wine-coloured frames for elderly white faces, dark rims for large faces and light ones for small, and low-set glasses for tall people, high-set ones for short.

In 1923 gold-filled spectacle frames, according to Ryland, were probably more widely used than either steel or gold. In this same year in *Antic Hay*, Aldous Huxley took a passing swipe at American promotion of spectacles :

'"The most masterly examples I can think of," Mr. Boldero went on, with growing enthusiasm, "are those American advertisements of spectacles, in which the manufacturers first assume the existence of a social law about goggles, and then proceed to make all the sanctions which fall on the head of the committee of a solecism upon those who break it. . . .

'"For sport or relaxation, they tell you, as though it was a social axiom, you must wear spectacles of pure tortoiseshell rims, and nickel earpieces lend 'incisive poise'; we must remember that for our ads., Mr. Gumbril. . . .

'"For semi-evening dress, shell rims with gold earpieces and gold nose-bridge.

Fig. 107 : Rudyard Kipling. Pen and ink
drawing by Massaguer, 1923

And for full dress, gold-mounted rimless pince-nez are refinement itself and absolutely correct.

"'Thus we see a social law has been created, according to which every self-respecting myope or astigmat must have four distinct pairs of glasses. Think if he should wear the all-shell sports model with full dress !

"'Revolting solecism ! The people who read advertisements like that begin to feel uncomfortable ; they have only one pair of glasses, they are afraid of being laughed at, thought low-class and ignorant and suburban. And since there are few who would not rather be taken in adultery than in provincialism, they rush out to buy four new pairs of spectacles.'"

Also in 1923 Bausch and Lomb were making what they called Crookes Glass lenses based on a formula supplied by Sir William Crookes. These were sun-glasses of a special kind, available in three shades—light, medium, and dark. Although the manufacturers claimed that Crookes Glass was 'worn by almost everyone during the summer', they were hopeful that opticians might persuade their customers to wear it in the winter as well—not only for winter sports but also 'to relieve the eyes from the glare of indoor lighting during the dull afternoons and long evenings of the winter season'.

Two years later a contributor to the *Deutsche Optische Wochenschrift* pointed out that Germany seemed to be threatened with an invasion of monocle wearers. But far from being disturbed, he thought it rather a good thing since the *Einglas* provided, in addition to its optical correction, good discipline for the wearer, who would be obliged to master his facial expression in order to prevent the glass from becoming independent and causing 'a derisive, mischievous laugh from bystanders. The monocle is, then,' he concluded, 'a good educative medium which would not prove hurtful to all those in public life, as diplomats, officers, actors, merchants, etc.'

Fig. 108 : Harold Lloyd, silent screen comedian, whose horn-rimmed glasses were his trademark. After a drawing by Wynn, *c.* 1925

An article in *Le Temps*, reported in the *Literary Digest* in June 1925, exhibits a certain puzzlement about contemporary fashions in spectacles :

'An attentive observer of our fashions, M. de Trevières, has characterized the present generation as the "tortoise-shell-spectacle generation". Spectacles, indeed, are a very significant peculiarity of our time. One might believe that the post-war humanity were composed wholly of the near-sighted, the far-sighted, and the astigmatic. A fashionable youth must now shave his face carefully, plaster his hair back, leave off his hat, and protect his eyes with two aggressive lenses like automobile lamps—such is a synthetic portrait of the Americanized European.

'There was a time when the masterpieces of medical optics were more discreet. The weaknesses of the eye were hidden as much as possible. Light glasses were worn, spectacles with almost imperceptible bows. The lenses were as small as possible. Care was taken not to change the appearance of the face, and the nose was pinched as delicately as it could be.

'Today such scruples are not the mode. Tortoise-shell spectacles with enormous lenses and solid frames are affected even by youths and maidens. Formerly a young person wearing spectacles would have been regarded as ridiculous. Today a Harold Lloyd and a Buster Keaton sport their heavy eyepieces as buoyantly as a cavalry officer manœuvering his troop.

'It is perhaps not very easy to explain this evolution in our manners. Doubtless American influence has played a great part in it, but this is not enough to justify such universal adoption. In reality, we have become accustomed to study the infirmities of vision without reserve. For many years we have now been examining very attentively the eyes of children. Methodical tests are required in the schools. It is sought at the earliest possible moment to ameliorate and cure certain cases that formerly aroused no interest. The important part now played in our lives by reading and the intensive study required of modern pupils, tends assuredly to fatigue the optic nerve. . . . We are no longer ashamed to call at an optician's to procure supplementary eyes.

'Finally, it has been quickly seen that on the fresh face of a girl the heavy spectacles of our grandparents create a piquant and amusing contrast, which simply goes to emphasize the triumph of youth. This argument was certainly not the least compelling among those that decided the arbiters of our fashions to replace the invisible pince-nez with this robust optical apparatus.'

In the late eighteenth century, as we have seen, eyeglasses became works of art, and vast sums were spent on them. Their practical function seemed to be secondary. But in the nineteenth century, when the need to see overcame the requirements of fashion, especially among men, spectacles became largely functional. The rich man's spectacles differed from the poor man's only in that the frames might be of gold instead of steel. Ladies' lorgnettes and opera glasses were often elegant and expensive ; but their spectacles, if they condescended to wear them at all, were as plain and unbecoming as their husbands'.

It was not until the third decade of the twentieth century that much thought seems to have been given to beautifying spectacles instead of merely making the best of them, and it was still some years before much progress was made. In 1925 John F. Hill, in a radio address on 'Glasses and Appearance', had this to say :

'Optical men of late have been giving a vast amount of attention to improving eyeglasses and spectacles, not alone from the standpoint of optical science, but also from the viewpoint of beauty of design and perfection of workmanship. The past year or two has witnessed a great stride forward in the art of producing glasses that combine beauty with practical service. Some of the new designs really possess artistic merit of a high order. . . . Perhaps the idea of making glasses beautiful may strike some of you as a little faddish, a bit extreme. Glasses, you perhaps say, are purely utilitarian. . . . Is there any reason why your glasses, the most prominent detail in your whole costume, should not be selected with as much care and as much attention to design, material, harmony of color, and, most important of all, becomingness ? . . . People are demanding higher quality, more beautiful materials and finer workmanship in their glasses. You would be surprised to know how many solid gold frames we see. Not long ago a lady gladly paid $65 (about £23) for a beautifully engraved pair of oxford eyeglasses, with which she was delighted, especially after many of her friends admired them and asked her where they, too, could get such beautiful glasses.

'Some of the great costume designers in France, as well as in this country, are beginning to study this question seriously. Not long ago I saw illustrated in one of our leading fashion magazines a group of beautiful glasses of most artistic design and charming decoration, which had been created by a great French designer. And recently a lady showed me an article in another fashion magazine dealing entirely with the artistic and cosmetic effect of glasses as an accessory of dress which has been long neglected. . . .'

The curious thing about Mr Hill's address, at least in retrospect, is not that he urged an improvement in the appearance of glasses but that the idea was evidently so revolutionary that he felt called upon to justify it to his listeners.

In September 1927 the Associated Press reported that President Coolidge had apparently abandoned his old black-rimmed spectacles in favour of a new pair of pince-nez with a gold nosepiece and a long black cord. He wore the new glasses for the first time in public in reading his formal conversation with President Calles of Mexico over the long-distance telephone. In the November issue of their magazine, Bausch and Lomb, noting the development, could hardly contain their delight : 'Like a snow ball rolling down hill the sale of White Gold Frames and Rimless constantly gathers momentum and volume. . . . One by one the leaders of today, in business, politics, society, and fashion are lending the weight of their influence to the style movement by selecting for their personal use handsome eyeglasses and spectacles, with or without rims, made up in the beautiful new White Gold designs. What a splendid thing for the good looks and the good vision of a Nation ! And how fortunate that you and we can have a part in bringing about this significant change.'

No doubt the increased emphasis on the appearance of glasses had a good deal to do with the increase in sales. According to a survey made by an American optical company in 1929, fifty-three per cent of the people interviewed, though perhaps not enthusiastic, believed that their glasses were more or less becoming to them. A number of the others thought glasses were never becoming to anybody, and one man said he didn't give a damn. The company concluded, prophetically, that 'there is hope that in the not too far distant future it may be possible to make glasses stylish and to sell them as jewelry. That is what we have got to come to.'

In the spring of this same year Bausch and Lomb reported on the current styles in frames : 'Nearly everyone who takes his or her glasses seriously wears white gold in some form or other. Shell is being sold less and less although it is still seen all too frequently. Yellow gold is almost never seen any more. But white gold is as commonly used for frames and mountings as leather is for shoes.'

## THE THIRTIES

In 1930 P. G. Wodehouse listed the rules for novelists relevant to the wearing of glasses :

'(*A*) Spectacles : These may be worn by (1) good uncles, (2) clergymen, (3) good lawyers, (4) all elderly men who are kind to the heroine ; by (5) bad uncles, (6) blackmailers, (7) money-lenders. (*B*) Pince-nez : These may be worn by

Fig. 109 : German General von Seeckt.
From a photograph

good college professors, bank presidents, and musicians. No bad man may wear pince-nez. (*C*) Monocle : This may be worn by (1) good dukes, (2) all Englishmen. No bad man may wear a monocle. (*D*) These beastly tortoise-shell-rimmed things : Never worn in fiction. It is time that a stop was put to this arbitrary state of affairs. . . .

'It is futile to advance the argument that glasses are unromantic. They are not. I know, because I wear them myself, and I am a singularly romantic figure, whether in my rimless, my gold-bordered, or the plain gent's spectacles which I wear in the privacy of my study. It is useless to say that they are becoming. You have only got to look at me to see that. They are the very swagger. They lend an air, a zip, so to speak, to the appearance.

'Besides, everybody wears glasses nowadays. That is the point I wish to make. For commercial reasons, if for no others, authors ought to think seriously of this matter of goggling their heroes. It is an admitted fact that the reader of a novel likes to put himself in the hero's place—to imagine, while reading, that he is the hero. What an audience the writer of the first romance to star a spectacled hero will have ! All over the country thousands of short-sighted men will polish their glasses and plunge into his pages. It is absurd these days to go on writing for a normal-sighted public.'

In April 1931 Fassett Edwards wrote in *Hygeia* about the glasses that were being worn :

'The current style is spectacles in various forms, although we do see persons wearing pince-nez, or eye glasses. . . . Many persons have different sorts of glasses for varying types of work. For instance, it is entirely out of the question to play

Fig. 110 : Hugh Walpole.  Lithograph by Eric Pape, 1930

Fig. 111 : Leon Trotsky.  Drawing by Annenkov, 1927

Fig. 112 : Leon Trotsky.  Drawing for the cover of *Time*, 1937

the piano while wearing bifocal glasses to read the music.  One's neck will not long endure the discomfort.  For such persons vocational glasses are a frequent necessity. The big library glasses are comfortable to use while perusing a favorite volume. Of course such frames are too bulky to be used in the street or carried about. . . .

'Opticians are making considerable ado these days about white gold frames for glasses, and indeed they are excellent, perhaps the best of all.  Sometimes they are not quite so becoming as shell frames, but that is a matter of personal taste.  A metal frame is more persistently serviceable than a shell mounting.'

In 1936 it was estimated that in the United States alone there were 10,000 oculists and 22,000 optometrists and that more than 100 million dollars was spent annually for glasses.  While the designers, who were undoubtedly responsible for much of the boom in eyeglasses, were working to make them even more appealing, the technicians were working equally hard on making them more practical.  In addition to improvements in frame construction, bifocals were technically better, and even trifocals had been introduced.  Great progress was also being made in the perfection of contact lenses.

With the increased emphasis on style in glasses, fads inevitably developed. 'About fifteen years ago,' wrote Meta Rosenthal in 1937, 'it was utterly useless to try to sell a Princeton man a pair of glasses that were not white gold.  If he could not afford them, white gold-filled was substituted, or even steel—but white they had to be. At the same time, Yale was wearing shell glasses, and no sales talk could put over another kind.' Miss Rosenthal also mentioned the curious fad, early in the thirties, for wearing heavy shell-rimmed glasses, even by young women in formal dress at the opera. In an article the following year she pointed out that the pince-nez was still being worn by dowagers, headwaiters, old men, and a few others. Even young ladies wore it in the oxford style. Ketcham and McDougall were still advertising the automatic eyeglass holder, available in many of the same designs sold in the late nineteenth century. And the *Portsmouth Evening News* described Mr Chamberlain 'driving home points by thrusting gently with his pince-nez. He has a mannerism whereby he adjusts his glasses carefully, consults his notes, and immediately whips them off before speaking.'

The monocle was still sufficiently in evidence to be thought worth satirizing. In 1936, in *The Monocle*, Aldous Huxley wrote of a young man named Gregory and his monocle :

'His eye-glass had done nothing to increase his self-confidence. He was never at ease when he wore it. Monocle-wearers, he decided, are like poets : born, not made. . . . He could not get used to his monocle. Most of the time . . . it dangled at the end of its string, a pendulum when he walked and involving itself messily when he ate, in soup and tea, in marmalade and the butter. It was only occasionally, in specially favourable circumstances, that Gregory adjusted it to his eye ; more rarely still that he kept it, once adjusted, more than a few minutes, a few seconds even, without raising his eyebrows and letting it fall again. And how seldom circumstances were favourable to Gregory's eye-glass ! Sometimes his environment was too sordid for it, sometimes too smart. To wear a monocle in the presence of the poor, the miserable, the analphabetic is too triumphantly pointed a comment on their lot. Moreover the poor and analphabetic have a most deplorable habit of laughing derisively at such symbols of superior caste. Gregory was not laughter-proof ; he lacked the lordly confidence and unawareness of nature's monocle-wearers.'

Whereas monocles, even in England, were worn by only a small minority, sun-glasses, at least in the United States, seemed to be worn by almost everyone. According to the *Popular Science Monthly* of July 1939, 'the craze for gayly colored sunglasses that swept across the country last year and is booming again with even greater fervor as summer comes on again, has revived to full capacity one of the most remarkable and least-known branches of the glass-making industry. Although tens of thousands of the familiar "smoked" and amber glasses, for beach and sport-ing wear, had been made and sold regularly each year, the new fad sent the demand skyrocketing to millions, while lens glass of half a dozen new tints and colors had to be created almost overnight.' The solution lay in making huge 'goggle-balls', fantastic bubbles of blown glass, polished by fire and later cut by means of heated electric wires and diamonds into the small convex disks and other shapes required for lenses.

Fig. 113 : George Arliss.  Drawing by Major, 1938

The whole thing seems to have been started by a Belgian master glass worker. 'Beginning with amber, he later developed blue, green, fieuzal, smoke, and many special tints. . . . The goggle balls . . . are nearly three feet in diameter. . . . Sliced into halves by the electrically heated wires, they are further subdivided by cutting into curved plates with diamond tools. From these, girls cut lenses of the desired shapes with rotary scoring machines. The last stage of the process is to insert the lenses into heated frames. As the frames cool and contract, the lenses are gripped firmly.'

Despite the enormous advances in optical science, non-prescription glasses were still available at very low prices, and there was obviously a market for them. G. P. Hunt commented in verse on the sale of cheap spectacles :

> Sing a song of six pence,
> What a price to pay
> For a heap of spectacles
> Piled on a tray.
> When the store was opened
> People would surge in.
> Some would buy the wretched specs.
> Isn't that a sin ?

## THE FORTIES

By the early forties a variety of contact lenses was available—blown glass, ground glass, moulded glass, plastic and glass, and all plastic. But all were still comparatively large and could not normally be tolerated for long periods of time. In 1943 an advertisement in the *Optical Journal* offered spherical contact lenses, moulded contact lenses, tinted contact lenses, contact lens holders, contact trial sets, plastic moulding sheets, buffer solution, moulding equipment, and plastic hooks.

Euin Steele, writing in London in 1951, speculated on the reason for the decline in the use of contact lenses in the late forties following the second World War, pointing out that towards the end of the war contact lenses received a great deal of publicity in the United States. 'This aroused considerable interest in the spectacle-wearing public, many of whom were at that time in a financial position to satisfy a natural desire for these invaluable aids to vision. This interest on the part of the public was, unfortunately, equally matched by that of a considerable number of unscrupulous promoters who saw in the fitting of contact lenses the opportunity of making very substantial incomes. The result is only too well known. Many patients were supplied with unsuitable and ill-fitting lenses and . . . were vehement in their condemnation of this new technique.' Mr Steele went on to point out that

Fig. 114 : Decorative American glasses, 1947

if contact lenses were to achieve any lasting popularity, new techniques were essential to increase the comfort and the tolerance period.

In the summer of 1947 *Business Week* turned its attention momentarily to fashions in sun-glasses : 'Dark glasses were once the badge of the blind man. Hollywood turned them into a fad ; today they are a definite style item in avid demand by young and old. Along with plastic frames came an avalanche of weird shapes and tints. To be really smart, a girl must have not only the type and shade to suit her face-shape and coloring ; she requires a different pair for sports, every day, and even—in some extremes of the dark glasses fad—for evening wear. Sometimes there are individual frame designs for special costumes.'

The magazine pointed out that the change was forced by the fashion designers on the naturally conservative industry dominated by optical scientists and technicians, resulting, predictably, in a sharp rise in sales. 'Today,' *Business Week* continued, 'sun glasses in fancy frames are being pushed by five-and-dime stores, drug stores, and department stores as well as by the special optical outlets. They retail for from 25¢ (for grades which the scientific producers ignore) to $25 (for those having personally fitted lenses). As yet, the volume of sun glass sales at retail amounts to a possible $18 million in a total for spectacles of $250 million. But sales executives say that sun glass promotion is only in its infancy. . . .'

The general trend, reported *Business Week*, was towards more variety in lens shapes. In one model the temples were laminated 'with plaid and other textiles sandwiched inside'. The yarn was permitted to extend slightly in order to prove that the textiles were genuine. It was possible to have fabrics in the laminated temples match the fabric of a dress. Even lace was sometimes used. The retail price was from $6 to $8 (2 guineas and up). Sometimes broad black temples were decorated with small gold stars, which were especially recommended for grey-haired ladies. Some temples had openwork designs; others were flecked with gold for a touch of chic.

Changes in lens shapes resulted, according to *Business Week*, from 'teen-age rebellion against the solemn, round, owl-eyed type of horn-rims'. The most popular innovation was the harlequin shape—'a long lens with the upper and outer end slightly lifted. Since the note it added was decidedly cheerful, present designs are mostly modifications of the harlequin.' *Business Week* also reported that contact lenses were still in the experimental stage and that trifocals were a recent innovation. Actually, trifocals were available in 1936.

It was not until the forties that designers of spectacle frames began to take note of fashion trends and to relate their designs to current fashions. This seems to have taken place in Germany and in the United States at about the same time. There was considerable controversy at first as to whether frames should match the complexion or the costume, but eventually that was left for the individual wearer to decide.

Emphasis on fashion resulted, as always, in fads. In the summer of 1948 there appeared for the first time sunglasses which, rather disconcertingly, appeared to the observer as mirrors, completely obscuring everything which lay behind them. For the wearer they had several practical advantages. Since they reflected thirty per cent of the sun's infra-red rays, they gave better protection to the eyes, they provided handy makeup mirrors, and they made it possible to give the effect of focusing rapt attention on a long-winded companion while actually observing everything else that was going on.

## THE FIFTIES

The revolutionary idea that eyeglasses could be stylish seemed to be achieving some sort of fulfilment in 1951 in an optometric fashion show, narrated by Margaret S. Dowaliby:

'Naomi is wearing a beautiful, pure silk two-piece shantung suit. The tangerine color . . . is repeated and accented by the plastic frame she wears. The color of the frame and suit are well suited to her warm-toned complexion and contrasted by her lovely hair. Because the suit has a detailed top and peplum, the applique on the frame is simple in design. Silver jewelry accents this costume, both by the earrings worn and the silver trim on the upper rim of the frames. . . .

Fig. 115 : Leaguे Print. Engraving by Reginald Marsh, 1949

'Even our younger patients love wearing frames that are designed especially for them. Here is Dickie June with a lovely tan skirt, blue blouse, and pearl blue frame to match. And these frames were made especially to delight the hearts of little children. The shields on the end-pieces and temples are in the shape of horses' heads. Her friends are really envious when they see her cowboy glasses.'

From the Glasses-Are-Fun department Dr Dowaliby shifts to a male model named Lee wearing a brown suit and brown glasses. A few minutes later Lee is back in his same brown suit dressed up with amber frames appliqued in gold. Then Joyce (age unspecified) appears in white pique: 'The smart simplicity of white is contrasted by the bright green and white frames and green accessories worn with it. The frame has scalloped edges on the temporal sides, which adds a note of interest to its design. . . . Her attractive long hair is set back so as not to detract from the beauty of her frames.' Later Joyce comes back in a banana-coloured cocktail dress with a veil 'designed especially to be worn with spectacles'. Her gold-coloured, all-metal frames, Dr Dowaliby insists, add the final note of glamour.

Then it's Lee's turn again. He has had time now to change to a grey suit with which he wears matching grey frames trimmed in silver. Perhaps to offset his determined conservatism, Lee is followed by Dickie June and Anne:

'Well, it looks like Dickie June is all dolled up to go to a party! The pink in her very sweet dress is repeated in the frame she wears. The shields of this frame, especially designed for children, are in the shape of little dogs. The upswept lines in the lens shape are very flattering to a little girl with a round face like Dickie June's. . . . Here is Anne in a stunning pink nylon tulle ball dress. Her glasses present a very novel idea in rimless spectacles. The mounting is constructed to give the effect of twisted gold. The appliques have been attached directly to the lenses rather than the mounting. The pink flowers surrounded by gold match the loveliness of the pink tulle. Now, ladies, look at your husbands and ask yourself, "Will men make passes at girls who wear glasses?"'

In this same year two French coiffeurs designed, for fancy-dress balls, masks of lace, sequins and feathers to be worn over eyeglasses.

Going along with the trend, Lenore Hailparn wrote in 1953 in the *Independent Woman*: With a little care in selection, anyone can find the pair of glasses that does the most for her particular facial shape and coloring; no one need assume any longer that her glasses will detract from her good looks in any way. . . . Who knows, the time may come when the woman with perfect vision who would like to alter the contours of her face slightly, may take to wearing a pair of new smart frames with just a piece of plain glass in them.'

But in January 1954 Bernice Peck, writing in *Mademoiselle*, pointed out that the girl who wore glasses usually had only one pair—a serious limitation, Miss Peck felt, since glasses, carefully chosen, 'can vary and improve your style, expression, personality, complexion, and general attractiveness. . . . Lately frames have

Fig. 116 : Fashionable glasses for American
women, mid–1950s

become so much handsomer than they ever were. New colors never before seen,
vivid, delicate, strong, or muted, in undreamed-of variety. New materials,
plastics, metals, and new ways to work them into unusual textures and finishes.
New shapes combining the nicest flattery with that practical essential—good
design.'

Miss Peck reported happily that 'violently cutesy' frames (horses' heads and
little dogs, perhaps?) and those overloaded with ornamentation were a thing of the
past. The idea had been 'that if you were jokey enough, you wouldn't mind
having to wear glasses'. But Miss Peck felt that the line between being amusing and
being laughable had grown rather thin, and she welcomed a change : 'Today all
the emphasis is being put where it really belongs : on good design, on taste, on
color used for its fashion or its cosmetic value, on variations of line so small as to
be unnoticeable when you look at six pairs on a tray, but different enough from
one another to provide the utmost personal becomingness to individual facial
structures. There's a certain vivid gaiety *but* a nice restraint and subtlety.' Available colours mentioned in *Mademoiselle* were frosty blue, fresh violet, bronze,
mauve, gun-metal, grey, amethyst, and moonstone white.

In July the *Woman's Home Companion* reported on frames of a new Celanese
plastic, mother-and-daughter matching frames, lenses which could be easily and
quickly transferred from one frame to another by the wearer, plaid frames for sunglasses (Figure 116), and a folding lorgnette 'for reading menus or looking up
telephone numbers' (Figure 116).

The May 1958 issue of *Vogue* shows models wearing large, fake-tortoise frames. 'The idea,' says *Vogue*, 'is simply to treat your spectacles as you would a diamond bar pin; they go with *practically* anything if they're worn with dash.'

Men were also affected by the style changes, some less than others. According to Hugh Foster, writing in *Holiday*, 'Dwight D. Eisenhower saw himself through eight years in office on only two changes of glasses. He came in wearing the gold-rimmed Dean-of-Men model he had acquired at Columbia University and went out in a pair of clear plastic Dynamics. President Truman went through three changes, beginning with Missouri Gothic, switching midway through his first term to the rimless, octagonal Merchant Prince and finally to the modified Clubman.'

## THE SIXTIES

Early in 1960 a staff writer for the *New Yorker*, his curiosity aroused by contemporary trends in eyeglasses, made a brief survey—in New York, of course. Optometrists reported that about sixty per cent of their customers requested 'something sturdy' in the way of frames; that the dark, heavy models were preferred by actors, teenagers, and longshoremen; that wives often 'urged their husbands to buy dark frames, because they're supposed to produce a youthful effect'; and that style was more important than comfort.

From the executive of an advertising agency associated with the Better Vision Institute (he was wearing heavy plum-coloured frames at the time) the *New Yorker* learned that the French had initiated the fad for heavy frames after the second World War. Frames were being imported not only from France but also from Italy, Germany, Mexico, and Japan. Two-thirds of American adults, it was estimated, wore glasses, accounting for the sale of twenty million frames a year, excluding sunglasses. In 1961 the Institute estimated that 77 million Americans were wearing glasses. More than 20 million dollars worth of non-prescription sunglasses were sold in the United States that year—most of them in drug stores, dime stores, supermarkets, and gasoline stations.

Metal frames and rimless glasses were not, as a New Yorker might suppose, disappearing from the land. The heavy frames were too sophisticated, too intellectual for the average wearer. The most popular frame, the executive noted disapprovingly, had plastic or coloured-aluminium temples and rolled-gold eyepieces.

In May 1960 *McCall's* reported on 'featherweight aluminium frames in silver pastels: frames with removable tops, tiny specs to slip in a bag, frames in a diamond shape'. As in other magazine articles, emphasis was placed on choosing eyeglasses to go with the face and to correct facial as well as visual defects—to give angles to the round face, to shorten the long nose and lengthen the short one, to soften the angles of a square face, to narrow a too-wide forehead.

Fig. 117 : French styles in sunglasses, 1964. Exported to other European countries and the United States. Available in as many as 14 lens colours

Women over forty, according to Hugh Foster, writing in 1961, tended to gravitate towards fancy frames—'the Frou-Frou, the Cha-Cha in taffy with a hint of mint, the Starry-I in the mood of champagne and candlelight'. What he called 'Mood' frames were preferred by women between 25 and 35, the mood perhaps all too frequently being one of 'erotic languor' expressed through 'the Florentine, Madame X, and Tango models, in colors like wild mink, espresso, and pecan'. Women under 25 preferred more severe frames such as Miss Exec, a modified version of the manly Top Brass. Mr Foster closed his article with the fascinating information that in glasses for young girls the successor to Pixies was a new design called Pookies. Shirley Temples, he added with evident relief, were no longer being stocked.

About this same time *Good Housekeeping*, steering clear of eccentric styles and placing the emphasis on the face, offered some sensible advice on choosing glasses :

'Choose the color of your frame as you'd choose an accessory. Select a neutral shade, or a flattering hue you wear often, to complement your wardrobe.

'If you have a small, pixie face or one that's delicately thin, steer away from large, heavy frames in dense navy, black, or brown. They are overpowering, may steal the show. For either a normal or a large face, avoid tiny severely shaped specs. They make themselves even more noticed by their size contrast. A narrow or a perfect oval face may be prettier with the accent of a horizontal line. However, if you do have an oval face, you're free to choose almost any flattering shape.

'A long, thin face is happy wearing harlequin-shaped frames. This slight upward tilt will make your face seem shorter. Or choose oval or slightly square frames with a straight brow line. A round or square face seems larger when frames are wider at the top than at the bottom, forming an angle at the temples.

'Noses need consideration too. Make the most of a small nose with a high bridged frame. A long, slender nose seems shorter when frames have a low bridge. Heavy, slightly squared frames narrow a broad nose. Close-set eyes look wider spaced with spectacle frames ornamented at the outer corners. Shallow lenses with heavier lower rims hide under-eye pouches. Upswept lines tend to give a youthful look.'

In the autumn of 1962 *Holiday* reported agreement in the trade that the harlequin-shaped glasses, which had begun with a gentle, Mongoloid uptilt and then began 'flaring farther outward and upward, like the old Moulmein Pagoda', were on their way out. The magazine also called attention to the quickness of the optical companies to capitalize on other new and successful products—the Seven-O-Seven, for example, named after the sleek jet liner and constructed, appropriately, of aluminium.

In this year of rapid style changes *Redbook* illustrated sunglasses in a variety of colours (both frames and lenses) to harmonize with eyeshadow and lipstick shades : 'Golden-hued, wrap around frames with dark green lenses . . . sea-green frames with medium green lenses—both are effective with green, golden brown, or aqua eyeshadow. . . . Azalea-colored frames harmonize with all pink, coral, or light red lipstick shades. . . . Turquoise frames and brown lenses blend with pale blue or turquoise eyeshadow. . . . Mauve frames and blue lenses deepen the effect of violet or blue shadow.'

In 1964 it was reported that Carmine de Sapio, a New York politician, had lightened the dark tint of his glasses to improve his public image. Evidently he didn't lighten them enough, for he lost the election.

The average price for American lenses and frames in the mid-sixties was estimated at about \$25 (about £9), considerably lower (often less than \$10) at certain well-patronized optical houses offering quick service at bargain prices. Contact lenses, which had shrunk to what appeared to be a minimum size, covering only the cornea, remained fairly expensive (\$100–\$300 or even higher in the United States). They were available in a variety of colours for those who felt the need of a change. Laurence Olivier, to whom no detail of character creation was unimportant, kept a number of pairs in various colours to suit whatever character he might be playing.

*Time* reported that in 1964 six million Americans were wearing contacts, sixty-five per cent of them women—this despite certain disadvantages in addition to cost, pointed out by *Time* : 'Then there is the matter of removing them, a highly complicated process involving a series of postures (feet planted firmly on the floor before the mirror, back hunched, one palm cupped below the eye, the other fanned out beside it) that might seem the essence of grace in a Kabuki dancer but stir less enthusiasm when performed in a crowded ladies' room, look downright insane in

Fig. 118 : Style of glasses affected by some American
girls in 1965

a restaurant'. *Time* also pointed out that lost lenses were likely to disappear down
drains, into swimming pools, off ski slopes, behind radiators, or even between the
pages of a book. They could also get stuck, one inside the other, as the wife of a
Peace Corpsman stationed in Peru discovered to her dismay after waiting months
for a replacement of what she assumed to be a lost lens. It turned out that the one
she had been wearing in the meantime was really two.

The great majority of people with vision problems still relied on conventional
lenses, often in unconventional frames. In the window of what appeared to be an
average optician's in New York there were 113 styles of frames displayed and inside
the shop more than 400 for the customers to choose from.

The designers of frames, faced with the necessity of supplying an endless stream
of new designs at as rapid a rate as possible, inevitably turned back in history and
revived some old styles in contemporary materials. The lorgnette, a very practical
form of eyeglass for casual use, was to be found in all the opticians' shops in a variety
of styles, mostly plastic (Plate 72). Half-moon pulpit spectacles, usually in dark
plastic frames, were in vogue for both men and women. The frame designer of the
American Optical Company credited Fred Astaire with reviving the style once
popular among preachers. A Milwaukee optician who had formerly sold no more
than two pairs a month, reported *Time*, began selling at least a pair a day. He gave
television the credit: 'The half-spec enables people who only need glasses for
reading to go through the evening paper and watch TV at the same time without
taking their glasses off'. This may well be; but had they not seen them *on* TV
(or on Fred Astaire), they might not have been quite so quick to adopt them.

In line with the reaching into the past for ideas, there was in the mid-sixties a fad, probably started by young people and encouraged by the designers and optical shops, for wearing aggressively old-fashioned spectacles—excessively large horn rims (Figure 118), small gold or steel oval frames, octagonal frames in white gold or silver, small rectangular metal frames in imitation of nineteenth-century styles. Optical shops took to displaying old, even antique, frames, and the designers turned out new frames in imitation of the old styles. This seemed to follow a general resurgence of interest in the past—in hair styles, in clothing, in architecture—and was part of the general concept of 'camp', a concept so esoteric that it could not really be explained to outsiders but had to be intuitively understood.

By 1966 'granny' glasses, most of them with tinted lenses (Plate 75), were flooding the market. In November 1965 the *New York Times* speculated on the new fashion:

'The trend to elderly eyegear seems to be the final stage in the campaign to disprove Dorothy Parker's axiom to the effect that bespectacled females do not evoke passionate impulses in the opposite sex. The conscious propaganda of the opticians was never responsible for the result.

'First there was Gertrude Lawrence's "Lady in the Dark", which made elegant

Fig. 119 : Inexpensive wrap-around sunglasses, 1965

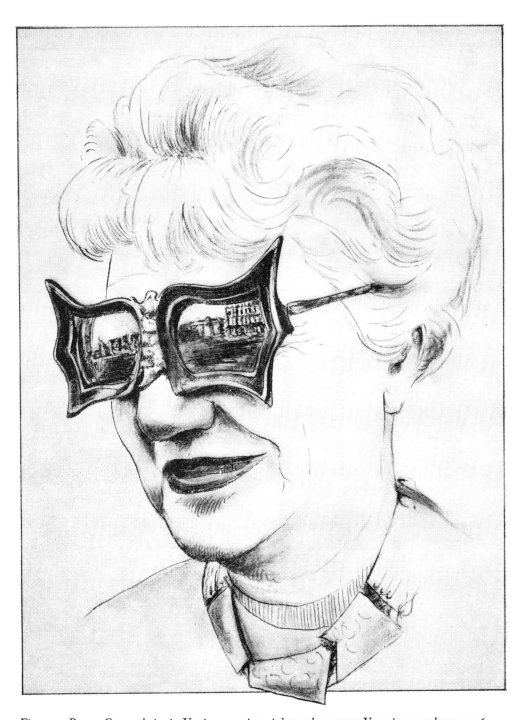

Fig. 120 : Peggy Guggenheim in Venice, wearing eighteenth-century Venetian sunglasses, 1965

career women in colored eye frames seem palatable, to middle-aged executives at least. Then, unintentionally, Mrs John F. Kennedy sent younger hordes in search of oversize sunglasses. Courrèges pushed that principle to the extreme with his humorously conceived slit sunglasses (Plate 74-A).

'But the latest fad had more eccentric origins. A dozen years ago, Serendipity, the boutique-coffeehouse, acquired the stock of an old-fashioned optometrist who was going out of business. The shop resold them, slowly and quietly, to visionary customers.

'Three years ago the traffic in Benjamin Franklin spectacles and the round, steel-rimmed style admired by Soviet politicians started booming.'

At this same time high-fashion eyewear by Oliver Goldsmith of London included both narrow steel-rimmed sunglasses and enormous plastic-rimmed ones. Wooden frames 'in teak, rosewood, and charcoal with swept-back lugs' were advertised in *The Optician*. In January 1966 woodgrain eyewear for men was being publicized —'Superbly fashioned in the currently popular woodgrains much admired today by men of good taste. The WOODMAN is made in ROSE BRIAR and CHARCOAL colours.' Ladies could buy frames hand-covered in lizard skin to match handbags. Even Op art (Plate 75-E) invaded eyewear design. But many Englishwomen, impervious to lizard and woodgrain and Op, still wore pink translucent plastic frames prescribed by the National Health (Plate 74-D).

The idea of making glasses fashionable, not just acceptable, was given new impetus in the United States by the formation in November 1964 of the Fashion Eyewear Group of America. One of the main purposes of the organization was to promote American-designed frames as a fashion accessory (see page 241). In 1965 an article in *Vogue* featured a number of frames from the Eyewear Group. Publicity photos subsequently sent out by the Group showed a number of frames in mother-of-pearl, most of them conspicuous by virtue of either size, decoration, or shape. One of the most conspicuous was a pair of wide-rimmed triangular glasses (Plate 74-C) in mottled mother-of-pearl, 'so absolutely neutral', according to the publicity blurb, 'it looks just right with any color'. What sort of face would be improved by the addition of enormous triangular glasses was not specified.

The *Vogue* article pointed out that in regard to eyeglasses there are basically two types of women—those who resent having to wear glasses and want them to be as inconspicuous as possible but still attractive and those who, whether they really enjoy wearing glasses or not, figure there's no use trying to hide them. These are the women who go in for the extreme styles which change from season to season.

For the conservative woman (conservative, that is, from *Vogue's* point of view), the editors recommended half-spectacles, the one-eyed lorgnette, perfectly round lenses with frames of tortoise or wood-grain, and for the sun, a pair of 'superb dark glasses'. *Vogue* also emphasized the importance of correct fit and having the right kind of glasses for the use to which they are to be put.

For the fashion-conscious (or, perhaps, fad-conscious) woman *Vogue* listed its

predictions for the coming season : 'You'll want, we predict, the one-eyed lorgnette—or the monocle-turned-lorgnette. . . . For people who like spectacular
spectacles, immense square-eyed frames and great oval owl eyes ought to be
enjoying near hysteria. . . . Frames in shades like Kelly green, true violet, Pucci
sky-blue, bright lacquered shades, should be ragey. . . . So should frames carved
by jewellers out of coral, jade, or lapis lazuli. . . . Hexagonals, "the hottest thing
in the market today", may still be one of the several pairs of spectacles you'll want
to own a year from now. Ditto, the horizontal ovals, like a pair of child's barrettes
(we see these as a basic shape ; next year they might be done in real ivory or jade
or gold). . . . Non-sunglass lenses may pick up a fair amount of tint and at their
most charming may put over the eyes the most perfectly-applied eye shadow—
a watercolour transparency of pale-green grey.'

By the spring of 1966 glasses seemed to have gone just about to the limit of
faddishness. Not only were there large squares, rectangles, octagons, and ovals in
stripes, checks, and plain colours (not necessarily the same colour for both eyes),
but even one-way-mirror lenses were sometimes patterned in checks or stripes.
And 'just for fun', as *Time* put it, 'some glasses come armed with roll-up awnings
and huge fake eyelashes ; others sport spectacular papier-maché designs glued on
to the frames ; still others have movable lenses that lift up into a coy wink'. For
the moment, at least, eyeglasses seemed to be not so much for seeing as for being
seen.

For those who wanted none of these, and there were a good many, contact lenses
seemed to provide the answer. The report in *Holiday* in 1962 that four million
people, most of them under forty, were wearing contact lenses, representing an
increase of 3,800,000 during the preceding six years, suggests that a 700-year cycle
was perhaps nearing completion. In that time man had progressed from heavy,
rigid, almost unmanageable spectacle frames holding in place crude lenses suitable
only for close vision, to tiny, feather-weight bits of plastic which floated on the
eyeball, were very nearly invisible when worn, and could, if one wished, change
the colour of the eyes to suit the costume or a passing whim.

It should, perhaps, also be noted that in the mid-sixties Americans were able to
order extremely inexpensive reading glasses by post. The correct lens could be
obtained, they were assured, merely by stating their age.

Fig. 121 : High-fashion frames of marbellized mother-of-pearl, 1965.  Design from the Fashion
Eyewear Group of America

PLATE 51 : THE TWENTIETH
CENTURY 1900–1910

A  *c.* 1905, probably French. Folding lorgnette entirely in gold, suspended from long, delicate, gold chain. Used in New York. (*Museum of the City of New York*)

B  1900, American. Automatic reel for eyeglass chain. Made by Ketcham and McDougall, New York.

C  1905, American. Automatic reel in gold for eyeglasses or pencil.

D  1900, American. Lorgnette (closed), available in sterling silver and plated sterling.

E  1900, French. Sold in the United States. Mother-of-pearl opera glasses with side handle. Shown in folded position.

F  1910, American. Lorgnette made by Zondel Manufacturing Company, New York.

G  *c.* 1900, French. Folding lorgnette (closed) in pink translucent enamel and gold.

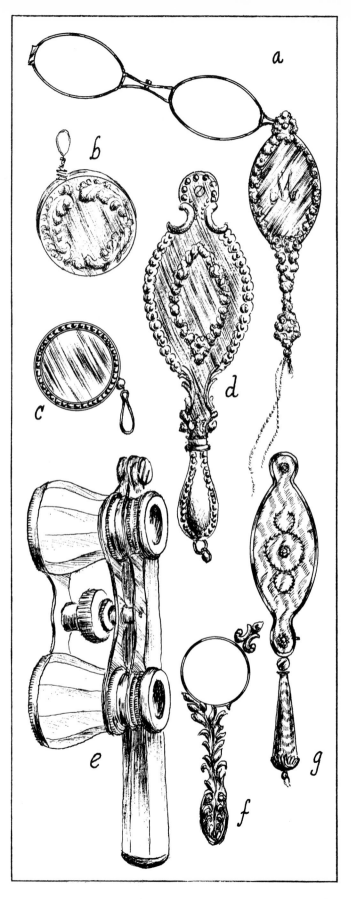

Plate 52 : The Twentieth
          Century 1900–1915

A  *c.* 1910, probably American. Rimless pince-nez with gold finger-pieces. Lenses down-set for reading.

B  *c.* 1914, American. Worn by Albert Henry Washburn, New York lawyer.

C  *c.* 1914, American. Rimless pince-nez worn by Peter Gansevoort Ten Eyck, New York congressman.

D  *c.* 1914, American. Silver or steel rimmed pince-nez worn by Watson M. Rogers, New York supreme court justice.

E  *c.* 1914, American. Rimless pince-nez worn by Reverend Edgar M. Thompson of Brooklyn.

F  *c.* 1900, probably American. Solid gold pince-nez with gadroon engraved rims.

G  1904, American. Automobile goggles.

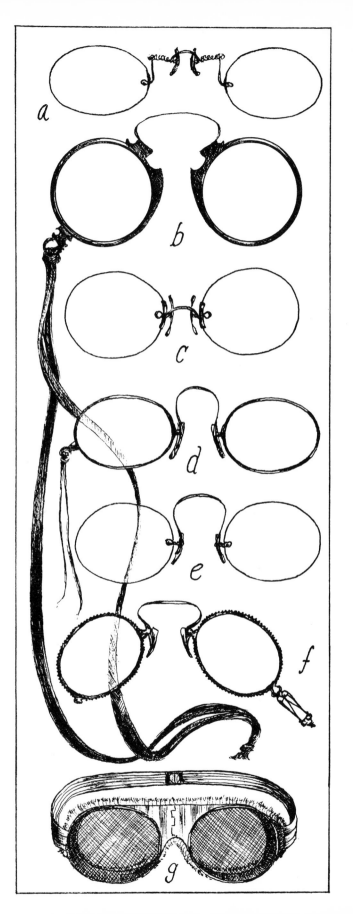

PLATE 53 : THE TWENTIETH CENTURY 1900–1915

A  *c.* 1914, American.  Worn by Henry Ward Ranger, New York artist.

B  *c.* 1914, American.  Worn by Thomas Hunter, New York educator.

C  *c.* 1914, American.  Steel rims.  Worn by Algernon S. Frissell, New York banker. In the 1890s Mr Frissell wore pince-nez.

D  *c.* 1914, American.  Shell rims.  Worn by Dr A. W. Herman, New York.

E  1914, American.  Worn by Daniel Frohman, New York theatre manager.  Mr Frohman wore a similar style in the 1890s (see Figure 83-F).

F  American.  Half-glasses for close vision.  This style was worn for many years. (See also H below.)

G  After 1903, American.  Designed by Charles Douglas Hilabald.

H  After 1903, American.  Designed by a Dr Briggs.

I  *c.* 1903, French.  Ribard glasses for close vision, permitting easy distance vision without removing the glasses.  These preceded G and H above.

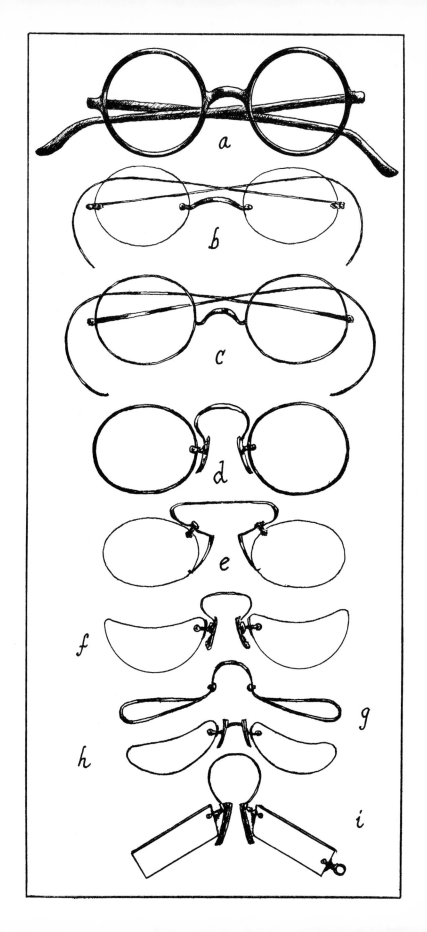

PLATE 54 : THE TWENTIETH
CENTURY 1914–1920

A  1914, American.  Rimless spectacles.

B  1914, American.  Rolled gold folding oxfords.

C  1917, American.  Rolled gold frame with inlaid 'Shellikit Bevel Rims'.

D  1917, American.  Rolled gold folding oxfords with inlaid Zylo rims.

E  1918, American.  Crystal cherry imitation shell frames.  Available with amber or smoke lenses as well as clear.

F  1918, American.  U.S. Army standard frames of Alumnica.

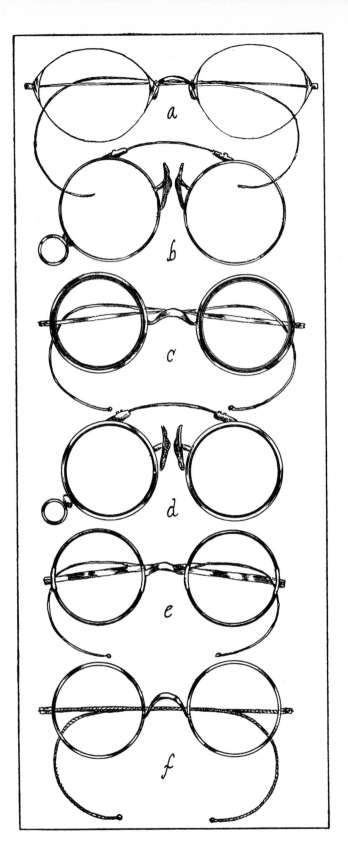

PLATE 55 : THE TWENTIETH
CENTURY 1920–1925

A  1922, American.  Shell oxfords.

B,  1922, American.  Oxfords in closed
C  position.

D  1922, American.  Oxfords.  Suitable
for men or women.

E  1920, American.  Automatic eyeglass holder.  Black enamel on
metal.  Ketcham and McDougall,
New York.  This model was still
being sold in 1935.

F  1925, American.  Lorgnon (closed)
in sterling silver.  'Engine-turned
pattern with fancy eye-wires'.  Frank
Krenentz Company, New York.

G  1925, American.  Lorgnette (closed)
in rolled gold.

H  1922, American.  Automatic eyeglass holder in gold.  Ketcham and
McDougall, New York.

I  1925, American.  Automatic eyeglass holder.  White rolled plate
front.

J  1922, American.  Automatic eyeglass
holder.

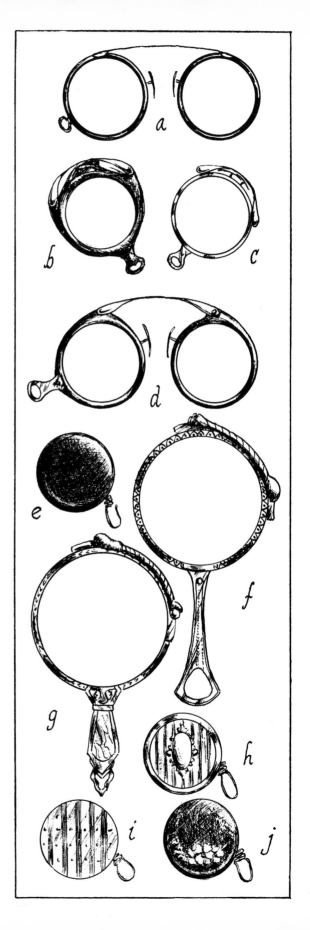

PLATE 56 : THE TWENTIETH
CENTURY 1920–1930

A 1925, American. Folding oxford style in silver. 'Grecian' spring.

B 1921, American. Available in white or yellow gold.

C Monocle.

D 1925, American. Shopping oxfords for women, in sterling silver, white gold, or 14 carat rolled gold.

E Folding spring lorgnettes for
-G women.

H 1920. Available both earlier and later. Spring reel for eyeglasses or pencil.

I c. 1920, American. Although this pair was in use in Salt Lake City about 1920, it was old-fashioned by then and was worn by an elderly gentleman. The style was worn by both men and women. (*Pioneer Museum, Salt Lake City*)

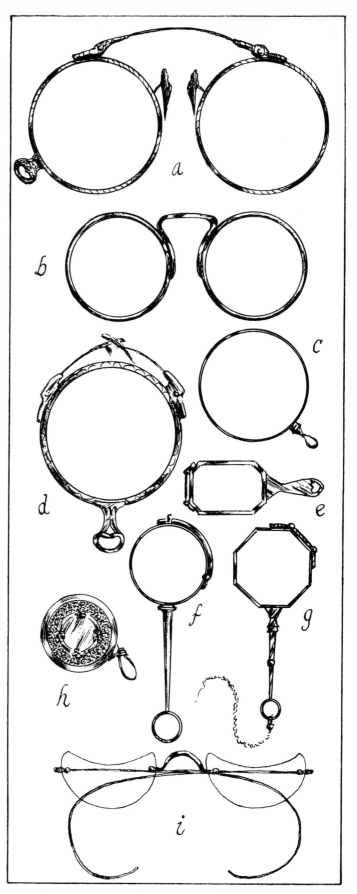

PLATE 57 : THE TWENTIETH
CENTURY 1920–1930

A 1924, American. Rimless pince-nez.
Solid white gold mountings.

B 1925, American. Xylonite rims.
-D

E 1924, American. Rimless.

F 1924, American. Xylonite rims.

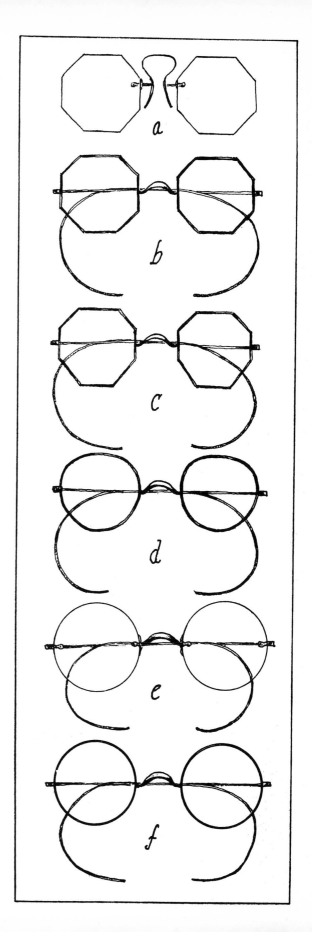

PLATE 58 : THE TWENTIETH CENTURY 1920–1930

A-D   1923, American.   Bausch and Lomb 'Artshell' frames, for men and women.

E   1924, American.   Spring bridge and flexible cork guard designed to adjust to any nose. Frame of shell-coloured or crystal Xylonite. Introduced by Bausch and Lomb in January.

F   1924, American.   Gold-rimmed pince-nez.   A no-longer-fashionable style still popular with older people.

G   1924, American.   Pince-nez with very thin dark rims.

H   1924, American.   Rimless pince-nez.

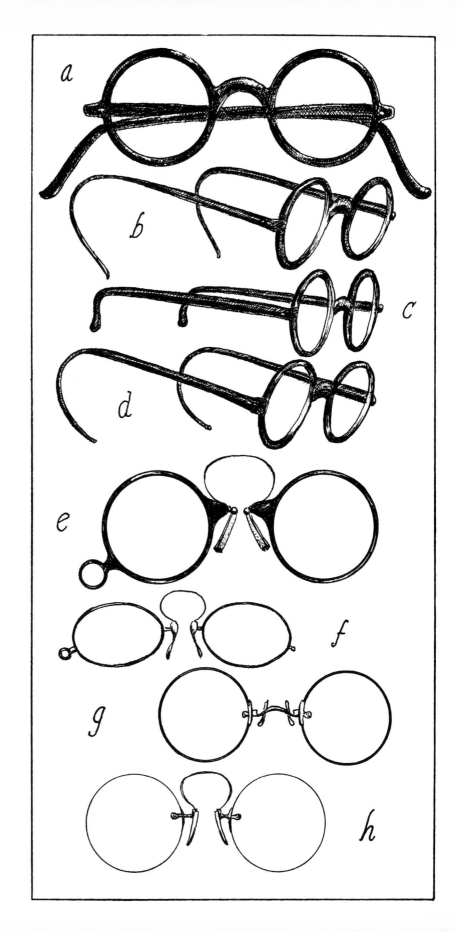

PLATE 59 : THE TWENTIETH
         CENTURY 1925–1930

A  1928.  Pince-nez, available in white, yellow, or green gold, with crystal, black, or cherry shell rims.

B  1928.  Rolled gold or solid gold rims. Made by Bausch and Lomb.

C  1929.  White gold frames with inner rims of black xylonite.  Made by Bausch and Lomb.

D  1928.  Rimless glasses with nose-piece and temples of gold.

E  1928.  Oxford glasses, available in white or yellow gold with crystal, black, or cherry shell rims.

F  1928.  Pince-nez.  Available in white, yellow, or green gold with crystal black, or cherry shell rims.

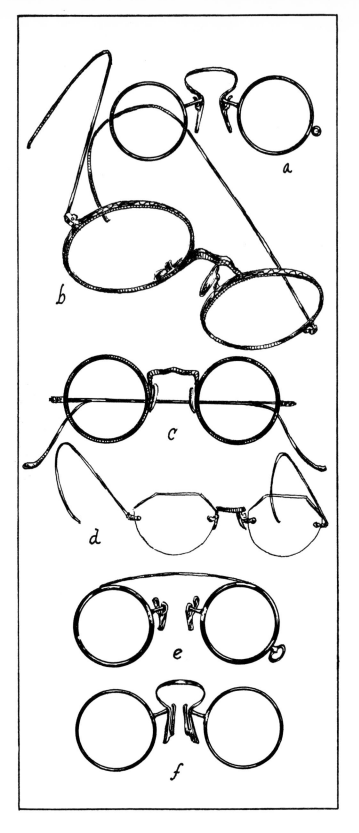

PLATE 60 : THE TWENTIETH CENTURY 1930–1940

A 1938, American. Rimless sunglasses.

B 1938, American. Sunglasses with translucent frames.

C English. Sportsman's glasses with splinter-proof lenses. Made by Theodore Hamblin, London.

D 1936, American. Sunglasses with metal frames.

E 1932, American. Magnifying glass available in 6 colours. Made by Bausch and Lomb and sold for 60 cents (about 4s. 4d.).

F 1932, American. Folding pocket magnifying glass with zylon mounting, available in 4 colours. Made by Bausch and Lomb.

G 1932, American. Magnifying glass with metal handle, available in 3 sizes.

H 1935, American. Folding oxford glasses. The lenses lock together on being closed and can be released with a slight pressure on the small decorative handle.

PLATE 61 : THE TWENTIETH CENTURY 1930–1940

A–C  1933, American.  Rimless with rolled gold fittings.

  D  1938, American.  Rimless with rolled gold fittings.

  E  1938, American.  Rimless.  Rolled gold arm follows top edge of lens.

  F  1938, American.  Rimless with rolled gold fittings.

  G  1931, English.  Collapsible spectacles known as 'Speclettes'.  Made by Theodore Hamblin, London.

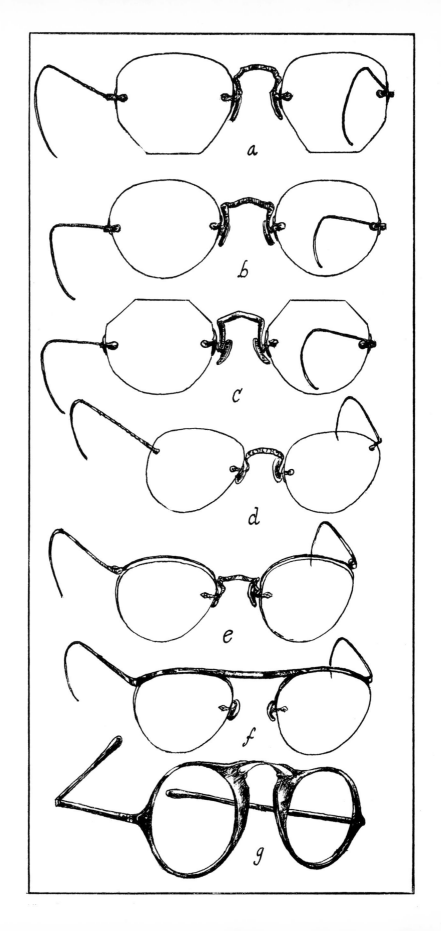

PLATE 62 : THE TWENTIETH
        CENTURY 1940–1950

A   1942, American.   Rimless.

B   1942, American.   Rolled gold
    frames.

C   1948, American.   Plastic frames.

D   1949, American.   Plastic frames.

-F

G   1947, American.   Plastic frames.

H   1947, American.   Sunglasses.

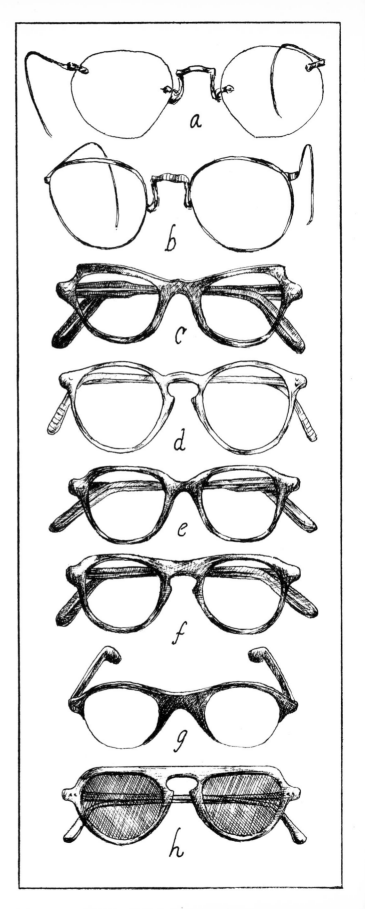

PLATE 63 : THE TWENTIETH
CENTURY 1940–1950

A   1948.  Folding lorgnette.

B   1949, American.  Pink rolled gold frames with green lenses.

C   1949, American.  Clip-on sunglasses with green lenses.  For men and women.

D   1949, American.  Pink rolled gold frames with brow bar and green lenses.  Aviation style for men.

E   1945, American.  Black plastic frames for women.

F   1945, American.  Imitation tortoise plastic frames for men.

G   1947, American.  High fashion black plastic sunglasses for women.

H   1943, American.  Plastic frames for women, available in a variety of colours.

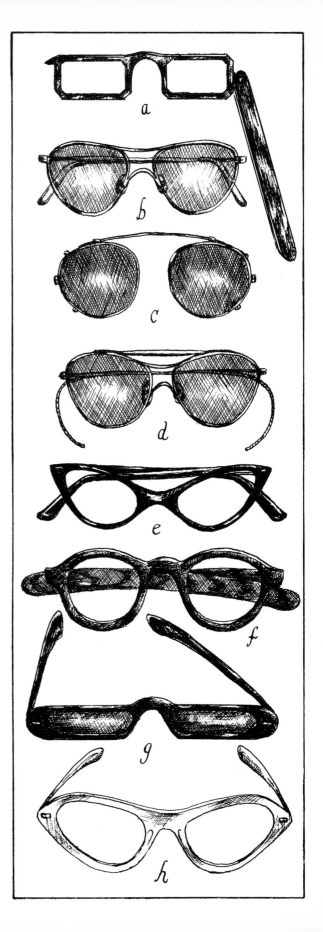

PLATE 64 : THE TWENTIETH
CENTURY 1950–1955

A  1953, American. Plastic frames for women.  Also used for clear pre-scription lenses.

B,  1954, American.  Plastic frames for
C  women in assorted colours.

D  1954, American.  Imitation tortoise shell with metal nosepiece.

E,  1952, American.  Light imitation
F  tortoise - shell  frames for women. Also used for clear prescription lenses.

G  1952, American.  Plastic frames for men and women.

H  1954, American.  Plastic frames in assorted colours.

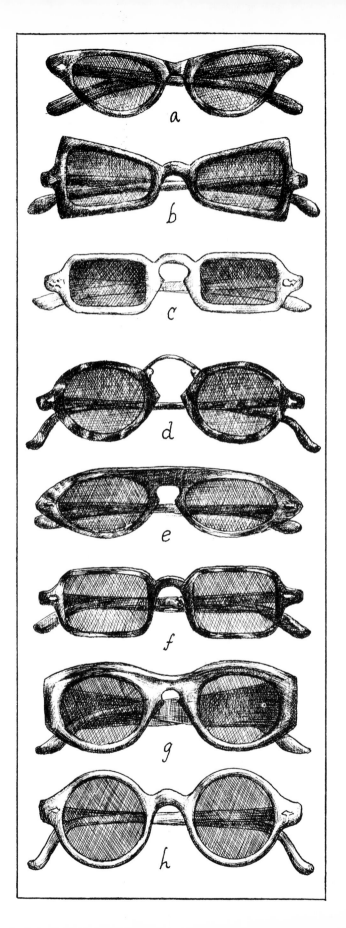

PLATE 65 : THE TWENTIETH
CENTURY 1950–1955

A 1953, American. Sunglasses for women. Metal frames. Made by Bausch and Lomb.

B 1953, American. Plastic and metal frames for women.

C 1953, American. Conservative semi-rimless style for women. Rolled gold temples and eyewires. Plastic ends on temples.

D 1955, French. Black or brown plastic and gold frames for men. Also used for sunglasses.

E 1951, American. Rimless glasses with gold frames.

F 1955, French. Semi-rimless sunglasses for women.

G 1955, French. Semi-rimless sunglasses with gold eyewires and temples.

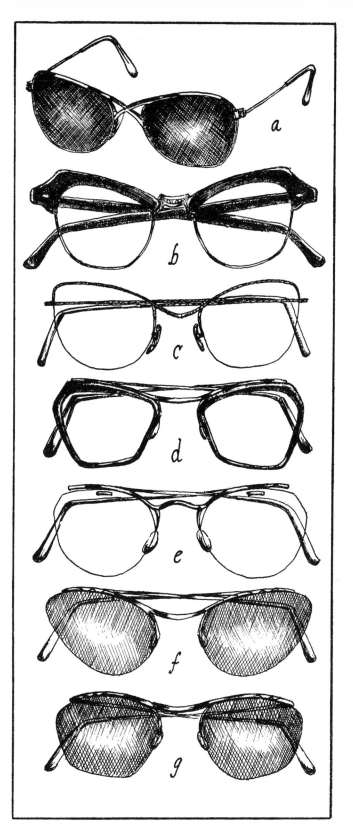

PLATE 66 : THE TWENTIETH CENTURY 1950–1960

A 1958. Dressy gold and pink frames for women.

B, C 1952. Women's black plastic frames with gold trim.

D 1958. Women's clear plastic frames with sparkles.

E 1958. Black plastic frames for women.

F 1958. Dressy gold frames for men.

G 1958. Sturdy plastic frames for children.

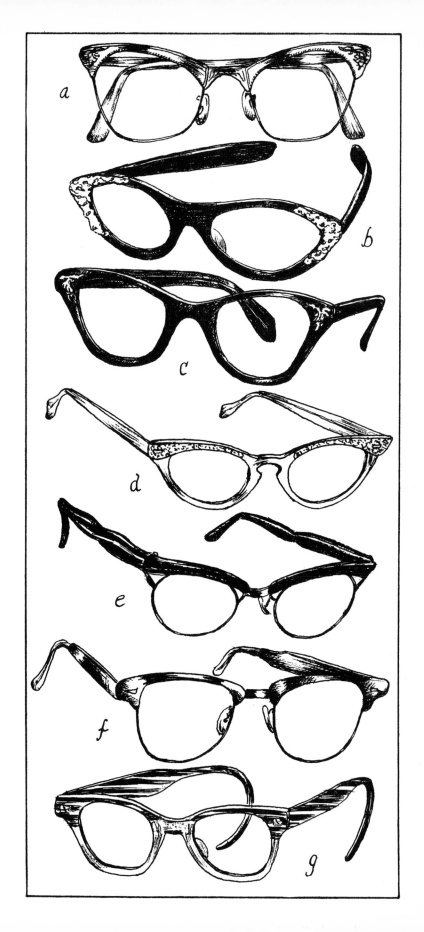

Plate 67 : The Twentieth Century 1960–1965

A   Plastic frames for men, available in onyx, grey, or amber.

B   Plastic frames for men, available in grey, brown, and onyx.

C   Combination frame for men, available in walnut, onyx, and blackwood.

D   Combination frame available in gun-metal, bronze, and brownstone.

E, F   Conservative rolled gold frames.

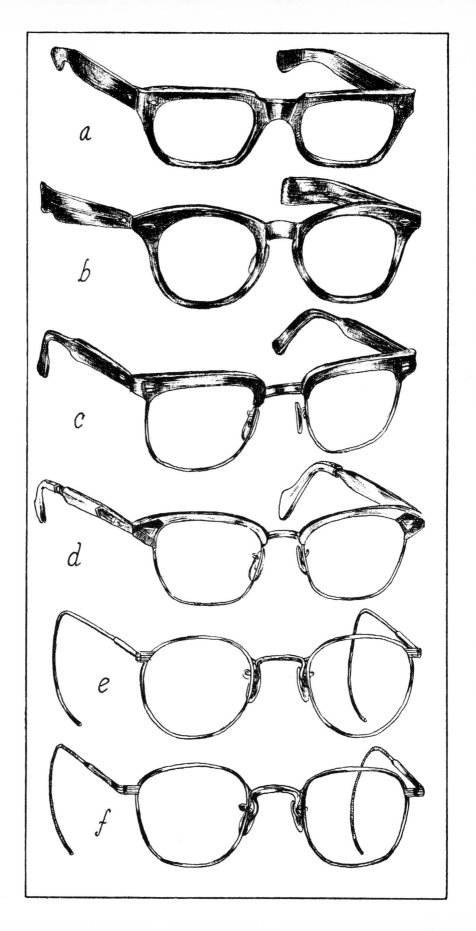

PLATE 68 : THE TWENTIETH CENTURY 1960–1965

Fashionable American styles.

A    Available in 5 colours—onyx, sable, slate, amber, and white pearl.

B    Plastic frame available in onyx, amber, and brown.

C    Two-tone colours—feather brown, snow raven, feather grey, brown haze, grey haze.

D    Available in onyx, brown, and mink haze.

E    Combination style available in jet (silver motif), brown (gold motif), blue (design in silver), champagne (design in brown).

F    Combination style available in pink or white rolled gold chassis with plastic top rims and temples in black star, brown star, silver onyx, silver slate, onyx, and blue mist.

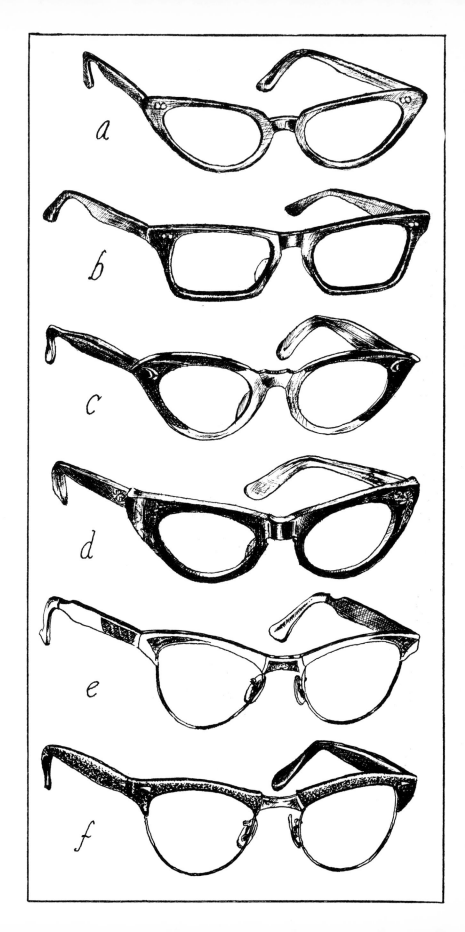

PLATE 69 : THE TWENTIETH CENTURY 1960–1965

A, B   Conservative, semi-rimless styles for men and women. Rolled gold temples and eyewires.

C   Fashionable half-eye style for men and women. Designed for people requiring glasses only for near viewing. This style available in grey and brown. Similar designs from other manufacturers available in black and colours.

D   Conservative flesh pink clear plastic frames for men and women.

E   Fashionable and very popular style for men. Plastic frames available in black, grey, and brown, black being the most popular. Other styles of temples available.

F   Fashionable style for women. Plastic frames available in onyx, wine, and slate.

G   Sturdy plastic frames designed for very young children. Brown tops fade into clear plastic.

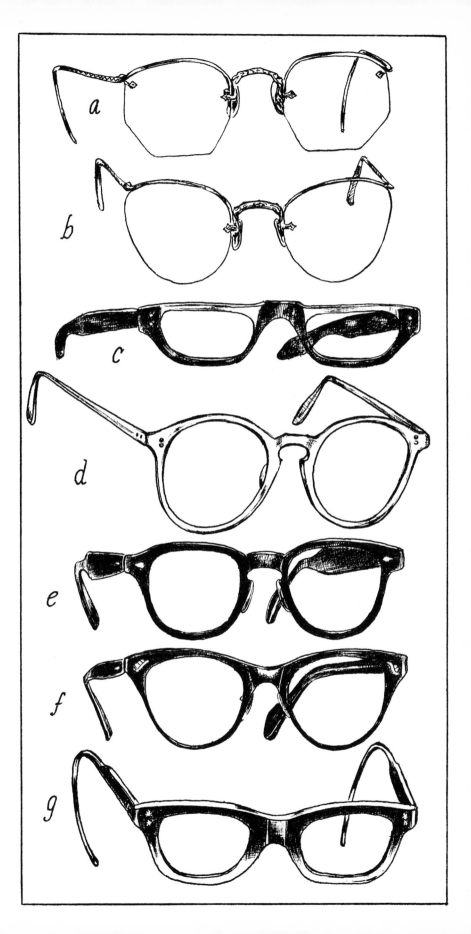

PLATE 70 : THE TWENTIETH CENTURY 1964, 1965

A   French.  Beige, pearl finish, with rhinestones.  Sold in Amsterdam.

B   Eccentric sunglasses.  Gold and black.  Sold in London, New York.

C   French.  Pearl grey finish with rhinestones.  Sold in Amsterdam.

D   Double eyeglasses for distance and reading.  Or one half could be used for sunglasses.  Black plastic with clear edges.  Sold in London.

E   Teakwood frames.  Sold in Amsterdam, London, New York.

F   Dark brown plastic and gold frames.  Sold in Amsterdam.

G   Italian.  Black plastic frames with bronze-finish temples.  Sold in London.

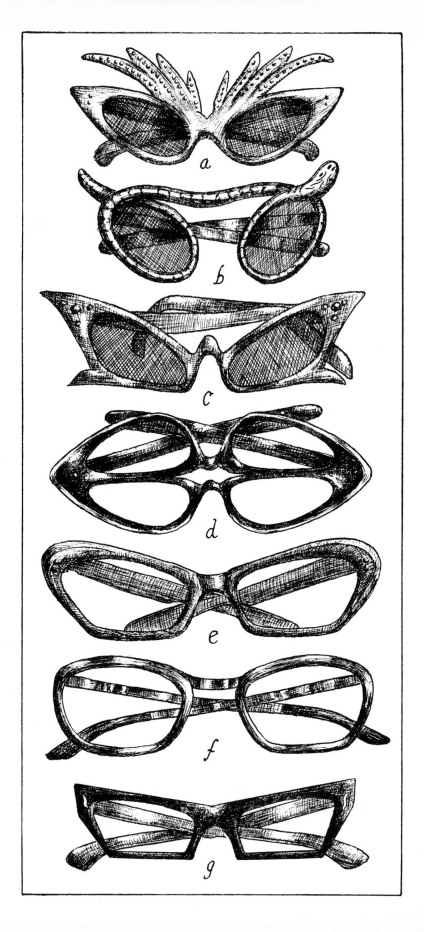

PLATE 71 : THE TWENTIETH
CENTURY 1964, 1965

A New York. Women's imitation mother-of-pearl frames with clear and ruby-red rhinestones.

B New York. Women's eccentric sunglasses, available in imitation mother-of-pearl, gun-metal, or black with miniature gold-coloured key.

C French. Sold in New York. Women's eccentric frames in black or white with rhinestones and decorative gold lines.

D French. Sold in New York. Women's eccentric frames in imitation tortoise shell with tiny rhinestones.

E Mexican. Sold in New York. Slightly eccentric men's frames in black plastic.

F Sold in New York. Black plastic frames for women.

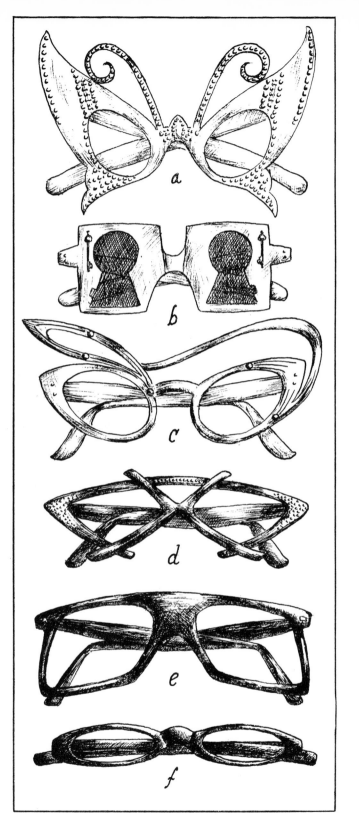

PLATE 72 : THE TWENTIETH
        CENTURY 1964, 1965

A London. Folding lorgnette.

B London and Amsterdam. Black plastic lorgnette with rhinestones.

C New York. Folding lorgnette.

D New York. Tortoise-shell lorgnette.

E New York. Reading glass. Gold colour with rhinestones.

F New York. Single glass in different positions. Tortoise shell.

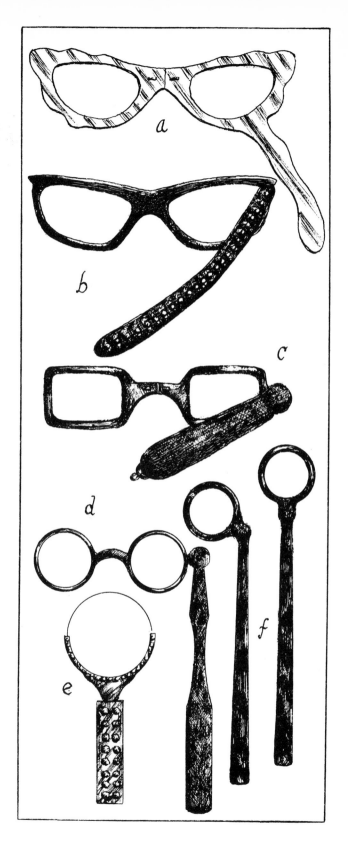

PLATE 73 : THE TWENTIETH CENTURY 1964, 1965

A   French.   Sold in New York.

B   French.   Sold in New York.

C   American.   Semi-rimless half-glasses with black plastic frames.

D   American.   Gold wire frames.   Temples have flesh-coloured plastic ends.

E   French.   Brown plastic.

F   Italian.   Black plastic.

G   French.   Black plastic.

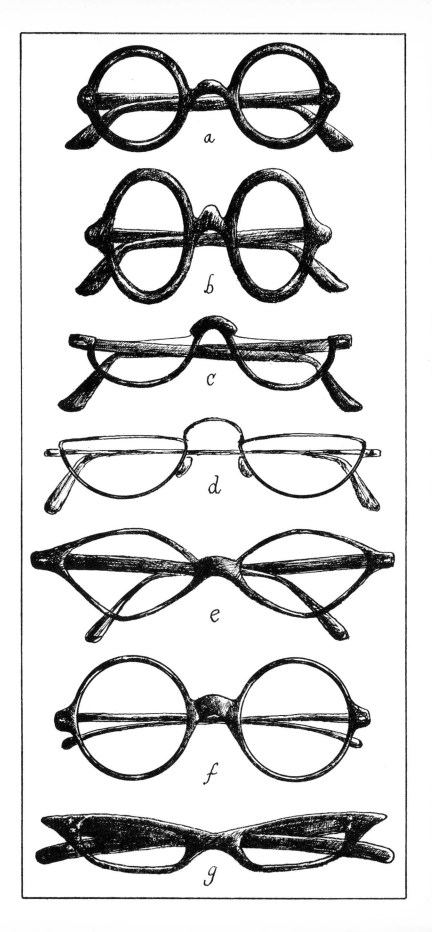

PLATE 74 : THE TWENTIETH
CENTURY 1965

A   Opaque white sunglasses with eye-slits.  Plastic frames.

B,  High-fashion frames for women in
C   mottled mother-of-pearl.

D   English.  Conventional pink translucent plastic frames in style prescribed by the National Health.  The most commonly worn style in England.

E   Women's frames inspired by the film *Goldfinger*.

F   Leopard print sunglasses. Also available in zebra and giraffe.

G   Japanese.  Vertical reading glass for use with characters running up and down the page.  Frame of tortoise shell.

H   English.  'Magna-Add', near-vision half-lenses designed to be clipped on the front of plano or distance sunglasses.

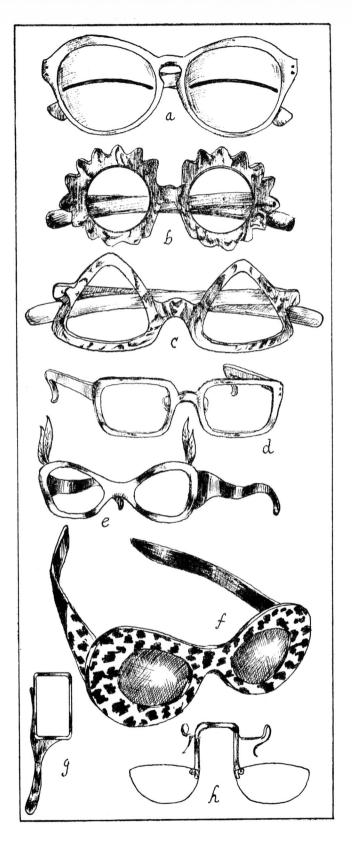

PLATE 75 : THE TWENTIETH
CENTURY 1966

A  Granny glasses. Sunglasses avail-
-D  able in a variety of lens colours—
pink, yellow, blue, green, grey,
brown. Metal frames. Less expensive models available in frames
of coloured plastic.

E  Sunglasses with plastic frames in-
fluenced by fad for Op art. These
are called 'Op checkerboard'.

F  Sunglasses with wrap-around plastic
frames.

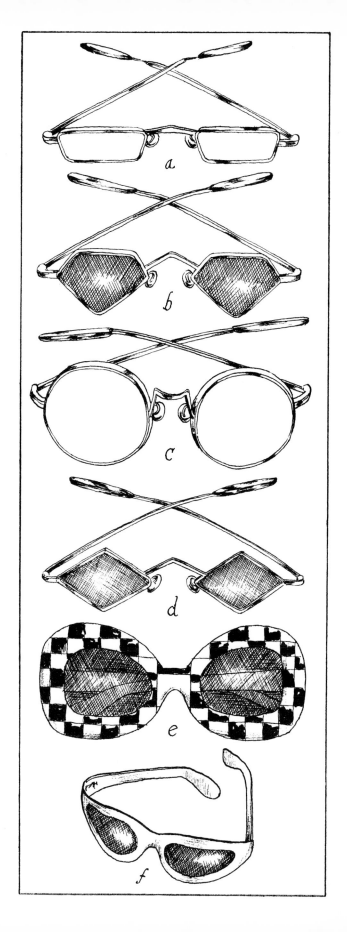

Fig. 122 : High-fashion sunglasses, 1967

PLATE 76 : THE TWENTIETH
CENTURY 1967-1970

A   Black plastic frames.

B   Plastic frames.

C   Sunglasses with white plastic frames.

D   Plastic frames.

E   Sunglasses with white plastic frames.
Faddish style.

F   Plastic frames.   Popular style, available in black, tortoise-shell, and other colours.

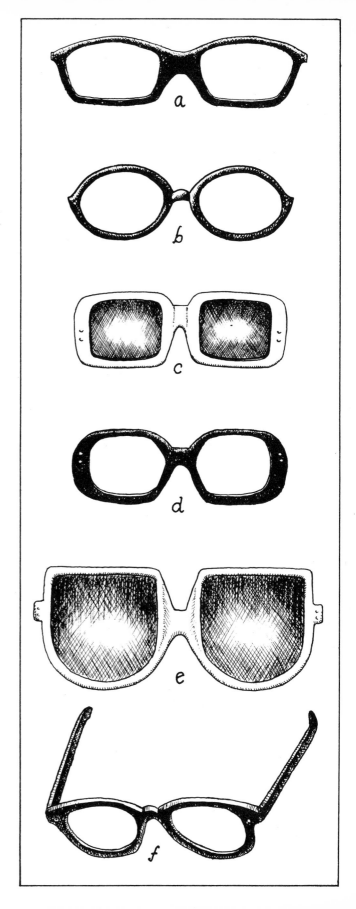

A   Fashionable sunglasses, 1970.

B   Tortoise-shell frames with tinted lenses.

C   Amber plastic frameless sunglasses, 1970.   Faddish style.

D   Gold frames with tinted lenses.

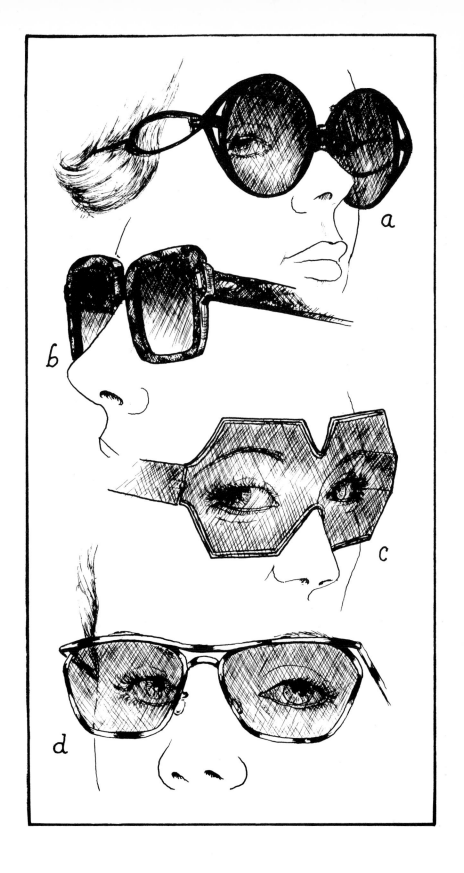

a

b

c

d

PLATE 78 : THE TWENTIETH CENTURY 1967-1970

A   Plastic frames.   Fashionable style, available in various colours.

B   Black and white frames for women's sunglasses.   Faddish style.

C   Plastic frames for women.

D   High-fashion sunglasses with two-tone frames.

E   Popular style for women.   Plastic frames, available in various colours.

F   Plastic frames, available in various colours.

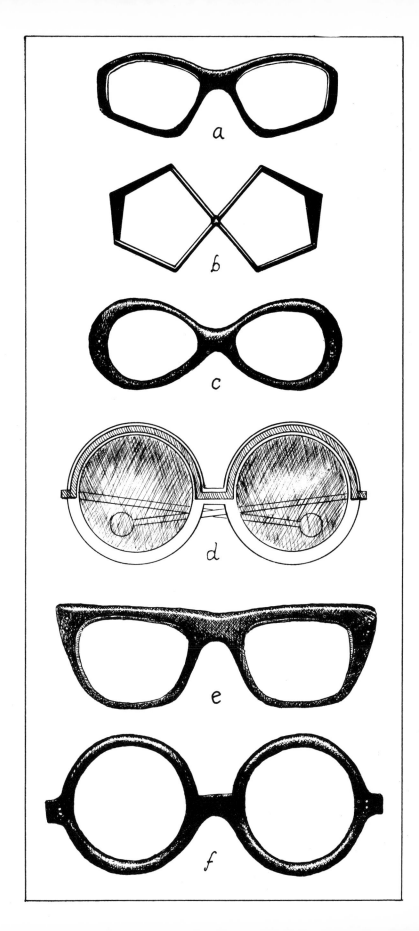

Plate 79 : The Twentieth Century 1970-1975

A   Metal frames for men.

B   Metal frames.

C   Metal frames.

D   Plastic frames for women.

E   Metal frames.   Popular style for men.

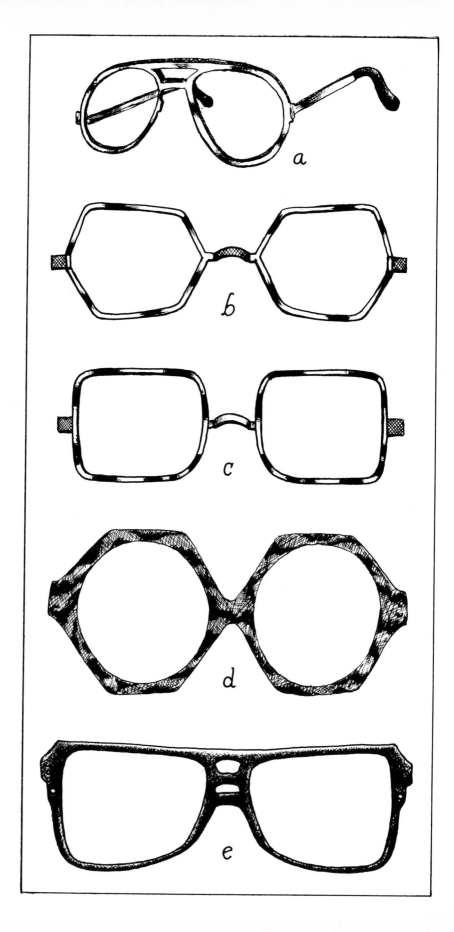

PLATE 80 : THE TWENTIETH
          CENTURY 1970-1975

A   Wire frames.

B   Gold frames.

C   Gold frames.

D   Gold frames.

E   Plastic frames for women.

F   Black plastic half-glasses for reading.
    Available in other colours.

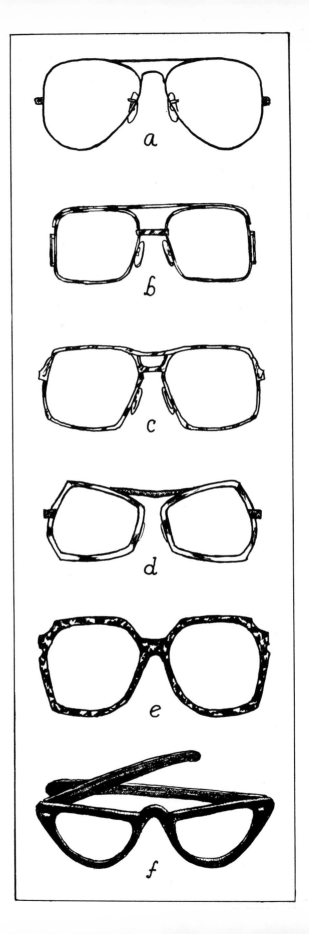

A   Folding lorgnette.

B   Folding plastic frames.

C   Gold lorgnette.

D   Half-glasses for reading.

E   Rhinestone-studded frames.

F   Magnifying glass.

G   Plastic frames with low-set temples.

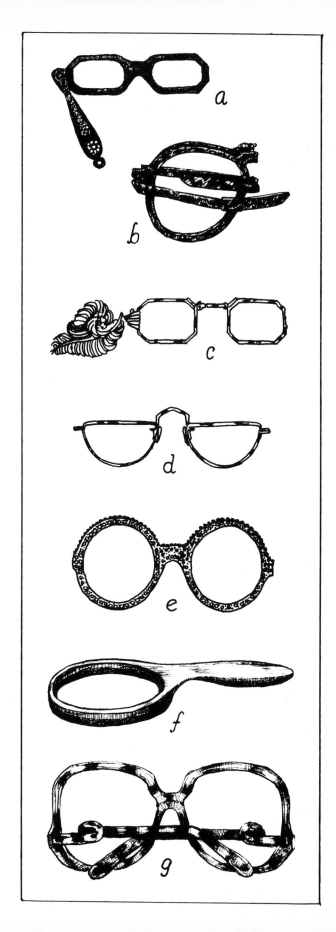

PLATE 82 : THE TWENTIETH CENTURY 1975-1979

A   Plastic frames.

B   Shaded plastic frames with low-set temples.

C   Plastic frames.   Popular style.

D   Sunglasses.

E   Plastic frames.   Popular style for men.

F   Plastic frames with low-set temples.

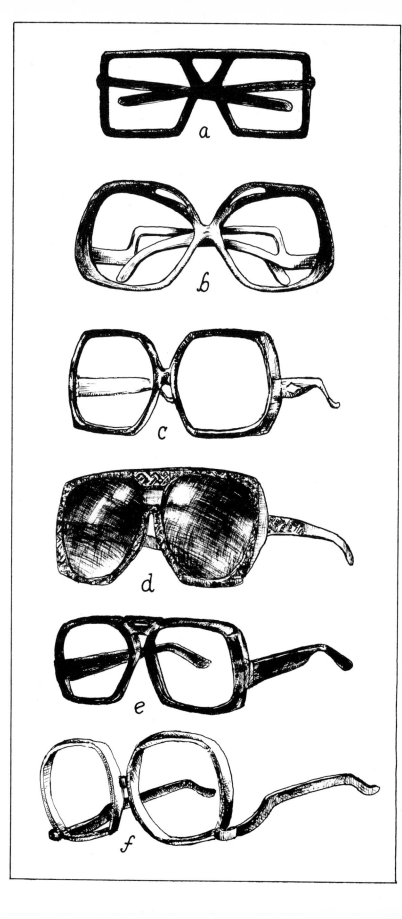

PLATE 83 : THE TWENTIETH
CENTURY 1975-1979

A    Plastic frames.  Popular style for
     men.

B    Metal frames.

C    Plastic frames.  Popular style, avail-
     able in various colours.

D    Gold frames.

E    Metal frames.

F    Plastic frames, available in white or
     colours.  Faddish style.

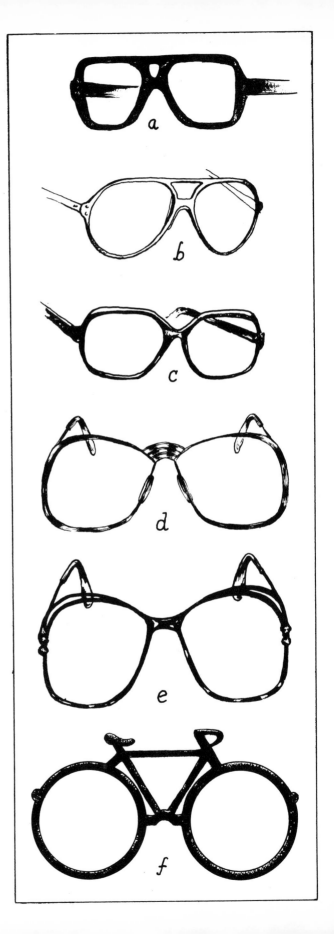

PLATE 84 : THE TWENTIETH
CENTURY 1975-1979

A  Half-glasses for reading. Plastic
frames.

B  Plastic frames for women.

C  Plastic frames.

D  Gold frames for women.

E  Metal frames.

F  Metal frames.  Popular style.

G  Plastic frames for women.

H  Plastic frames.  Popular style.

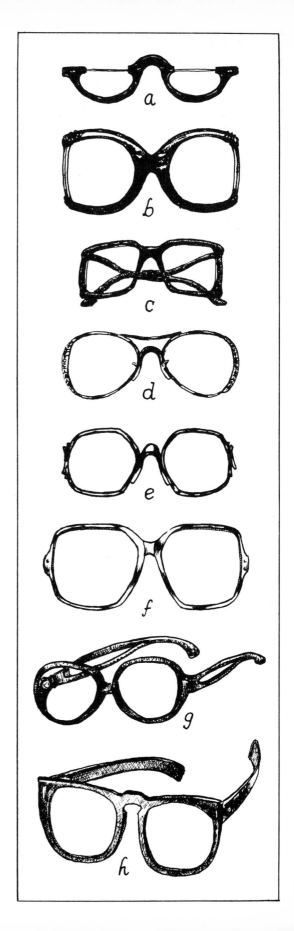

PLATE 85 : THE TWENTIETH CENTURY 1975-1979

A   Opera glasses.

B   Frames decorated with rhinestones.

C   Plastic frames with flip-down lenses to permit making up the eyes without removing the glasses.

D   Magnifying glass for reading menus, programmes, etc.

E   Lorgnette.

F   Lorgnette.

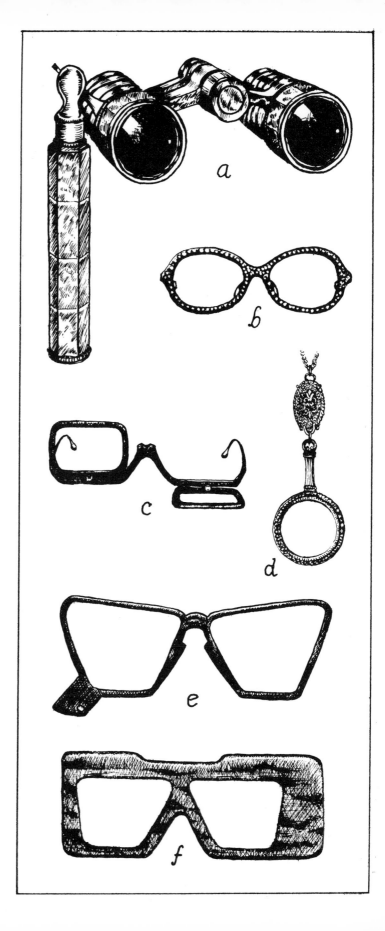

*a*

*b*

*c*

*d*

*e*

*f*

A   White plastic frames with blue stripe. Available in other colour combinations.

B   Plastic frames.   Faddish style.

C   Plastic frames.   Available in various colours.

D   Plastic frames.

E   Men's sunglasses with plastic frames.

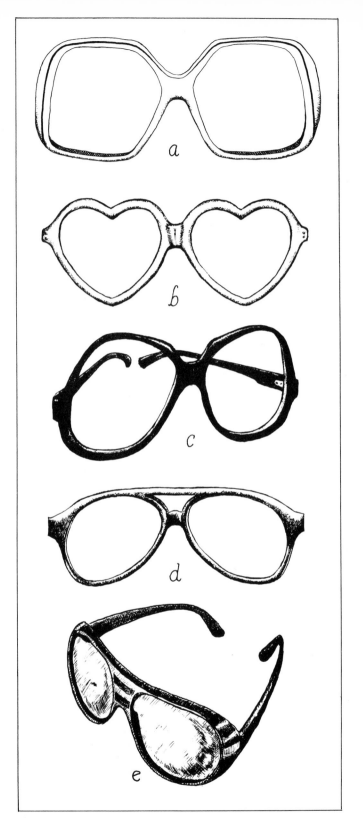

## Museums and Libraries

Aix-en-Provence—Musée
Amsterdam—Rijks Museum
Florence—Palazzo Pitti, Galleria Uffizi
London—British Museum, Science Museum, Victoria and Albert Museum
New York—Academy of Medicine Library, Metropolitan Museum, Museum of the City
    of New York, New York Historical Society, New York Public Library, Brooklyn
    Museum
Nürnberg—Germanisches Nationalmuseum
Paris—Musée de Cluny, Musée du Louvre
Salt Lake City—Pioneer Museum
Stockholm—Nordiska Museet

## Books and Periodicals

'Age of Spectacles' (in *Literary Digest*, 13 June 1925)
Allemagne, Henry René d'—*Les Accessoires du costume et du mobilier depuis le XIII^e
    siècle jusqu'au milieu du XIX^e* ; Schenier, Paris, 1928
*All the Year Round*
Andrew, Llewelyn—'Some Notes on the History of Spectacles' (in *Transactions of the
    Lancashire and Cheshire Antiquarian Society*, 1925)
*Annals of Medical History*
*Atlantic Monthly*
Aulnoy, Marie de Berneville, Comtesse d'—*Relation du voyage d'Espagne*, Paris, 1874–6
Barck, Carl—'The History of Spectacles' (in *Open Court*, April 1907)
*Bausch and Lomb Magazine*
*Boston Evening Post*
Bourgeois, A.—*Les Besicles de nos ancêtres* ; Maloine & Fils, Paris, 1923
Bull, George—*Lunettes et pince-nez* ; Librairie de l'Académie de Médecine, Paris, 1889.
*Business Week*
Carroll, Lewis (Charles L. Dodgson)—*The Hunting of the Snark* ; Macmillan, London,
    1876
Carroll, Lewis—*Phantasmagoria* ; Macmillan, London, 1869
Carroll, Lewis—*Sylvie and Bruno Concluded* ; Macmillan, London, 1893
*Chambers's Journal*
*Chicago Tribune*

Cockayne, Rev. Thomas Oswald—*Leechdoms, Wortcunning, and Starcraft of Early England*; Longman, Green, Longman, Roberts, and Green, London, 1864

Court, Thomas H., and Rohr, Moritz von—'On the Development of Spectacles in London from the End of the Seventeenth Century' (in *Optical Society Transactions*, London, 1928–9)

Cuming, H. Syer—'On Spectacles' (in *Journal of the British Archaeological Association*, 1855)

Dickens, Charles—'Dr Marigold's Prescriptions' (in *All the Year Round*, 1865)

Dickens, Charles—*Little Dorrit*; Riverside Press, Cambridge, 1869

Diderot, Denis—*Encyclopédie ou Dictionnaire raisonné des sciences, des arts, et des métiers*
*Dioptric Review*

Dowaliby, Margaret S.—'The Fashion Factor in Optometric Practice' (in *Optical Journal*, 1951)

Eckermann, Johann Peter—*Conversations with Goethe*; J. Munroe and Company, Boston, 1852

Edwards, Fassett—'Those Glasses We Wear' (in *Hygeia*, April 1931)

Flick, Cecil Stanley—*A Gross of Green Spectacles*; Hatton Press, London, 1951

Foster, Hugh G.—'A Capsule History of Eyeglasses' (in *Holiday*, September 1962)
*Frasers Magazine*

Gardner, Albert—'Lenses and Spectacles' (in *Outlook*, 5 August 1895)

Ginsburg, Samuel D.—'The History of Spectacles' (in *Optical Journal*, 13 April 1922)

Goldsmith, Oliver—*The Vicar of Wakefield*; James Cochrane and Company, London, 1832
*Good Housekeeping*

Grand-Carteret, John—*L'Histoire, la vie, les mœurs, et la curiosité*; Librairie de la Curiosité et des Beaux Arts, Paris, 1927

Greeff, Dr R.—'Evolution of Spectacle and Lens Forms' (in *Optical Journal*, 15 January 1925)

Hailparn, Lenore—'Your Face and Your Glasses' (in *Independent Woman*, October 1953)

Hart, Ernest—'Spectacled Schoolboys' (in *Atlantic Monthly*, November 1893)

Hemingway, William—'Putting on Specs' (in *Harper's*, 15 February 1913)

Herbert, Pitt H.—'An Eye on the Monocle' (in *Optical Journal*, 1 April 1950)

Heymann, Madame Alfred—*Lunettes et lorgnettes de jadis*; J. Leroy et Cie, Paris, 1911

Hill, John F.—'Glasses and Appearance' (in *Optical Journal*, 5 February 1925)
*Holiday*

Holme, Randle—*Academy of Armoury*; Chester, 1688

Horne, Richard H.—'Eyes and Eye-glasses' (in *Frasers Magazine*, December 1876)

'How to Look Well in Glasses' (in *Literary Digest*, 1 October 1921)

Huxley, Aldous—*Antic Hay*; George H. Doran, New York, 1923

Huxley, Aldous—'The Monocle' (in *Two or Three Graces and Other Stories*; Chatto and Windus, London, 1926)
*Hygeia*
*Independent Woman*

James, R. Ruston—*Studies in the History of Ophthalmology in England Prior to the Year 1800*; Cambridge University Press, Cambridge, 1933

Joly, Jean-Paul—'Petite Histoire des lunettes' (in *Revue de Deux Mondes*, 1 April 1954)

*Journal of the British Archaeological Association*

*Journal of the History of Medicine and the Allied Sciences*

*Kansas City Star*

Kitchiner, William—*Economy of the Eyes*; London, 1824

Kitchiner, William—*Practical Observations on Telescopes, Opera-Glasses, and Spectacles* (3rd edition); London, 1818

Kitchiner, William—*Precepts for the Improvement and Preservation of the Sight*; London, 1824

Layard, Austen H.—*Discoveries among the Ruins of Ninevah and Babylon*; G. P. Putnam and Company, New York, 1853

Lebensohn, James E.—'The History of Spectacles' (Paper read before the Society of Medical History of Chicago, 6 January 1925)

Lebensohn, James E.—'The Selling of Glasses' (in *Hygeia*, October 1936)

*Life*

*Literary Digest*

*Mademoiselle*

Martin, Benjamin—*An Essay on Visual Glasses* (5th edition); printed for the Author, 1760

*McCalls*

Moore, T. Haines—'Evolution of a Pair of Glasses' (in *Optical Journal*, 25 August 1921)

*Newsweek*

*New Yorker*

*New York Herald Tribune*

*New York Times*

*Open Court*

*Optical Journal and Review*

*Optician, The*

*Outlook, The*

Pansier, Pierre—*Histoire des lunettes*; A. Maloine, Paris, 1901

Peck, Bernice—'Look at it This Way' (in *Mademoiselle*, January 1954)

Pepys, Samuel—*Diary and Correspondence*; Bell and Daldy, London, 1867

Pflugk, A.—'Die Meisterzeichen der Nürnberger Brillenmacher' (in *Arch. f. Aughlkde.*, 1922)

*Popular Science Monthly*

Phillips, Richard Jones—*Spectacles and Eyeglasses*; P. Blakiston's Son and Company, Philadelphia, 1908

Rasmussen, O. D.—*Old Chinese Spectacles*; North China Press, Tientsin, North China, 1915

*Redbook*

*Revue des Deux Mondes*

Rohr, Moritz von—'Additions to our Knowledge of Old Spectacles' (in *Optical Society Transactions*, London, 1924–5)

Rohr, Moritz von—'Contributions to the History of English Opticians in the First Half of the Nineteenth Century' (in *Optical Society Transactions*, London, 1926–7)

Rohr, Moritz von—'Contributions to the History of the Spectacle Trade from the Earliest Times to Thomas Young's Appearance' (in *Optical Society Transactions*, London, 1923–1924)

Rohr, Moritz von—'Lectures on Spectacle History' (in *Optical Journal*, 1921)

Rosen, Edward—'The Invention of Eyeglasses' (in *Journal of the History of Medicine and the Allied Sciences*, January 1956)

Rosenthal, Meta—'The Eyeglasses Mirror the Era' (in *Hygeia*, June 1937)

Rosenthal, Meta—'The Pince-nez' (in *Hygeia*, April 1938)

Ryland, Herbert S.—'The Manufacture of Gold-Filled Spectacle Frames' (in *Optical Society Transactions*, London, 1922–3)

Schnell, Ivar—'Notiser om Glasögonens Historia i Sverige' (in *Nordiska Museets och Skansens Årsbok*, 1934)

Sichel, J.—*Spectacles Their Uses and Abuses in Long and Short Sightedness*; Phillips, Samson and Company, Boston, 1850

'Spectacle Glasses' (in *Chambers's Journal*, 7 February 1891)

'Spectacles' (in *Chambers's Journal*, 15 August 1896)

Steele, Euin—'The Future of Contact Lens Practice' (in *Optical Journal*, 1951)

Sullivan, Charles H.—'Things Are Not What They Were' (in *Optical Journal*, 1951)

'Sun Glasses Bow to Fashion' (in *Business Week*, 12 July 1947)

Super, Charles William—'Sight and Seeing in Ancient Times' (in *Popular Science Monthly*, May 1907)

Sutton-Vane, Sybil—*The Story of Eyes*; Viking Press, New York, 1958

Swift, Jonathan—*Gulliver's Travels*; Houghton, Mifflin and Company, Boston, 1896

Sylvester, A. J.—*The Real Lloyd George*; D. C. Benson and Campbell Thompson Ltd, 1947

*Time*

Tomes, Robert—*The Bazar Book of Decorum*; Harper & Brothers, New York, 1870.

*Transactions of the Lancashire and Cheshire Antiquarian Society*; H. Rawson and Company, Manchester

*Transactions of the Optical Society, London*

*Vogue*

Voltaire, *Candide*; Boni and Liveright, New York, 1918

'Warning Against Eyeglasses, A' (in *Literary Digest*, 24 December 1921)

*Woman's Home Companion*

Wood, Casey A.—'The First Scientific Work on Spectacles' (in *Annals of Medical History*, volume 3)

# Index